PALÆONTOLOGY OF CALIFORNIA.

VOL. I.

GEOLOGICAL SURVEY OF CALIFORNIA.

J. D. WHITNEY, State Geologist.

PALÆONTOLOGY.

VOLUME I.

CARBONIFEROUS AND JURASSIC FOSSILS.

BY F. B. MEEK.

TRIASSIC AND CRETACEOUS FOSSILS.

BY W. M. GABB.

PUBLISHED BY AUTHORITY OF THE LEGISLATURE OF CALIFORNIA.

1864.

CAXTON PRESS OF
SHERMAN & CO., PHILADELPHIA.

TABLE OF CONTENTS.

PREFACE.

As it is presumed that the volumes of Palæontology, forming a part of the series of publications of the State Geological Survey of California, will come into the hands of persons who will not have the other parts of the work, it is deemed proper to preface this volume by a brief notice of the origin and organization of this Survey. This subject will be entered into more fully in the first volume of the geological portion of the Report; but it is suitable that a sufficient account of the course and plan of operations of the Survey should be prefixed to the first volume of each separate department, to enable those consulting the publications in that department to understand the scope of the work, and to give due credit to those engaged in bringing together the materials, of the special working up of which this volume is the first instalment.

The Act of the Legislature creating the office of State Geologist and authorizing a Geological Survey of the State of California, was approved April 21st, 1860; but operations were not commenced until about the 1st of December of that year; consequently the work has been in progress not quite four years.

The plan of the Survey, according to the requirements of the Act by which it was originally organized, demanded "AN ACCURATE AND COMPLETE GEOLOGICAL SURVEY OF THE STATE," and a Report, containing "a full and scientific description of its rocks, fossils, soils, and minerals, and of its botanical and zoological productions." Provision was also made for the collection of specimens in all departments of Geology and Natural History, which specimens were to be deposited "in such place as shall be hereafter provided for that purpose by the Legislature."

Under this Act, the Survey was carried on, with greater or less vigor, according to the varying amounts appropriated by each successive Legislature, until the spring of the present year, when the Act expired by constitutional limitation; the Legislature of California having no power to create an office which shall last over four years.

By an Act of the last Legislature, however, approved April 4th, 1864, the office of State Geologist was again created, and filled by the same person who had thus far held it, while the course of investigation to be pursued, under the new Act, was less distinctly marked out than in the previous one, leaving more to the discretion of the State Geologist, and the chances of smaller or greater appropriations from the next Legislature; but requiring him "to complete the Geological Survey of the State, and to prepare a Report of said Survey for publication, and superintend the publication of the same;" farther adding, that "such Report shall be in the form of a geological, botanical, and zoological history of the State."

The following persons have been employed on the Survey since its commencement: Professor W. H. Brewer has had charge of the Department of Botany and Agricultural Geology, and has also occupied the post of Principal Assistant, having had charge of the party in the field during my absence. We have been assisted in the field-work by Messrs. Clarence R. King and Auguste Rémond, both of whom have rendered efficient and valuable service as volunteers, the former during part of the last year and during the season of 1864; the latter at various times, and especially in the summer of 1862. It is hoped and expected that one or both these gentlemen will be permanently attached to the Survey during the remainder of its continuance. Mr. C. Averill was also connected with our work from its commencement up to February, 1863, as clerk, commissary, and barometrical observer. In the Topographical Department, Mr. C. F. Hoffmann has been employed from March, 1861, up to the present time, with the exception of a short interval during the early part of the current year. Mr. V. Wackenreuder has also rendered assistance in this branch of our work, during the seasons of 1862 and 1864. In the Palæontological Department, Mr. W. M. Gabb has been regularly employed as Palæontologist to the Survey, since the beginning of the year 1862; he also acted as Assistant in the field-work during a part of the season of 1862. Dr. J. G. Cooper has had charge of the Zoological Department, having been employed, with occasional intervals, since July 1st, 1861. Mr.

W. Ashburner served as Assistant in the field from the commencement of the Survey up to the spring of 1862, and was chiefly employed, during that time, in examining gold-quartz mines and machinery in the principal mining counties of the Sierra Nevada. To all these gentlemen my cordial thanks are tendered for their devotion to the interests of the Survey. Rarely can it have happened, that one in charge of a work of this kind has found himself more efficiently or more pleasantly supported by his associates.

We have also been greatly assisted by the use of collections and materials furnished by private individuals. I will only specify in this connection such help as we have had in what bears directly on the Palæontological Department, leaving that which is related to the other branches of the Survey to be fully set forth in other volumes.

In the first place, the California Academy of Natural Sciences has given us free access to its collections, among which are some things of interest, collected chiefly by Dr. J. B. Trask, which we should otherwise have failed of obtaining. Dr. Trask has also frequently and most effectually aided us by communicating valuable information as to localities, as well as in other ways. Dr. J. A. Veatch has supplied the Survey with extensive collections of fossils from various localities, especially from the prolific one of Lick Springs, or Tuscan Springs, as it is now called; he has also contributed valuable specimens from the Cerros Islands and from Clear Lake. Mr. Gorham Blake has also made important additions to our collections, by specimens contributed from various quarters, especially from the Humboldt Mining

Region, and from the auriferous rocks of the Sierra Nevada. Mr. R. Homfray kindly presented us with a valuable suite of fossils from Nevada Territory. Mr. Rémond has given the Survey the use of his collections, made chiefly in the vicinity of San Francisco Bay, previous to his joining our corps. Dr. George H. Horn, U.S.A., who was stationed at Fort Téjon for several months, collected assiduously in that prolific locality of Cretaceous fossils, and kindly placed all his materials at Mr. Gabb's disposal. Mr. E. Mathewson has collected with great zeal in the prolific localities around Martiñez, and has generously furnished the Survey with specimens of all such species found by him as were not already in our possession. Other persons have contributed one or more specimens each, some of which, belonging to the larger mammalia, are of considerable value: these will be noted in the volume in which they will be described, and due credit given to the persons by whom they were presented.

As the general plan of operations of the Survey, and the progress made in each department up to the present time, will be fully set forth in the volume of Geology, which will soon follow this, it will only be necessary here to give such a sketch of the extent and order of our field-work as may be necessary to enable those consulting this volume to understand what parts of the State and the adjacent Territories we have visited, and what districts are represented by the materials elaborated in this portion of the Report.

During the winter of 1860–61, the field-work having commenced December 12, 1860, we explored San Bernardino and Los Angeles counties; then the region of the Coast ranges, from Los Angeles to Santa Barbara; thence to San Luis Obispo; thence down the Salinas Valley and across to San Juan; thence down the Mount Diablo range to New Idria, back to San Juan, and up through Alameda and Contra Costa counties, on the west side of the range, to Mount Diablo; thence across the Straits of Carquines and up Napa Valley as far as the Geysers, which point was reached just at the setting in of the rainy season of 1861–2. The party then returned to San Francisco, having been in the field just a year. The chief palæontological collections made during this time were of Tertiary age.

The explorations of the year 1861 having revealed the presence of Cretaceous rocks in the Mount Diablo range, and various circumstances making it apparent that the vicinity of Mount Diablo itself, by a detailed and careful study, would throw much light on the structure of the Coast ranges, and furnish a key to what had previously been more or less obscure in the stratigraphical position of the rocks south and west of the San Joaquin, we devoted a month, at the commencement of the season of field-work for 1862, to making a detailed examination of the region between Martiñez, on the Straits of Carquines, and Marsh's ranch, ten miles east of the mountain.

This accomplished, the party, in charge of Professor Brewer, continued their explorations along the Mount Diablo range towards the southeast as far as Pacheco's Pass, working up the geology and topography of an extensive district, of which almost nothing had been previously known. Having completed this task, it had been my intention to have the party cross the San Joaquin River, and meet me at Snelling's, on the Merced, and then to devote the remainder of the season to working up the geology of the foot-hills of the Sierra Nevada, going as far north as time would permit, and then returning on the west side of the Sacramento, along the foot-hills of the Coast ranges north of the Bay of San Francisco. It appeared, however, that all the ferries of the San Joaquin had been broken up by the unprecedented storms of the previous winter (1861–2), so that there was no possibility of crossing at any point, the river continuing greatly swollen by the melting of the snow of the Sierra until late in the season. This rendered a change in our plans necessary, as the party had to return up the San José Valley and cross at Benicia. It was then determined to continue the work up the valley, along the Coast ranges west of the Sacramento River, with the view of reaching Mount Shasta before it would be too late in the season for its ascent. This plan was partially carried out, and the region north of Benicia explored as far as Rag Cañon; but the severe sickness of several of the party during the summer, seriously interfered with our progress. After reaching and ascending Mount Shasta, additional explorations were made in that vicinity, in Shasta, Siskiyou, and Trinity counties, and afterwards along the east side of the Sacramento Valley, in the foot-hills, for the purpose of ascertaining more clearly the relations of the Cretaceous formation to the auriferous slates of the Sierra Nevada. Still later in the season, the field-work being continued to the end of November, the vicinity of the

Bay of San Francisco was more thoroughly examined by small parties on foot, especially portions of Santa Clara, Contra Costa, and Alameda counties. During this season the larger portion of the Cretaceous fossils described in this volume were collected, a large number of the most prolific localities having been discovered in the course of the summer. The Carboniferous limestones of the Sierra Nevada, from Pence's ranch north to Bass's ranch, were also carefully examined during this season, and the collections made which are reported on by Mr. Meek in this volume.

During the season of 1862, we were fortunate enough to secure Triassic fossils from several different portions of the Territory of Nevada, especially a valuable collection made by Gorham Blake, Esq., in the Humboldt Mining Region.

In 1863, the region about Fort Téjon, the Cañada de las Uvas, and that portion of the State which lies about the head-waters of the San Joaquin, was made the object of a reconnoissance by Messrs. Brewer and Gabb. and a considerable number of new Cretaceous species discovered. After this was accomplished, the work of the Survey was, during the remainder of the season, mainly confined to the high Sierra, and consequently but little was added to our stock of fossils. In September, however, Messrs. Brewer and King made the interesting discovery of a locality of Triassic, and also one of Jurassic fossils, in and near Genessee Valley, in Plumas County; the latter constitute the material worked up by Mr. Meek in Section III, of this volume. The Triassic fossils from Genessee Valley, together with those collected by Mr. G. Blake, and by the Survey as previously noticed, and to which was afterwards added a valuable suite of specimens from the Humboldt eastern range, made by Mr. Homfray, have been elaborated by Mr. Gabb, in Section II.

In the autumn of 1863, Mr. Gabb was engaged by me to conduct some explorations outside of California and the regular work of the Survey. He made a trip, of three months' duration, through Oregon and Washington Territory to Vancouver Island, and collected a considerable number of Tertiary and Cretaceous fossils, making important additions to the little previously known of the geology of that extensive region. He has now joined an exploring party through South-eastern Oregon, emphatically a geological *terra incognita*, from which region he can hardly fail to bring back facts of importance. The expedition started from Fort Klamath, at the north end of Klamath Lake, about the 20th of June.

During the spring of the current year Mr. Clarence R. King made some valuable explorations in the Humboldt ranges of Nevada Territory; he also, previously to that, had made an interesting contribution to the geology of the Sierra Nevada, by the discovery of *Belemnites* in close contact with one of the great auriferous quartz veins of the central gold mining region (on the Mariposa estate), thus adding a very important link to the chain of evidence going to show that the auriferous slates and metamorphic rocks of California are, to a large extent at least, of Secondary age, and not Palæozoic, as had heretofore always been assumed, without evidence. Messrs. Brewer, King and Hoffman are now, or have been up to a quite recent period, engaged in the high Sierra, around the head-waters of King's River, and the other streams between that and the Merced,—a region from which we can hardly expect any considerable additions to our palæontological materials, while, on the other hand, their geographical discoveries, and their additions to our knowledge of the topography of the State, have been of great importance.

Mr. Rémond, having been for some time detached from the Survey, has resided in Sonora, Mexico, and has made numerous geological observations, an abstract of which will be communicated in the forthcoming volume of this Report especially devoted to Geology.

The observations of the Survey, taken in connection with those already and hereafter to be made on the north, south, and east of California, will enable us to form a general idea of the geological structure of a vast area of country bordering on our Pacific coast, and we trust that we shall be able, in due time, to furnish a geological map of a large portion of the western side of our continent; a map which, it may with truth be added, will have little resemblance to those heretofore published. Such a map, however, will of course only present an outline of the geology of this region; for anything like a thorough exhibition of its structure we shall have to wait many years, since it is a field sufficiently extensive, and difficult of exploration, to require an almost unlimited amount of labor before its details shall have been fully wrought out.

It will be proper, in this connection, to mention, in as concise a manner as possible, some of the principal results of our Survey, and particularly those which relate to the character and distribution of the different subdivisions of the geological series, as developed on and near the Pacific coast.

Perhaps the most striking fact we have to present is, the immense development on the western edge of our Continent of rocks equivalent in age to the Upper Trias of the Alps, and palæontologically closely allied to the limestones of Hallstadt and Aussee and the St. Cassian beds, that extremely important and highly fossiliferous division of the Alpine Trias.

This great Triassic belt of the Pacific coast has been most fully explored by the Survey in the latitude of 40°, and over a width east and west of nearly four degrees of longitude (117° to 121°). It is from this region that the largest portion of the Triassic fossils described in this volume have been obtained, namely, from the three parallel ranges, in longitude 117° to 118°, in Nevada Territory, known as the Humboldt Mountains, or the Humboldt Mining Region, and from localities in Plumas County, California. But sufficient palæontological evidence has been obtained to enable us to state that this formation extends from Mexico to British Columbia, and that it occupies a vast area, although much broken up, interrupted by eruptive rocks, and covered in many places by heavy accumulations of volcanic materials.

Among the specimens from the Humboldt ranges, as also from Plumas County and other localities in the Sierra Nevada, Mr. Gabb recognizes at least four species as identical with European, while the whole aspect of our Triassic collections is strikingly like that of the Hallstadt and St. Cassian beds, there being the same remarkable intermixture of Orthoceratites, Ceratites, Goniatites, Nautili, and Ammonites, the latter frequently of those peculiar globose forms occurring in the Alps, together with *Halobia*, *Monotis*, *Avicula*, *Pecten*, and other species, a *Monotis* being the most abundant and most widely diffused of all.

Accompanying this Triassic formation in the Sierra Nevada, and probably also in the Humboldt ranges, is an extensive development of rocks of Jurassic age, usually highly metamorphosed and extremely barren of fossils. Enough of these, however have been found to warrant the assertion, that the sedimentary portion of the great metalliferous belt of the Pacific coast of North America is, to a large extent, made up of rocks of Jurassic and Triassic age, with a comparatively small development of Carboniferous limestone, and that these formations are so folded together, broken up, and metamorphosed in the great chain of the Sierra Nevada, that it will be an immense labor, if indeed possible at all, to unravel its detailed structure. While we are fully justified in saying, that a large portion of the auriferous rocks of California consist of metamorphic Triassic and Jurassic strata, we have not a particle of evidence to sustain the theory which has been so often brought forward, that all, or even a portion, of the auriferous rocks are older than the Carboniferous, not a trace of a Devonian or Silurian fossil ever having been discovered in California, or indeed anywhere to the west of the 116th meridian. It appears, on the other hand, that no inconsiderable amount of gold has been obtained from metamorphic rocks, belonging as high up in the series as the Cretaceous.

The fourth section of this volume furnishes evidence of the wide-spread occurrence of the Cretaceous system on the Pacific coast. The Coast ranges of California and Oregon are, indeed, to a large extent, made up of rocks of this age, usually somewhat metamorphic in their condition, and often highly so; but still, on the whole, forming the richest fossiliferous formation of California, having furnished already, in the course of our necessarily rapid explorations, a more or less extensive series of species at over thirty localities. The Cretaceous formation is also extensively developed on the flanks of the Sierra Nevada, in the northern part of the State, and in this position being less metamorphosed than in the Coast ranges, several of the localities discovered have proved to be prolific in well-preserved as well as interesting and novel forms. According to Mr. Gabb, it appears that the Cretaceous, so far as is yet known, is represented on the Pacific coast by but a single member,—the Upper or White Chalk,—and that it may be divided into two well-marked groups, the lower of which corresponds to the No. 4 of Meek and Hayden, or the Fort Pierre group. This division (Div. A.) of this volume, has yielded 152 species in California, out of about 260 collected in the Cretaceous, and of these only about half a dozen are common to this and the upper division (Div. B.). This latter should, probably, judging from its stratigraphical position, correspond with the Fox Hill group, or No. 5 of Meek and Hayden; although all the species, with a single doubtful exception, are peculiar to California, and that species is referred to one described from No. 4 in New Jersey and Tennessee.

Rocks of Tertiary age are extensively developed in the Coast ranges, and especially in that portion of them which lies between the parallels of 34° and 35°. Although fossiliferous in many localities, these beds do not usually retain their organic remains in as good a state of preservation as the Cretaceous, while the number of distinct groups of species in the Tertiary rocks is considerable, indicating the existence of several subdivisions of the system, the exact relations of which to each other, and to those recognized in the Eastern States and in Europe, are not yet fully wrought out. Besides the marine mollusca of the Tertiary, to be worked up by Mr. Gabb during the coming winter, there are, in the collections of the Survey, large numbers of fossil plants, as well as of mammalian remains, from the later Tertiary and Post-tertiary of the Sierra Nevada and the Coast ranges, which will be elaborated by competent authorities, and which will furnish, as is expected, the materials for a second volume of the palæontological portion of our Report.

For a full description of the Stratigraphical Geology of the State, so far as developed, and for farther details as to the distribution and relations of the fossils described in this volume, the reader is referred to the forthcoming volume of General Geology, which is intended to follow the one herewith presented without delay.

J. D. WHITNEY.

OFFICE OF THE GEOLOGICAL SURVEY
OF CALIFORNIA, Sept. 1864.

PALÆONTOLOGY OF CALIFORNIA.

VOL. I.

SECTION I.

DESCRIPTION OF THE CARBONIFEROUS FOSSILS.

BY F. B. MEEK.

FORAMINIFERA.

GENUS FUSULINA, Fischer.

FUSULINA ROBUSTA, Meek.

Pl. 2, Fig. 3, and 3 *a*, *b*, *c*.

SHELL oval-subglobose, the longer diameter being to the shorter about as 26 to 20. Surface with longitudinal linear, slightly impressed furrows, placed at regular intervals, one over each septum, and extending from end to end,—becoming a little twisted as they approach the extremities. Volutions five or six, the last or outer one being usually less capacious than one or two of those immediately within. Septa about thirty to forty in the last or outer turn of adult shells; nearly straight at their outer edges, but becoming waved and distorted within, so as to give the interior a complex cellular appearance, particularly near each end of the shell. Mesial fissure apparently short and very narrow or linear.

Greatest length of one of the largest specimens, 0.40 inch; breadth of do., 0.32 inch. Average size, about one-fourth less.

Compared with the published figures of the Russian species, *F. cylindrica* of Fischer, this species will be found larger and greatly more ventricose. Notwithstanding its larger size, however, it usually has about one volution less, while its septa, and the coincident striæ of the exterior, are less numerous and more distant. It agrees more nearly in form and size with a variety of a shell found in the Coal-measures of Kansas and Missouri,—usually referred to *F. cylindrica*,—for which Dr. Hayden and the writer proposed the name *Ventricosa*. (Proceed. Acad. Nat. Sci. Philad. 1858, p. 261.) It is uniformly much more gibbous, however, and generally attains a larger size; while transverse sections show that even much smaller sized individuals of the Kansas shell have two or three more volutions than the species under consideration, and several more septa in each turn.

Locality. Bass's Ranch, Shasta County.*

FUSULINA GRACILIS, Meek.

Pl. 2., Fig. 1, and 1 *a*, *b*, *c*.

Shell small, very slender, cylindrical; volutions five to six. Surface marked longitudinally by slight linear furrows, or faintly impressed striæ coincident with the septa within. Fissure unknown. Septa about twenty-five in the last or outer turn, very strongly undulated laterally so as to come nearly or quite in contact at regular intervals, thus giving the interior, as seen in longitudinal sections, a distinctly reticulated cellular appearance.

Length, 0.20 inch; breadth, 0.05 inch.

This is by far the most slender and regularly cylindrical species of the genus I have seen,—its sides being parallel and without the slightest tendency to swell out in the middle. It will be readily distinguished, by its form alone, from the most slender individuals of *F. cylindrica*, or of any other known species, excepting perhaps *F. elongata* of Shumard; and from that by its comparatively minute size, since Shumard's species attains a length of one to two inches.

Occurs associated with *F. robusta*.

FUSULINA CYLINDRICA, Fischer?

Pl. 2, Fig. 2, and 2 *a*.

Fusulina cylindrica, Fischer. Oryct. Moscow, 1837, p. 126, pl. 18, fig. 1–5.
Fusulina depressa, Fischer. Ibid., pl. 13, fig. 6–11.
Fusulina cylindrica, Murchison, De Verneuil and Keyserling. Geol. Rus. &c., vol. ii, pt. 2, p. 16, pl. 1, fig. 1, a, b, c, d.

Along with the foregoing there are a few weathered silicious specimens, having exactly the form and agreeing in size with the above-cited species; but the specimens are not in a condition to warrant a very positive opinion in regard to their identity with the Russian form. I suspect they will probably be found to be distinct, but being unable, from the imperfect specimens examined, to point out any characters by which they can be distinguished, I refer them provisionally to that species.

Length of a medium-sized specimen, 0.28 inch; thickness of do., 0.10 inch.

Occurs in a silicious mass with *F. robusta*.

---

* All the species described or noticed in this section are from the limestone belt, which crops out, forming a range of hills, east and northeast of Bass's Ranch, Shasta County. J. D. W.

ZOOPHYTA.

Genus LITHOSTROTION, Fleming.

Lithostrotion mamillare (?), Castlenau, (sp.)

Pl. 1, Fig. 4, and 4 *a*, *b*.

Stylina, Lesueur. 1832.
Astræa mamillaris, Castlenau. Ter. Sil. de l'Amerique du Nord, pl. 24, fig. 5. 1843.
Axinura Canadensis. Ibid., fig. 4.
Acrocyathus floriformis, d'Orbigny. Prod. de Palæont., t. 1, p. 160. 1850.
Lithostrotion basaltiforme, Owen. Rept. Wiscon., Iowa, and Min., tab. iv, figs. 5 and 6. 1852.
Lithostrotion mamillare, Edwards and Haime. Monog. Polyp., p. 400, pl. 13, figs. 1 and 1 a, b.
Lithostrotion mamillare, Hall. Geol. Rept. Iowa, vol. i, part 2, p. 667, pl. 24, fig. 5, a, b.

I have referred this coral to the above species with some hesitation, because the specimens are imperfect fragments, not giving a very satisfactory idea of the general appearance of the entire corallum, nor of the calices. As near as I have been able to determine, however, from sections, it agrees well in its internal structure with fine specimens of *L. mamillare*, now before me, from Missouri and Illinois. There can be no doubt in regard to its generic characters; and, if not specifically identical with the common species of the Mississippi valley, it is certainly a closely allied representative form.

As in that species, the specimens present two modes of growth, one in which the corallites are in closely aggregated masses, and assume an angular prismatic form, and another in which they are less crowded, cylindrical, and grow in tufts. These two forms may be distinct species; but they seem to present the same internal structure, and it is not improbable that additional specimens would show intermediate gradations in the mode of growth, as we see in authentic examples of *L. mamillare* from the Western States.

In both of the forms alluded to above the rays vary from about twenty to thirty-eight, most of which extend to the columella. Alternating with these is another series of much shorter, or rudimentary rays. The tabulæ pass obliquely upwards and inwards from the outer vesicular zone on all sides to the columella, and occasionally divide, so as to impart a somewhat vesicular appearance to the interior area. The outer vesicular zone consists of small vesicles, arranged in irregular oblique rows, sloping inwards from the surrounding external wall.

In the tufted specimens with cylindrical corallites, where the epitheca is well preserved, the surface shows no traces of costal striæ, such as we see so well defined on similar varieties of *L. mamillare* from the subcarboniferous rocks of the Mississippi valley. From this fact, and the slightly more flexuous appearance of the corallites, I am led to suspect that this form may possibly prove to be a distinct species. If so, I would suggest for it the name *L. sublæve.* Whether the other form, with crowded angular corallites, presents smooth or striated surfaces, when the corallites separate, I have no means of knowing, there being no specimens in the collection in a condition to show these surfaces.

Lithostrotion? Californiense, Meek.

Pl. 1, Fig. 2, and 2 *a, b, c.*

Corallum apparently growing in small tufts, or probably sometimes produced and branching into dendroid forms. Corallites large, cylindrical, or cylindrico-conical, and more or less flexuous. Surface marked by small but distinct wrinkles of growth, and, where the epitheca is well preserved, scarcely visible traces of costal striæ. Calices rather deep, circular or a little oval, and bearing within a moderately prominent, somewhat compressed columellar boss. Rays from fifty to sixty-eight, a little flexuous; about half of them extending to the columella, while the intermediate smaller ones only pass about one-third of the way in from the outer wall. Vertical section showing the outer vesicular zone to be bounded by a thin, irregular, inner wall, and composed of small, unequal vesicles, arranged in oblique, irregular rows, sloping inwards; each row consisting of about six to eight of the vesicles. Tabulæ ascending and much divided, so as to form large, irregular vesicles, sloping outwards from the axis.

The specimens of this species yet obtained are mostly detached corallites, embedded in hard limestone, and consequently are not in a condition to show very clearly its mode of growth. As near as can be determined, however, it would seem to have grown in small tufts of a few large diverging corallites,—at first subconical in form, but becoming elongated and cylindrical with age. Whether or not they continued to branch, so as to present a dendroid aspect, cannot be determined from the specimens yet collected. The rather large size and subconical form of some of the corallites, as seen detached, might lead to the supposition that they belong to the genus *Clisiophyllum*, from which they do not differ materially in their internal structure. The compound mode of growth, however, of the entire corallum, would exclude it from that genus as defined by Edwards and Haime. Until better specimens can be obtained for study, its generic relations must remain somewhat doubtful.

The large size, and more conical form of the calices, as well as their more widely divergent mode of branching, will readily distinguish this species from any variety of the common *L. mamillare*. The surfaces of its calices are also more wrinkled by the marks of growth, while it wants the rather distinct costal striæ of that species. Again, the large vesicles of its middle area, as seen in a vertical section, are more numerous and irregular, and do not slope with a downward curve, as in *L. mamillare*.

LITHOSTROTION ——— ?

Pl. 1, Fig. 3, and 3 *a*.

Corallum loosely fasciculate. Corallites slender, cylindrical, more or less flexuous. Calices unknown. Rays twenty to twenty-four, rather strong, straight, and apparently extending nearly or quite to the columella; sometimes alternating with short rudimentary rays. Tabulæ thin, arranged more closely than the rays, and curving strongly upwards as they approach the axis. Outer vesicular zone, as seen in vertical sections, very narrow, and occupied usually by a single series of small, very oblique vesicles.

Only knowing this coral in the condition of very imperfect specimens, I do not feel warranted in identifying it with any known species; nor would it be desirable to attempt to describe it from such material under a new name. It may be compared with such forms as *L. irregulare*, Phillips (sp.), *L. Martini*, Edwards and Haime, &c., though it seems to differ in its internal structure from these and all the other species with which I have compared it.

Genus CLISIOPHYLLUM, Dana.

Clisiophyllum Gabbi, Meek.

Pl. 1, Fig. 1, and 1 *a*, *b*.

Corallum elongate, or becoming at maturity cylindrico-conical, attaining a large size; smaller extremity rather pointed, and more or less abruptly curved. Surface with small obscure wrinkles of growth, and rather faintly marked longitudinal or costal striæ, coincident with the rays within, which are regularly arranged, about six to eight in the space of 0.25 inch. Rays forty to sixty, moderately strong, nearly straight, and in part extending to and ascending the central boss of the calices with a slight twist. Alternating with these principal rays there is another series of short rudimentary ones, rarely extending beyond the inner margin of the outer vesicular zone. Calices deep, and nearly or quite circular, with a thin rim, and a rather prominent, acutely conical, central protuberance. Outer vesicular zone, as seen in a vertical section, composed of very small, regular, subrhombic vesicles, ranging with their longer axis nearly vertical, but disposed so as to form oblique rows sloping inwards. Middle area between the pseudo-columella and the outer vesicular zone, occupied by large, irregular, elongated, more or less arcuate, transverse vesicles. Pseudo-columella composed of irregular, elongated vesicles, inclined obliquely downwards and outwards, parallel to the outer slope of the central boss.

Length of a rather small conical specimen, 2.50 inches; breadth of ditto, at larger extremity, 1.45 inches. Fragments of large subcylindrical specimens in the collection indicate their entire length to have been six to eight inches, and their transverse diameter near two inches.

This fine coral is perhaps more nearly related, both in form and internal structure, to *Clisiophyllum bipartitum*, McCoy (Palæozoic Fossils, p. 93, pl. iii c, fig. 6), than to any other known species. It attains a larger size, however, and has a more acutely conical, central protuberance; while it presents differences in the details of its internal structure. As in that species, a vertical section shows its outer vesicular area to be comparatively thin, and composed of very small vesicles, the middle zone between this and the pseudo-columella of coarser, transverse vesicles; and the false columella itself of elongated, slanting vesicles. In our species, however, the comparative breadth of these zones is different; its middle one, of transverse vesicles, between the false columella and the outer area, being proportionally much broader, or nearly equalling the breadth of the pseudo-columella; while, according to Prof. McCoy's figures, the columellar space is ten to twelve times as broad as the middle zone in his species. Again, the outer vesicular zone in the species under consideration is proportionally a little broader where fully developed.

It is worthy of note that the outer area is merely rudimentary in small specimens, and probably entirely wanting in very young examples of our species. In specimens of one inch to one and a quarter inches in length there is usually but a single series of these small outer vesicles, rising like little blisters on the inner side of the epitheca between the rays. Farther up from the smaller extremity of the corallite another alternating series is developed upon these, and still higher another, and so on until ten or twelve series are produced in large specimens; beyond which there would seem to have been no farther increase. The vesicles themselves of the outer zone appear to be of uniform size at all stages of growth; their height being about 0.04 inch, and their breadth about 0.02 inch. No well-defined walls were observed separating the outer and middle zones, nor the latter from the pseudo-columella.

The specific name is given in honor of Mr. W. M. Gabb, Palæontologist of the State Geological Survey of California.

MOLLUSCA.

BRACHIOPODA.

Genus ORTHIS, Dalman.

Orthis (sp. undt.)

Pl. 2, Fig. 5, and 5 *a, b. c.*

Compare *Orthis Michelini*, L'Eveille (sp.). Davidson, Carb. Brach. Grt. Brit., pl. 30, Figs. 6 to 11.

Shell small, suborbicular, or a little oval, the length being greater than the breadth; hinge-line very short, or less than one-third the breadth of the valves, and not imparting any angularity to the lateral margins. Valves nearly equal, without any mesial depression. Ventral valve somewhat flattened in front, but more convex than the other in the umbonal region; beak prominent and incurved; area small, regularly arched; foramen higher than wide. Dorsal valve more regularly convex than the other, most prominent between the middle and the cardinal margin; beak rather prominent, but less so than that of the other valve, moderately incurved. Surface of both valves ornamented with fine threadlike radiating striæ, which increase by division and intercalation; crossing these are a few distant, obscure, concentric marks of growth. Striæ of both valves showing the bases of minute, scattering, hair-like, tubular spines.

Length, 0.35 inch; breadth, 0.32 inch; convexity, 0.17 inch.

This little shell seems to be an exact miniature of *Orthis Michelini*, L'Eveille, excepting that its beaks are more prominent and arched than is common in that species, particularly that of the ventral valve. In the prominence of its beaks it agrees more nearly with *O. Michelina*, var. *Burlingtonensis*, Hall; but it is a much smaller shell, with a shorter hinge, and more rounded cardinal extremities. Mr. Davidson, I understand, considers the form figured under the name *O. Michelina*, var. *Burlingtonensis* (after a careful comparison of authentic specimens), identical with British examples of L'Eveille's species. This being the case, I cannot see how the form under consideration can be distinguished from that species, unless by its much smaller size. If the only two specimens I have seen are not young shells, or accidentally dwarfed individuals, they may belong to a distinct species; but, until other specimens can be procured for comparison, I prefer to leave the question in regard to their relations to *O. Michelini* for future consideration.

GENUS PRODUCTUS, Sowerby.

PRODUCTUS SEMIRETICULATUS, Martin (sp.)

Pl. 2, Fig. 4, and 4 *a*.

Anomites semireticulatus, Martin. Petrefact. Derb., pl. 32, figs. 1 and 2, and pl. 33, fig. 4. 1809.
Anomites productus, Martin. Ibid., 22, figs. 1 and 2.
Anomites Scoticus, *Martini*, and *antiquatus*, Sowerby. Min. Con. 1814 and 1821.
Anomites Martini and *antiquatus*, Phillip. Geol. Yorkshire, pl. 7, fig. 2. 1836.
Leptæna antiquata and *tribulifera*, Fischer. Oryct. Mosc., pl. 26, figs. 4 and 5, and pl. 26, fig. 1. 1837.
Productus Martini, De Koninck. An. Foss., pl. 7, fig. 2.
Productus Inca and *Peruvianus*, d'Orbigny. Voy. Am. Mer., pl. 4, figs. 1, 3, and 4.
Productus flexistriata, McCoy. Synopsis Carb. Foss., Ireland, pl. 17, fig. 1. 1844.
Productus semireticulatus, De Koninck. Monogr. Gen. Product, pl. 8, fig. 1.
Productus Calhounianus, Swallow? Trans. St. Louis Acad. Sci., vol. 1, p. 215. 1858.

THE specimens of the shell referred to the above-cited species are very imperfect, but seem to agree in all their visible characters with that well-known form. Still it is possible that better specimens, showing the entire shell and its internal characters, might present differences warranting its separation. It evidently attained a large size, some of the specimens indicating a transverse diameter of near three and a quarter inches.

GENUS RHYNCHONELLA, Fischer.

RHYNCHONELLA (sp. undt.)

SHELL small, subglobose, or subtrigonal. Dorsal valve more convex than the other, most prominent a little in advance of the middle, and rounding down to meet the other valve in front and on each side; ornamented with from nine to eleven simple, rather obtuse, plications, which extend scarcely half way up towards the beak from the front, three of them being raised anteriorly, so as to form a moderately prominent mesial ridge. Ventral valve somewhat compressed, most gibbous near the umbo; beak slightly arched, and extending a little beyond, and closely pressed upon that of the other valve; surface with plications and mesial depression corresponding with the mesial ridge and plications of the dorsal valve; anterior margin provided with a mesial projection, which fills a corresponding sinuosity in the front of the other valve when the shell is closed.

Length, 0.33 inch; breadth, 0.28 inch; convexity, 0.25 inch.

In a genus like this, where there are so many closely allied species, it would be folly to attempt to determine a species from a single imperfect specimen partly embedded in the matrix, especially when it comes from a distant and hitherto unexplored locality. I therefore merely give such characters and as good a figure as the condition of the specimen will admit of,* and leave the determination of its specific relations until we can have an opportunity to study better specimens.

---

* This shell is not figured on the plates furnished by Mr. Meek. J. D. W.

GENUS SPIRIFER, Sowerby.

SUBGENUS MARTINIA, McCoy.

SPIRIFER LINEATUS, Martin? (sp.)

Pl. 2, Fig. 6, and 6 *a*, *b*, *c*, *d*.

Conchiliolithus Anomites lineatus, Martin. Petrefact. Derb., tab. 36, fig. 3. 1809.
Terebratula lineata, Sowerby. Min. Conch. 4, p. 39, tab. 343, figs. 1, 2 (not fig. 1).
Terebratula imbricata, Sowerby. Ibid., 34, fig. 3.
Spirifera Martini, Fleming. Brit. An., p. 376. 1828.
Spirifera lineata, Phillips. Geol. York, p. 219, pl. 10, fig. 17. 1836.
Spirifera imbricata, Phillips. Ibid., fig. 20.
Spirifera mesiloba, Phillips. Ibid., fig. 14.
Reticularia reticulata, McCoy. Synop. Carb. Ireland, pl. 19, fig. 15. 1844
Reticularia imbricata and *lineata*, McCoy. Ibid., p. 143.
Martinia stringocephaloides, McCoy? Ibid., p. 144, pl. 22, fig. 8.
Spirifera elliptica, McCoy. Brit. Pal. Foss., p. 427. 1855.
Spirifera imbricata and *lineata*, McCoy. Ibid., p. 429.
Spirifer setigerus, Hall. Rept. Geol. Iowa, vol. 1, pt. 2, p. 705, pl. 27, fig. 4, a, b.
Spirifera perplexa, McChesney? New Species Palæozoic Fossils, p. 43.

THE shell I have referred to the above widely distributed species may possibly be found to present some internal or other specific difference from *Spirifera lineata*, when a series of good specimens, entirely detached from the matrix, can be examined. So far, however, as I have been able to determine from those in the collection before me, it seems to agree exactly with young examples of that species figured by Mr. Davidson in his "Monograph of the Carboniferous Brachiopoda of Great Britain." In size, and nearly all other respects, it likewise agrees well with *S. perplexa* of McChesney, which Mr. Davidson pronounces identical with *S. lineata*, after a careful comparison of authentic American specimens with British examples of Martin's species.

If our shell never attains a larger size than the specimens under examination, I should strongly suspect it to be distinct from *S. lineata;* but in that case it would be difficult to find characters to distinguish it from *S. perplexa*, McChesney, which from its uniformly smaller size may be distinct from *S. lineata.*

Genus SPIRIFERINA, Davidson.

Spiriferina (sp. undt.)

The specimen referred to the above-named genus is but a fragment of a dorsal valve. It is too imperfect to exhibit any reliable specific characters, and is only referred to this group from its coarsely punctate structure. It evidently belongs to the plicated section of the genus, and has an extended hinge-line, being apparently somewhat like *S. cristata*, Schlot. (sp.) Its mesial fold is larger than the lateral plications, of which there are four on each side.

Genus RETZIA, King.

Retzia compressa, Meek.

Pl. 2, Fig. 7, and 7 *a, b, c.*

Shell small, ovate, subtrigonal, rather compressed, showing no traces of a mesial fold. Beak of ventral valve moderately prominent, and but slightly arched; rounded, and truncated at the extremity by a small circular foramen. Surface ornamented by ten or eleven simple, rather narrow, prominent, radiating costæ, about equalling the deep furrows between, and extending nearly or quite to the beaks.

Length, 0.34 inch; breadth, 0.33 inch; convexity about 0.24 inch.

The specimens of this species in the collection examined are not in a condition to show the area, or any of the internal characters, yet they present peculiarities by which it may be distinguished from any other known carboniferous species. It is, perhaps, most nearly related to *R. Mormonii*=*Terebratula Mormonii*, of Marcou (Geol. North Am., pl. 6, fig. 11, a, b); but is a much less gibbous shell, with narrower and more sharply elevated plications. It may also be compared with *R. punctilifera*, Shumard (Trans. St. Louis Acad. Sci., vol. 1, p. 220), from which it also differs in being more compressed, and in having fewer and more prominent plications, as well as in being destitute of any traces of a mesial sinus.

The specimens being weathered, do not show the surface punctæ very distinctly, but, by the aid of a good magnifier, traces of them can be seen in a good light. They are very fine and regularly disposed.

GASTEROPODA.

GENUS EUOMPHALUS, Sowerby. = STRAPAROLLUS, Montfort?

SUBGENUS OMPHALOTROCHUS, Meek.

EUOMPHALUS WHITNEYI, Meek.

Pl. 2, Fig. 8, and 8 *a*.

SHELL large, rather thick, depressed-subtrochiform, widely umbilicated. Umbilicus deep and conical, nearly or quite equalling the breadth of the last whorl at the aperture. Volutions four to four and a half, sloping and concave above, and bicarinate around the outer side, the carinæ being separated by a wide, nearly vertical, flattened or concave space. Between the lower carina and the obtusely subangular margin of the umbilicus the under side of the whorls is nearly flat, or slightly convex; while the side forming the walls of the umbilicus is more or less flattened and very abrupt. Suture linear, but well defined. Aperture suborbicular, or transversely suboval, not modified by the preceding turn. Lip rather obtuse, and a little concave in outline on the inner side; while on the under side (judging from the curve of the lines of growth) it is oblique, and more or less sigmoid in outline. The same obliquity continues around the outer and upper sides, so that the margin of the lip must project forward considerably farther above than below. Surface marked only with lines of growth, which are most strongly defined on the under side and within the umbilicus.

Greatest breadth about 4.60 inches; height near 2 inches.

All the specimens of this shell in the collection are imperfect, but, taken together, they convey a correct idea of its form and most of its characters. Its biangular, broadly flattened periphery, and general outline, give it so much the aspect of some depressed subtrochiform species of *Pleurotomaria*, that it was not until fully satisfied that the lines of growth, in crossing the flattened space between the carinæ on the outer side of the whorls, as well as in passing over the carinæ, make not the slightest backward curve, that I could be convinced there might not have been a sinus in the lip, as in that genus. It differs from the type of Sowerby's genus Euomphalus (*E. pentangulatus*), as well as from the other typical species of that group with a more prominent spire, in having its whorls flattened or broadly concave around the outer side, and flattened with an outward slope above. It is also a much more ponderous shell, with a more oblique outline to its lip, in consequence of which it projects much farther forward on the upper than the lower side of the aperture. It also seems to have differed in having its peritreme scarcely continuous, or, at any rate, very thin on the side connecting with the preceding whorl.

I have some doubts in regard to the propriety of placing such shells in the same genus with *Euomphalus pentangulatus;* but do so from deference to the opinions of various authors, who insist upon making Sowerby's genus include a wide diversity of forms. It may be regarded as the type of a group for which I propose the name *Omphalotrochus*, including *O. antiquus*=*Solarium antiquum*, d'Orbigny, from the carboniferous rocks of Bolivia. (Voyage dans l'Amérique Mérid., p. 42, pl. 3, figs. 1, 3.)

The identity of Montfort's genus *Straparollus* with *Euomphalus*, Sowerby, would seem to be very questionable, if any reliance can be placed upon Montfort's figure and description of the type of his genus (*Straparollus Dionysii*). If they are congeneric, however, Montfort's name will have to take precedence, as it has priority of date; and the group to which our shell belongs would then stand as a subgenus under it, with the name of the type written *Straparollus* (*Omphalotrochus*) *Whitneyi.*

The specific name of this fine shell is given in honor of Prof. J. D. Whitney, State Geologist of California.

PALÆONTOLOGY OF CALIFORNIA.

VOL. I.

SECTION II.

DESCRIPTION OF THE TRIASSIC FOSSILS OF CALIFORNIA AND THE ADJACENT TERRITORIES.

BY W. M. GABB.

I am indebted to Mr. Meek, of Washington, to whom I sent sketches of some of these fossils, for comparing them with the works of European authors on the Trias, to which I could not at that time have access in California. Since then, I have been enabled to verify most of his opinions by reference to the fine monographs of Hauer. W. M. G.

ORTHOCERATITES, Breynius.

O. BLAKEI, n. s.

Pl. 3, Fig. 1.

SHELL slender, conical; apical angle in young specimens, 11°; diminishing as the animal increases in size, so that, in a fragment .7 inch in diameter, the sides are almost parallel. Septa placed at two-fifths the diameter of the shell apart. Siphon small, central. Surface plain.

There are no marked characters by which this species can be well distinguished. All the specimens are small. The figures are natural size.

Locality: Buena Vista District, Humboldt Mining Region. Collected by Gorham Blake, Esq., in honor of whom the species is named.

NAUTILUS, Breyn.

N. WHITNEYI, n. s.

Pl. 3, Figs. 2, 3.

SHELL moderate in size; last volution expanding somewhat rapidly towards the aperture, enveloping about two-thirds of the preceding whorl. Sides flat, converging towards the dorsum, and gradually rounding into it. Dorsum slightly arched. Umbilicus large, being nearly one-third the diameter of the whole disk; the umbilical margin slopes outwards and unites with the surface of the shell by a rounded angle. Septa deeply arched on the sides; separated from each other by about one-third the width of the volution. Surface marked by fine lines, which arise in the umbilicus; curve slightly backwards and then forwards on the side, and, as they pass over the angle between the side and back, again curve backwards, making a deep sinus on the dorsum.

This shell is allied in form to *N. bidorsatus*, Schlot. The sides are, in the present species, more strongly inclined towards each other; and the dorsum is convex, instead of being excavated. The umbilicus also is smaller.

Locality: With the preceding species.

N. MULTICAMERATUS, n. s.

Pl. 3, Figs. 4, 5.

SHELL broad, subglobose; whorls deeply embracing; sides compressed and rapidly converging; dorsum broadly grooved; umbilicus apparently quite small, partially obliterated in the specimen. Septa numerous, crowded, arching forwards on the sides, and curving slightly backwards on the back. Siphuncle unusually large. Surface marked by revolving, somewhat irregular elevated lines.

Figure, natural size.

Locality: A single specimen was found by Mr. R. Homfray at "Dun Glen," near the Auld Lang Syne Mine, Sierra District, Humboldt County, Nevada Territory.

GONIATITES, De Haan.

(? AGANIDES, Montf.*)

G. LÆVIDORSATUS, Hauer, sp.

Pl. 3, Figs. 6, 7.

(*Ammonites Id.*, Hauer; Sitzungsber. K. Akad. Wien, 1860. Pl. 3, figs. 9, 10 *b.*)

SHELL discoidal, whorls many; increasing very gradually in size; each volution enveloping about one-fourth of the preceding one. Umbilicus broad and shallow. Aperture sub-elliptical; sides sometimes nearly straight, emarginate on the ventral side. Surface sometimes plain, sometimes strongly ribbed. When the ribs are present, they arise on the margin of the umbilicus, and arch forwards as they approach the dorsum; but always become obsolete before reaching it.

They present every variety, from sharp, prominent ribs, to almost obsolete undulations, usually being more closely placed in proportion to their distinctness.

Septum composed of a dorsal and two lateral lobes, which, with their saddles, are all mere rounded undulations. Hauer, when he described this species, had not seen the septum.

Dimensions: Diameter across the body whorl, 1.05 inch. Width of body whorl, .32 inch. Width of aperture, .25 inch.

These measurements are from the specimen figured. It possesses five volutions. Another specimen, 1.75 inch in diameter, has eight whorls. The specimen figured differs somewhat from Hauer's figure in the transverse diameter of the whorls; but still greater differences exist between specimens found at our locality, both in this respect and in the prominence and distance between the ribs. Prof. Whitney collected in El Dorado Cañon, near Dayton, Washoe, a species which may be

---

* It is doubtful whether this name should be accepted. The description given by Montfort was so indefinite that it might be applied with equal or even greater propriety to the genus *Clymenia*. I prefer, therefore, to adopt the name given by the first author, who characterized the genus properly; especially since, with the exception of d'Orbigny, all subsequent authors have given it their sanction.

referred to the present one,—some specimens of which must have been a foot in diameter. From their state of preservation, however, it is impossible to decide on their identity, since they only occur as indistinct impressions on slate. Dr. Horn has more recently sent me a specimen, undoubtedly belonging to this species, found opposite the military station in Owen's Valley, Tulare County, California, about thirteen miles north of Owen's Lake, in the foot-hills on the east side of the valley.

CERATITES, De Haan.

C. Haidingerii.

Pl. 5, Figs. 8 and 10; and Pl. 4, Fig. 9.

(*Goniatites Haidingerii*, Hauer, Naturwiss., p. 264, Pl. 8, figs. 9-11.)

Shell compressed, lenticular. In the young state, the whorls entirely enveloping each preceding one; sides slightly arched, converging towards the dorsum, and then suddenly rounding towards it. Dorsum acutely carinate. Umbilicus very small. Aperture emarginate for nearly half its length. Septum, in a specimen about an inch in its greatest diameter, composed of a dorsal and seven lateral lobes.

More advanced individuals show a strong modification of these characters. In one, having the last whorl with a width of two and a quarter inches, the sides appear to be flatter, the umbilicus is proportionally larger, exhibiting a portion of some of the inner volutions, the dorsum has lost its central ridge, and becomes strongly bicarinate, and the lateral lobes of the septum are double in number those of the small specimen figured.

The septum consists, as remarked above, of a variable number of lobes and saddles. The saddles are simply rounded, though sometimes irregular; the larger lobes end abruptly, are deeply notched in the middle, and have one or two teeth on each side of the notch. In young specimens, the lobes nearest the dorsal margin are longest and widest, and show the denticulate termination most strongly. In the largest specimens examined, the lobes occupying the same position are a little the largest, but are very narrow, as are also their corresponding saddles. Their lower extremities are notched, but not dentate. Dorsal lobe unknown.

Locality: Humboldt Mining Region, Nevada Territory.

C. Whitneyi, n. s.

Pl. 4, Figs. 11, 12, 13.

Shell of moderate size; whorls five, enveloping about one-half. Surface of the whorls flattened on the sides for about two-thirds of their width, the dorsal third being inclined inwards. Dorsum grooved by a rounded channel, sometimes deep, at others nearly flat. Umbilical margin of the whorls abruptly truncated. Umbilicus broad and shallow; not quite a third of the greatest diameter of the shell. Sides ornamented by a variable number of arching ribs, which pass from the edge of the umbilical cavity to the margin of the dorsal groove. These ribs are sometimes dichotomous and bear a variable number of nodes. The largest number is four rows. They are placed, one row at the origin of the ribs, at the edge of the umbilicus; another row at the dorsal margin; a third on the middle of the whorl, at the point where the ribs bifurcate; the fourth row is placed between the last two. The two marginal rows are most constant, although sometimes only the dorsal row remains. The number of ribs is also variable, some specimens bearing twice as many as others of the same size. Occasionally numerous supplementary ribs occur; while in some specimens they are nearly or entirely absent.

Septum: Dorsal lobe divided at the end into two small, converging points, by a regularly rounded emargination; dorsal saddle wider than the lobe and simply curved; superior lateral lobe terminating in three small tooth-like processes, with an additional one on each side above. Remainder of the septum unknown. The part figured extends about half the width of the whorl. It is taken from a specimen one and a quarter inches in diameter. The figures of the shells illustrate the most marked forms of this somewhat variable species.

Named after Prof. J. D. Whitney, State Geologist of California.

AMMONITES, Brug.

A. Blakei, n. s.

Pl. 4, Figs. 14, 15.

Shell discoidal, compressed. Whorls five or six, truncated somewhat abruptly on the umbilical margin, usually flattened on the sides, rounded towards the dorsum, which is sometimes carinate, sometimes rounded. Body whorl enveloping about three-fourths of the preceding one. Umbilicus deep. Surface sometimes plain, or merely undulated; at other times, it is marked by numerous ribs, which cross the sides, arching forwards from the margin of the umbilicus to near the dorsum, where they generally become obsolete. These ribs sometimes commence with a strongly marked tubercle, although they are usually plain. There are also usually supplementary ribs at irregular intervals. These ribs arise in the middle or towards the ventral side of the whorl; and, at a short distance from their origin, become as large as the primary ribs.

Septum: Dorsal lobe divided, at the extremity, into two short branches, each ending in three teeth; above these branches are two notches on the side of the lobe; dorsal saddle about as wide as the lobe, and marked by three shallow notches; superior lateral lobe a third larger than the dorsal, bifurcate at the end and toothed at the sides; lateral saddle like the dorsal; inferior lateral lobe smaller than the dorsal, with two processes at the end and one on each side. Besides these there are two supplementary lobes and saddles much smaller than those described. Diameter, 1.85 inch. Width of body whorl, .85 inch. Width of mouth, .55 inch.

A specimen was collected by Mr. R. Homfray, near Star City, Humboldt, six inches in diameter, and with a row of large nodes on the middle of the whorl, from which the ribs bifurcated.

This shell is closely allied to *A. scaphitiformis*, Hauer; but the umbilicus seems to be larger; and the septum, which is of the same general style, is much more complex, especially in the dorsal and superior lateral lobes.

A. AUSSEANUS, Hauer.

Plate 3, Figs. 16 and 17.

SHELL subglobose; whorls deeply enveloping, increasing very gradually in size. Umbilicus small, profound. Surface smooth or striate by indistinct lines of growth. Cast marked at intervals of one-fourth of a volution by a deep groove, caused by a thickening of the shell. These constrictions bend slightly backwards at their origin, near the umbilicus, then arch forward on the side of the whorl and pass straight across, or curve a little backwards again on crossing the dorsum. This last character is not always constant. I have seen several specimens where it was entirely absent, and others in which it is but faintly exhibited. Aperture compressed crescentic, very deeply emarginate.

Septum: Dorsal lobe divided for half its length into two branches, each of which is subdivided into three smaller ones; two smaller spurs above the branches; dorsal saddle about as wide as the lobe, and trilobate at the end; superior lateral lobe divided into three branches at the end, with two above on each side, all variously toothed; superior lateral saddle like the dorsal saddle; lateral lobe like the preceding one, except that it has but two terminal branches, each of which is bifurcate; lateral saddle like the others, but smaller; inferior lateral lobe like the superior lateral, only differing in being smaller. There are, besides these, two smaller lobes and saddles.

Dimensions: Diameter, 2.45 inches. Height of aperture at the dorsum, .55 inch. Width of aperture, 1.5 inch.

This shell is so nearly like Hauer's figure that I have referred it to the same species. It is more compressed laterally, and there seems to be a little difference in the lateral lobes of the two forms; but these points are not of enough importance to warrant a separation.

A. Homfrayi, n. s.

Pl. 4, Figs. 18, 19.

Shell small, discoidal, deeply embracing; sides flattened, curving inwards towards the dorsal margin; umbilicus small, less than a fourth of the diameter of the shell; margin angular; dorsum bicarinate, channelled between the carinæ. Surface ornamented by numerous flexuous ribs, arising on the margin of the umbilicus, and crossing the sides in three broad curves, bending abruptly forwards when near the dorsum, and ending on the dorsal carina, which presents an undulated or tuberculated appearance. These ribs bear a variable number of rows of tubercles, the most constant of which are those nearest the dorsum and on the umbilical margin. Septum composed of a dorsal and three lateral lobes. The dorsal lobe is divided for about a third of its length, each branch bearing a couple of spurs, and with three or four simple tooth-like processes above; dorsal saddle narrow above and slightly notched at the end; superior lateral lobe broad above, narrow below, trifid at the extremity, and with three or four spurs above; lateral saddle shaped almost like two sides of an equilateral triangle, and slightly notched along the sides; inferior lateral lobe half the size of the superior lateral, with three irregular spurs at the end, and slightly toothed above; supplementary lobe much smaller, but nearly a miniature of the last.

Figures, natural size. Fig. *b*, septum.

Locality: E. Range, Humboldt, Nevada Territory. Collected by Mr. Richard Homfray, to whom the species is dedicated.

Some specimens, from the same locality, smaller than the one figured, are more convex on the sides, and with the ribs proportionally a little larger and less numerous; and with several rows of tubercles, in a few cases nearly as prominent as the ribs themselves.

A. Billingsianus, n. s.

Pl. 5, Fig. 20.

Discoidal, subcompressed; sides flattened, converging towards the dorsum, which is regularly rounded; umbilicus about a third of the diameter of the shell; margin rounded; whorls increasing very gradually in size in the young shell, afterwards more rapidly; aperture subcordate; surface plain; septum composed of a dorsal and two lateral lobes. From the condition of the specimens, I have not been able to obtain the details; but the lobes appear to be quite complex, with a tendency to throw out long slender spurs.

Figure, natural size; fig. *a*, section of the body whorl.

Locality: With the preceding. Collected by Mr. Homfray.

Named in honor of Mr. E. Billings, of the Geological Survey of Canada.

A. Ramsaueri? Quenst.

Pl. 3, Fig. 21, 21 *a*.

(*A. Ramsaueri*, Q. Hauer; Die Cephalopoden des Salzkammergutes, p. 22, pl. 8, figs. 1, 6.)

Two or three imperfect specimens of this Ammonite were found by Messrs. Brewer and King at Gifford's Ranch, Plumas County, the most perfect of which is figured. They agree in all external characters with figures 5 and 6 above quoted; and, in the absence of proof to the contrary, I have referred them to Quenstedt's species. The peculiar, irregularly placed, nodose ribs, the minute umbilicus, and the evidently subglobose form of the shell before distortion, forbid a separation; unless larger specimens should want the angle which forms on the dorsum of adults of the European form; or some difference should be detected in the septum.

Two or three fragments, showing merely a portion of the side of one volution, collected by Mr. Homfray, associated with *A. Homfrayi* and *A. Billingsianus*, should probably be referred to this species.

The identification of this shell—*A. Ausseanus*—and one or two other species, with known European forms, together with the close resemblance of others to their European congeners, as well as the great similarity of type between nearly all of the forms in the American and European deposits, point at once to a nearly, if not perfectly, complete synchronism between the Trias of the Sierra Nevada and that of the Alps.

MYACITES. Schlot.

M. (PANOPŒA ?) HUMBOLDTENSIS, n. s.

Pl. 5, Fig. 22.

SHELL equivalve (?), inequilateral; beak between a third and a fourth the length from the buccal end. Cardinal margin slightly elevated; posterior extremity broader than the anterior, and a little more regularly rounded. Surface marked by a few regular, prominent, rounded, concentric ribs. Length, 1.05 inch. Width from beak to base, .55 inch. Depth of valve, .1 inch.

This shell has only been found as internal casts. I refer it to Schlotheim's genus, *Myacites*, on the same grounds on which he founded the genus,—the external form. Later authors appear to doubt the validity of the genus. Be that as it may, it is very probable that among the antique forms, referred to the genus *Panopœa*, and of which the hinges have not been discovered, we may find not only one, but several distinct generic divisions.

Collected by G. Blake, in the Buena Vista District, Humboldt Mining Region, Nevada Territory.

PANOPŒA, Menard de la Groye.

? P. RÉMONDII, n. s.

Pl. 5, Fig. 23.

SHELL subelliptical, oblique, thin; beaks subcentral, prominent; anterior end rounded; posterior sometimes produced, sometimes regular; most prominent towards the base. Surface marked by concentric undulations and fine lines.

Figure, natural size.

Locality: From San Marcial, Sonora, Mexico. Collected by Mr. Rémond. Associated with two or three other bivalves, one apparently a Cardium, too imperfect for description. In the same formation were found fragments of fossil plants, probably Triassic.

CORBULA, Brug.

C. Blakei, n. s.

Pl. 5, Fig. 24.

Shell (right valve) subquadrate, convex; beak nearly central; umbone large, prominent. Anterior margin regularly rounded; posterior abruptly truncated. Umbonal ridge angular, distinct. Posterior to this ridge the surface slopes at an abrupt angle to the margin of the shell. Surface ornamented by irregular concentric lines. Length, .46 inch. Width from beak to base, .3 inch. Depth of valve, .12 inch.

A single specimen only has been found. Collected by Mr. G. Blake in the Humboldt Mining Region.

MYTILUS, Linn.

M. Homfrayi, n. s.

Pl. 6, Fig. 25.

Shell thick, oblique, convex; cardinal margin arched, posterior end convexly and obliquely truncated, anterior margin very slightly convex. Surface marked only by lines of growth.

Figure, natural size.

Locality: Two specimens from Dun Glen, Sierra District, Humboldt County, Nevada Territory, associated with *Nautilus multicameratus*. Collected by Mr. Homfray.

This shell belongs to the type of *M. vetustus*, Goldf., of the Muschelkalk, but is sufficiently distinguished by its outline, being longer, more slender and more oblique. It is also somewhat less convex than that species.

AVICULA, Klein, Lam.

A. Homfrayi, n. s.

Pl. 6, Fig. 26.

Shell trigonal, oblique; left valve convex, right valve unknown. Cardinal and posterior margins nearly straight, uniting by an obtuse angle; basal margin regularly rounded; anterior sinuous. Surface convex below, excavated towards the posterior wing; marked only by lines of growth. Anterior wing unknown.

Figure, natural size.

Locality: Star District, Humboldt County, Nevada Territory. Collected by Mr. Homfray.

A. MUCRONATA, n. s.

Pl. 5, Fig. 27.

SHELL small, compressed, oblique; beaks central; anterior basal margin rounded, obliquely truncated; posterior prominent; anterior ear unknown; posterior broad at the base, emarginate below, and produced at the extremity in the form of a slender spine-like process. Surface marked by fine, irregular, linear, radiating ribs, crossed by a few lines of growth.

Figure, natural size.

Locality: Gifford's Ranch, Plumas County.

HALOBIA, Bronn.

? H. DUBIA, n. s.

Pl. 5, Fig. 28, *a*, *b*.

SHELL equivalve, slightly oblique, very much compressed. Beak small, hardly projecting beyond the hinge margin; nearly (if not exactly) central. Cardinal margin straight. Surface marked by irregular, straight, or waved radiating ribs. These ribs are marked by fine impressed lines, one of which occasionally becomes deeper than the others, thereby causing a bifurcation. The spaces between the ribs are deep, and rarely more than half as wide as the ribs themselves. In most specimens the surface is crossed by oblique concentric undulations, as in some species of *Leptæna*.

The close resemblance of this shell to the genus *Orthis* is sufficient to throw some doubt on its correct generic determination. I have examined a large suite of specimens, and have not been able to detect any trace of an area: this fact, together with the resemblance of the outline, taken from the striæ of growth, to *Halobia Lomellii* of the Saint Cassian formation, renders it probable that they are generically related, especially when we take into consideration their geological relation.

Fig. *a*, represents the inside of a fragment of a valve, the largest specimen collected. Fig. *b*, is from the surface of one of the most perfect specimens. *c*, is a magnified view of the ribs.

Localities: Star Cañon, Buena Vista District, Nevada Territory, and Gifford's Ranch, Plumas County, California.

MONOTIS, Bronn.

M. SUBCIRCULARIS, n. s.

Pl. 6, Figs. 29, 29 *a*.

SHELL flattened, subcircular, produced behind; beaks placed between the middle and anterior end; anterior, basal and posterior margins forming nearly a perfect semicircle; the anterior margin curving regularly inwards, above, to the beaks. Wing short, broad, and obliquely truncated behind. Surface marked by from forty to fifty irregular, radiating ribs, alternating in size, and crossed by fine, squamose, concentric lines.

Figures, natural size, and a magnified view of the surface.

Locality: Gifford's Ranch, Plumas County, California; collected by Prof. Brewer; and Star District, Humboldt County, Nevada Territory, by Mr. Homfray.

This shell is very closely allied to *M. salinaria*, Bronn; but differs from that species, as figured by Goldfuss, in being less oblique, more prominent below, less produced behind; in the anterior end being regularly rounded above, instead of bearing a small angle, and in the ear being shorter and broader. The number of ribs is about the same, and they resemble each other in their being irregularly undulated and alternating, as well as in the cross striæ. The most obvious difference is in the rounded upper end of the anterior margin of this species, instead of the very distinct angle of *M. salinaria*, almost amounting to a second ear.

RHYNCHOPTERUS, N. Gen.

AVICULOID, hinge straight, no area; with a small acute ear anteriorly, posterior side not alate, rounding upwards and inward to the cardinal margin.

This genus bears almost the same external relation to *Avicula*, on one side, that *Monotis* does on the other. None of the specimens show more of the hinge than that it is straight and slightly thickened.

R. obesus, n. s.

Pl. 5, Fig. 30, *a*, *b*.

Shell oblique, very convex. Umbones prominent, placed at the centre of the cardinal line. Hinge straight, ear acuminate, small; posterior margin broadly and regularly convex. Anterior margin sinuous. Surface marked by irregular lines of growth, and occasionally by obsolete concentric undulations.

Figures, natural size.

Locality: Rattlesnake Point, near Humboldt City, Nevada Territory.

POSIDONOMYA, Bronn.

P. stella, n. s.

Pl. 6, Fig. 31.

Shell subcircular, convex, inequilateral; beaks prominent, anterior. Cardinal margin rounded in advance, straight and slightly sloping posteriorly, and uniting with the anal margin by a curve. Surface smooth, or marked by a few regular, concentric, rounded ribs.

Length, .9 inch; width, .75 inch; depth of valve, .18 inch.

Locality: Star Cañon, Humboldt Mining Region.

P. Daytonensis, n. s.

Pl. 6, Fig. 32.

Shell flattened, oblique; beak small, not prominent. Cardinal line straight, shorter than the greatest length of the shell. Buccal margin excavated below the hinge-line, convex below, merging insensibly into the base. Anal margin convex below, nearly straight above, and inclined inwards to meet the hinge-line. Surface depressed, marked on the cast by a few faint concentric undulations. Length, .3 inch from anterior to posterior extremities. Width, .28 inch. Smaller and more oblique than the preceding species: the central position of the beak and the straight hinge-line will serve at once to distinguish this little shell.

Width, .25 inch; length, .2 inch.

Locality: El Dorado Cañon, Nevada Territory, near Dayton.

Collected by Prof. Whitney. Probably of the same age as the preceding species.

MYOPHORIA, Bronn.

M. ALTA, n. s.

Pl. 6, Fig. 33.

SHELL small, inequilateral, higher than wide, abruptly truncated posteriorly; anterior end and base broadly rounded; beaks central, approximate, curved anteriorly; umbonal ridge acute, with a slight depression immediately in advance; surface posterior to this ridge abruptly descending to the posterior margin, and with a few radiating lines; anterior to it, the surface is marked only by faint concentric lines.

Figure, twice natural size.

Locality: Dun Glen, Sierra District, Humboldt County, Nevada Territory.

A single imperfect specimen, collected by Prof. Brewer, at Gifford's Ranch, Plumas County, has most of the characters of this species, and is about the size of the figure; but differs in having the beak more strongly curved forwards, and in the anterior margin being more prominent. These differences may be the result of the difference of age in the two specimens.

PECTEN, Linn.

P. DEFORMIS, n. s.

Pl. 6, Fig. 34.

SHELL small, thin, compressed, inequilateral, base oblique, ends subequal; sides sloping with a slight convexity from the apex; ears subequal, moderate in size. Surface marked by about twenty-five irregular, rather large, radiating ribs, a few of which arise at some distance from the beaks. These are crossed by very fine concentric lines.

Figure, nearly three times natural size.

Locality: A single specimen from Gifford's Ranch, Plumas County, California, associated with *Ammonites Ramsaueri, Monotis subcircularis,* &c.

TEREBRATULA, Lwyd, Auct.

T. Humboldtensis, n. s.

Pl. 6, Fig. 35, and 35 *a, b.*

Shell oval, elongate, smooth, sides regularly curved; base broadly truncated; lower valve, beaks prominent, incurved; base with a broad, rounded sulcus; upper valve rounded above, slightly elevated in the middle, below.

Figures, natural size. All of the specimens are so much distorted that their true outline is almost entirely destroyed. No two specimens are of the same shape, although the one figured appears to be nearly, if not quite, of the normal form.

Locality: Abundant in Star Cañon, Humboldt County, Nevada Territory. Collected by Mr. Homfray.

RHYNCHONELLA, D'Orb.

R. lingulata, n. s.

Pl. 6, Fig. 36, and 36 *a, b.*

Shell plicate, ventricose, sides sloping above, convex below, base subtruncated ; lower valve with three median ribs and three lateral ones on each side; base sulcate and prolonged into a long tongue-like process, edge serrate; upper valve with four median ribs, elevated above the general contour of the shell, and three lateral ones alternating with those of the opposite valve.

Figures, natural size.

Locality: With the preceding species.

Although this shell is also distorted, yet it retains much more completely its normal form than the Terebratula described above.

R. ÆQUIPLICATA, *n. s.*

Pl. 6, Fig. 37, and 37 *a*, *b*.

SHELL subglobose, convexity of the two valves equal. Beak large, prominent, incurved, sides sloping convexly to the ends of the hinge-line, beyond which they converge very gradually and merge into the nearly straight basal margin. Surface marked by fourteen nearly equal rounded ribs, which commence on the upper valve at about one-third of the distance from the hinge, and on the lower valve at a point opposite to the hinge. The two lateral ribs on each side are oblique, and end abruptly anteriorly, but are flat posteriorly. Between the rest are regular rounded grooves of about the same size as the ribs themselves. No median sinus. The four middle ribs extend a little further into the smooth part of the surface, but differ in no other respect from the adjoining ones. No surface markings have been detected.

Length, 1.1 inch. Width, 1. inch. Thickness, .85 inch.

From the "Cinnabar District," in the range east of the Humboldt Mountains. Collected by Gorham Blake, Esq.

SPIRIFER, Sow.

S. HOMFRAYI, n. s.

Pl. 6, Fig. 38.

SHELL long, narrow, ends rounded, most prominent below the hinge-line. Upper valve with a broad, regularly concave, median sinus, and six curved, subangular ribs on each side. Lower valve with a broad rib, corresponding to the sinus in the opposite valve, and five lateral ones. Area broad, shorter than the length of the shell. Beaks mutilated.

Figure, very slightly magnified.

Locality: A single distorted specimen found by Mr. Homfray in Star Cañon, Humboldt County, Nevada Territory, near his mill, associated with *Terebratula Humboldtensis* and *Rhynchonella lingulata.*

PALÆONTOLOGY OF CALIFORNIA.

VOL. I.

SECTION III.

DESCRIPTION OF THE JURASSIC FOSSILS.

BY F. B. MEEK.

CLASS BRACHIOPODA.

FAMILY RHYNCHONELLIDÆ.

Genus RHYNCHONELLA, Fischer, 1809.

Rhynchonella gnathophora, Meek.

Plate 8, Fig. 1, and 1 *a, b, c, d, e, f.*

Shell of medium size, subtrigonal or suborbicular, generally rather compressed, but sometimes gibbous in adult specimens; the greatest convexity being near the middle. Postero-lateral margins straight and diverging from the beaks at an angle of from eighty to one hundred degrees. Dorsal valve usually more convex than the other, particularly towards the front, where it rises into a low, rounded, mesial prominence, rarely traceable more than half-way back towards the incurved beak. Ventral valve with a moderately deep mesial sinus, occupying about half its entire breadth at the front, but narrowing and becoming more shallow as it recedes, so as to die out near, or a little beyond, the middle. Beak pointed, rather prominent, and moderately arched. Surface of each valve ornamented by sixteen to twenty simple, rounded, or subangular, radiating plications; three to four of which occupy the sinus of the ventral valve, and four to five the corresponding prominence of the dorsal valve.

Length (of a rather narrow specimen), 0.80 inch; breadth of do., 0.72 inch; convexity, 0.44 inch. Length (of wide compressed example), 0.76 inch; breadth, 0.83 inch; convexity, 0.36 inch. Convexity of a gibbous specimen, measuring 0.86 inch in breadth, 0.57.

None of the specimens of this species in the collection are in a condition to show the foramen, or fine surface striæ. They give a very clear idea, however, of all the other external characters, in which it appears not to vary greatly. It is evidently allied, judging from Mr. Davidson's excellent figures and description, to a shell from the Inferior Oolite, referred by him with doubt to *R. lacunosa*, Schlotheim, sp. I have not access to the figures of *R. lacunosa*, published by Schlotheim, or Von Buch; but on comparing our California species with those given by Mr. Davidson, it will be found that the latter represent a shell with more angular plications, and a less pointed and more incurved beak. They also represent the flattened space on each side the beak of the ventral valve, between the umbonal angles and cardinal margin, as being wider, and the umbonal angles more defined; while the front, as seen in a side view, is much less obliquely truncated.

Still it is by no means improbable our shell may prove to be identical with some of the forms referred to *R. lacunosa;* but until palæontologists have determined more clearly the limits of that species, and agree in regard to which of the several types, evidently included in it by some, is to retain the name, we shall probably be less liable to err, in distinguishing the form under consideration by another name, than if we were to identify it with Schlotheim's species.

It seems to be the most abundant species in the rock, and the specimens are generally little distorted.

FAMILY TEREBRATULIDÆ.

GENUS TEREBRATULA, Müller, 1776.

TEREBRATULA ———.

Pl. 8, Fig. 2, and 2 *a*, *b*.

SHELL subovate, gibbous, greatest convexity at or a little behind the middle; front faintly sinuous on each side of the slightly truncated middle. Ventral valve much more convex than the other posteriorly; forming a regular semi-ovate curve from near the beak to the front, where there is no mesial sinus, but sometimes an exceedingly faint longitudinal furrow on each side, corresponding to slight elevations in the other valve; anterior margin a little produced, so as to fill a shallow flattened recess in the edge of the other valve. Umbo gibbous, and rounding in on each side without defined lateral angles (point of the beak, in the only undistorted specimen in the collection, broken away). Dorsal valve less gibbous, and much shorter than the other, owing to the prominence and convexity of the umbo of the latter; forming a regular gentle arch from the beak to the front, where there is a low flattened mesial prominence, with a slight concavity on each side of it. Surface with moderately distinct concentric marks of growth.

Length, about 1.45 inch; breadth, 1 inch; convexity, 0.85 inch.

This shell bears considerable general resemblance to some varieties of *T. perovalis*, Sowerby; but is proportionally narrower, and has the umbo of the ventral valve much more gibbous, and more prominent, as well as less angular on each side. It would be idle, however, in a genus like this, to pretend to identify a species, from two or three mutilated and distorted specimens, with any known form; nor is it desirable, under such circumstances, to name it as a new species. It is more than probable, however, that it will prove to be new when a good series of specimens can be examined.

LAMELLIBRANCHIATA.

FAMILY OSTREIDÆ.

GENUS GRYPHÆA, Lamarck, 1801.

GRYPHÆA ———.

Pl. 8, Fig. 4, and 4 *a*.

SHELL thin, rather under medium size, varying from subovate to suborbicular. Under valve moderately deep, generally more or less lobed on the anterior side; beak not prominent, scarcely rising above the hinge. Upper valve flat, or slightly concave; beak not truncated. Surface of both valves apparently with only moderately distinct concentric marks of growth.

Length, about 1.68 inch; breadth generally less; convexity, about 0.45 inch.

The specimens of this *Gryphæa*, in the collection, are too imperfect to admit of a sufficiently satisfactory comparison with known species to determine whether or not it is new. So far as can be made out, from the imperfect specimens at hand, it seems to present somewhat the form of *G. vesicularis;* but is considerably smaller than the average size of that species, and more narrowed towards the beaks. It also differs in having the beak of the upper valve not truncated, but angular and curved a little to the left side. It seems to be more nearly allied to some Jurassic forms than to *G. vesicularis*.

FAMILY LIMIDÆ.

GENUS LIMA, Bruguière, 1792.

LIMA ? SINUATA, Meek.

Pl. 7, Fig. 4, and 4 *a*.

SHELL (left valve) broad, suborbicular; compressed and rounded in outline behind; moderately convex anteriorly; basal margin rounded; anterior side sinuous and distinctly gaping above, prominent and narrowly rounded below. Surface ornamented by from ten to twelve distinct radiating costæ, one-half to one-third as wide (at the border) as the depressions between. Costæ simple, extending to the beak, and more or less roughened or subnodose from the crossing of the concentric wrinkles of growth. (Ears and point of the beak unknown.)

Diameter, from the hinge to the ventral margin, 3.10 inches; antero-posterior diameter, 3.35 inches; convexity (left valve only), about 0.60 inch.

The foregoing description was drawn up from a cast of a left valve, with some remaining fragments of the shell attached, but not in a condition to show the finer surface-markings or ears. Indeed, until better specimens can be collected for examination, its generic relations must remain doubtful. In the forward curvature and attenuated character of the beak, it presents much the appearance of the curious Jurassic genus *Trichites*. The absence, however, of any traces of the prismatic shell-structure of that genus, if not due to metamorphic agencies, would alone exclude it from that group. In addition to this, it presents unquestionable evidences of having the anterior side distinctly gaping, as seen at *g*, in the profile, figure 4 *a*, plate 7; while in *Trichites* the valves are said to be closed all around. I suspect it will be found to present characters that will require for its reception the establishment of a new genus.

LIMA RECTICOSTATA, Meek.

Pl. 7, Fig. 5.

THE only specimen of this fossil in the collection is a cast of a right valve with the margin of the anterior side broken away. I was at first inclined to think it might be the right valve of the last-described species; but, on a more careful comparison, it was found to differ so materially in form, the straightness of its costæ, &c., as to lead to the conclusion that it can scarcely be the right valve of that shell, unless it belongs to an undescribed genus. Hence it has been thought better to view it, provisionally, as a distinct species.

It is much compressed, and presents a rhombic-oblong outline, as seen with a portion of the anterior margin broken away; the length being considerably less than the diameter from the hinge to the ventral margin. Its hinge-line is rather short, and ranges at right angles to the longer diameter of the shell. No remains of ears are visible, the posterior margin rounding apparently into the hinge-margin above. The beak is located anteriorly, and surface ornamented by eleven simple, straight costæ, which radiate backwards and downwards from the beak. The costæ are rather prominent, a little narrower than the depressions between, and present (in the cast) a roughened, irregularly subnodulose appearance, produced by concentric markings, which are also visible in the depressions between the ribs.

LIMA? CUNEATA, Meek.

Pl. 7, Fig. 6, and 6 *a*.

SHELL (right valve) obliquely subtrigonal, or suborbicular; moderately convex, particularly in the central and posterior regions, but cuneate anteriorly; posterior side obliquely truncated? anterior margin concave in outline above, where it is truncated obliquely forward and downward, to near the prominent middle, from which point it rounds into the rounded base; posterior umbonal slope prominent, and very distinct from the flattened ear above, in consequence of the abrupt inflection of the truncated posterior side. Beaks curving forward. (Hinge and ears unknown.) Surface ornamented with about twelve to fourteen strong, simple, obtuse, radiating plications, which are rather wider than the furrows between, and all curve regularly forward as they approach the beak; those on the anterior side descend from the beaks with an oblique forward curve. (Finer surface-markings unknown.)

Diameter from the beaks to the most prominent part of the ventral margin, about 2 inches; antero-posterior diameter, about the same; convexity (of right valve), 0.46 inch.

The only specimen of this shell in the collection is a right valve, which has the point of the beak, both ears (if there were two), and some of the posterior margin broken away. Hence it is with considerable doubt that I have ventured to refer it to this genus; and it is quite probable the above description may be found to require modification, when entire specimens can be obtained. Its most marked peculiarities, supposing it to be a true *Lima*, are the forward curvature of its beaks and costæ, and the prominence of its posterior umbonal slopes.

These characters, together with the strong radiating costæ, give the shell much the aspect of some types of *Cardita*, to which genus I should have been inclined to refer it, provisionally, were it not for the fact that it shows unmistakable remains of a flattened ear behind the beak. The specimen is not in a condition to show the size or form of this ear; but it was evidently very flat, and separated from the prominent posterior umbonal slopes by an oblique sulcus, formed by the inflection of the truncated posterior side of the valves. The specimen gives no indications of an anterior gap, or of a defined lunule.

In some respects, this species resembles *L. striata* of Deshayes, and *L. radiata*, Goldfuss, from the Muschelkalk; but it differs from both in the anterior curvature of its beaks and costæ, as well as in its cuneate anterior side, prominent posterior umbonal slopes, and flattened posterior ear.

If we go back of the date of the binomial system of nomenclature established by Linnæus, in carrying out the law of priority, Klein's name *Radula* would have to be adopted for the genus *Lima*; and the names of this and the foregoing species would become *Radula sinuata*, *Radula cuneata*, and *Radula recticostata*. Or, if it is considered desirable to separate such fossil species from the typical Limas of more modern date, Sowerby's name *Plagiostoma* would have to be adopted, and the names would be *Plagiostoma sinuata*, *P. cuneata*, and *P. recticostata;* unless some of our shells, as elsewhere suggested, may constitute a new genus.

FAMILY PECTINIDÆ.

GENUS PECTEN, Müller, 1776.

PECTEN ACUTIPLICATUS, Meek.

Pl. 8, Fig. 3.

THE only specimen of this species in the collection consists of an impression of apparently a left valve, in the hard matrix. Owing to the fact that the ears are imperfect, it is very difficult to determine, beyond doubt, whether it is a left or a right valve, though the slight obliquity of the plications, and the appearance of the remaining portions of the ears, indicate that it is the former; while its very slight convexity goes rather against this conclusion. It may be characterized as follows:

Subovate, compressed, longer from the hinge to the ventral margin than the antero-posterior diameter; sides converging from near the middle to the beaks, at an angle of about 80°; ventral and ventro-lateral margins regularly rounded; ears flattened, anterior? one with two or three small radiating costæ, and the posterior with one rib near the hinge margin; both marked with fine striæ of growth. Body of the valve ornamented by fourteen to fifteen regular, simple, sharply elevated, angular, radiating plications, equalling in size the angular furrows between; crossing the whole are numerous very fine, crowded striæ of growth, which are deflected so as to follow a zigzag direction, as they pass over the plications and across the depressions between.

Diameter from the hinge to the ventral margin, 2.50 inches; antero-posterior diameter, 2.15 inches; convexity (left valve?), 0.35 inch.

This species belongs beyond doubt to the genus *Pecten*, as usually understood by most authors; but does not, however, belong to that genus, as properly restricted by Lamarck, in 1799, to such types as *P. jacobæus*, which must be regarded as the type of the genus. Having no means of knowing to which one of Prof. Agassiz's unpublished genera of *Pectenidæ* it belongs, it is placed here for the present in the genus *Pecten*.

FAMILY PTERIIDÆ.

GENUS INOCERAMUS, Sowerby, 1814.

INOCERAMUS? OBLIQUUS, Meek.

Pl. 7, Fig. 2, and 2 *a*.

SHELL small, (right valve) much compressed, obliquely sub-ovate, sub-mytiliform; beak attenuate, oblique and nearly or quite terminal; anterior side a little sinuous, and sloping backwards above, sloping and a little convex in outline below; postero-basal margin narrowly rounded; posterior margin nearly straight, ascending forward so as to intersect the short hinge at a very obtuse angle. Surface apparently nearly smooth, or with slight tracings of concentric markings.

Length from the point to the beak, obliquely to the posterior inferior margin, 1.14 inch; antero-posterior diameter, 0.68 inch; convexity of left valve, 0.07 inch.

Knowing nothing of the hinge of this little shell, nor of the nature of its left valve, it is with considerable doubt I have ventured to refer it provisionally to the genus *Inoceramus*. If it belongs to that group, it would fall into the section *Mytiloides* of Brongniart, unless the other valve is much more gibbous.

INOCERAMUS? RECTANGULUS, Meek.

Pl. 7, Fig. 1, and 1 *a*.

SHELL (right valve) oval-oblong, higher than wide, much compressed, anterior side straight, and almost vertically truncate above, rounding into the rounded base below; posterior side forming a broad semi-elliptic curve, rounding to the hinge above; hinge short, and ranging very nearly at right angles to the truncated anterior margin; beak placed directly over the anterior edge, not prominent, or projecting above the hinge-line. Surface with small, obscure, concentric wrinkles.

Height, 1.17 inch; breadth, 0.97 inch; convexity (of right valve only), 0.13 inch.

I am equally in doubt in regard to the generic relations of this species, having seen but a single specimen, which gives no idea of the nature of the hinge, or of the form of the opposite valve. It differs from the last in being less oblique, proportionally broader, and in having the beak less prominent, while its hinge ranges more nearly at right angles to the longer axis of the shell. It is replaced by a greenish choritic substance, showing no traces of the shell structure.

FAMILY TRIGONIIDÆ.

Genus TRIGONIA, Bruguière, 1789.

Trigonia pandicosta, Meek.

Pl. 8, Fig. 7.

Shell small, rhombic subquadrate? moderately convex; beaks prominent, oblique, and nearly terminal; anterior side very short, rounding obliquely backwards into the rather short, rounded base; posterior side comparatively broad, compressed, and nearly vertically truncated. Corselet wide, compressed, occupying nearly half the surface of each valve, only marked with distinct, regular thread-like lines of growth, separated from the flanks by a linear ridge extending from the back part of each beak, with a gentle curve, obliquely backwards and downwards to the postero-basal margin. Flanks and anterior side ornamented by six to eight costæ, which extend from the margin of the corselet, first obliquely backwards and downwards, after which they are deflected very abruptly forwards and upwards.

Length, about 0.55 inch; height, about 0.37 inch; convexity, 0.35 inch.

Of this little *Trigonia* there is but a single specimen in the collection, and it is so firmly embedded in the exceedingly hard matrix, that it is not possible to determine very exactly its outline, or as clearly as is desirable some of its other characters. Its costæ seem to be without nodes, but it is possible that better specimens might show them to be faintly nodose or crenate. It seems not to be very closely allied to any species with which I am acquainted.

There are in the collection fragments of apparently two other species of this genus. One of these is considerably larger than that described, and has the costæ distinctly nodose. They are, however, not angularly deflected, but curved gradually forward.

FAMILY MYTILIDÆ.

GENUS MYTILUS, Linnæus, 1758.

MYTILUS MULTISTRIATUS, Meek.

Pl. 7, Fig. 7, and 7 *a*.

SHELL narrow, subovate, arcuate, moderately convex; the greatest convexity near the middle, or between it and the beaks; antero-ventral margin sloping backwards from the beaks, and a little arched; postero-basal extremity rather narrowly rounded; dorsal margin moderately arcuate, and passing rather gradually into the sloping posterior border. Beaks curved a little, more or less obtusely pointed, and not compressed. Surface with fine regular radiating striæ.

Length from beaks to postero-basal margin, 1.23 inch; greatest diameter at right angles to the same (below the middle), 0.55 inch; convexity, 0.36 inch.

This species bears some resemblance to *Mytilus pectinatus* of Sowerby, from the Kimmeridge clay; but is less convex, and has less prominent anterior umbonal slopes, while its radiating striæ do not divaricate. Its beaks also appear to be more pointed, and its postero-basal margin is more rounded.

FAMILY CRASSATELLIDÆ.

GENUS ASTARTE, Sowerby, 1816.

ASTARTE VENTRICOSA, Meek.

Pl. 8, Fig. 5, and 5 *a*.

SHELL of medium size, suborbicular, gibbous; basal and lateral margins rounded; beaks moderately prominent, subcentral, or a little in advance of the middle, obtuse and rather tumid; lunule apparently rather large. Surface ornamented with regular, distinct, concentric ridges, about equalling the furrows between.

Length and height about 1 inch; convexity near 0.55 inch.

It is with some hesitation this species is placed in the genus *Astarte*, since the specimens do not show the muscular or pallial impressions, nor very satisfactorily the nature of the hinge; while it is a more gibbous shell than is common in that genus. One of the specimens, however, shows an imperfect impression of the hinge of a right valve, which, so far as can be determined, seems to be like that of *Astarte.*

There are several more or less analogous European Jurassic species; but none of them appear to be more closely allied to our shell than *A. elegans* of Sowerby, which is less convex, and differs in outline. Our shell also differs in having more convex beaks.

FAMILY LUCINIDÆ.

GENUS UNICARDIUM, D'Orbigny, 1852.

UNICARDIUM? GIBBOSUM, Meek.

Pl. 8, Fig. 8, and 8 *a*.

SHELL thin, rhombic-suborbicular, very gibbous; length somewhat greater than the height; greatest convexity a little above the middle; beaks nearly central, rather prominent and gibbous;

anterior side somewhat narrowly rounded; dorsal side sloping and concave in front of the beaks, declining with a slightly convex outline posteriorly from the beaks to the middle of the anal margin, which is subangular; postero-basal margin truncated obliquely forward and downward to a point a little behind the middle of the base; ventral margin rounding down from the front, and extending backwards with a slight descent to its intersection with the obliquely truncated postero-basal margin, at which point there is a slight angularity of outline. Each valve provided with an obscure posterior umbonal ridge, which descends with a gentle curve from behind the beak to the postero-basal angle. Surface with moderately distinct, irregular, concentric striæ.

Length, 1.62 inch; height, 1.45 inch; convexity, 1.10 inch.

As we know nothing of the hinge, or muscular and pallial impressions of this shell, its generic relations cannot be determined beyond doubt. From its thinness, however, and general appearance, we have been led to refer it provisionally to D'Orbigny's genus *Unicardium.* Its most marked characters are its posterior umbonal ridges, and truncated postero-basal margins. We are not acquainted with any closely allied species.

FAMILY ANATINIDÆ.

Genus MYACITES (Schlot.), Munster, 1840.

Myacites depressus, Meek.

Pl. 8, Fig. 6, and 6 *a.*

Shell rather small, depressed, narrow-subelliptic, moderately gibbous in the middle, and along the flanks obliquely backwards and downwards from the umbones; slightly compressed in the antero-ventral region. Extremities very narrowly rounded,—the most prominent part of the anterior being below the middle, and of the posterior above it; anterior side nearly or quite closed, and the posterior a little gaping. Beaks depressed, approximate, located a little nearer the middle than the anterior margin. Dorsal outline declining obliquely in front of the beaks, nearly straight and horizontal behind them, where the margin is inflected so as to form a narrow false area. Base presenting an irregular, semi-elliptic outline, being rather more prominent behind the middle than in front, where it is even slightly sinuous. Surface ornamented with small, rather irregular, concentric costæ or ridges, which diminish in size to mere lines on the umbones.

Length, about 1.26 inch; height, 0.56 inch; convexity, 0.45 inch.

This species is perhaps most nearly allied to a shell described from the Lower Oolite by Munster, in Goldf. Petref. Germ. ii, p. 257, under the name *Lutraria tenuistriata*, and subsequently included by Prof. Agassiz in his genus *Pleuromya* (see Etud. Crit. sur les Mol., tab. 24). It differs, however, from all the forms of that rather variable species of which I have seen figures or specimens, in being more depressed, or longer in proportion to its height, and in having its extremities more narrowly rounded; while its beaks are less prominent and placed farther back. That these differences are certainly not due to accidental distortion is evident from the condition of the specimens. Should the name *Pleuromya* be substituted for *Myacites*, this shell should be called *Pleuromya depressa*, since it is a typical *Pleuromya*.

CLASS CEPHALOPODA

FAMILY BELEMNITIDÆ.

GENUS BELEMNITES, Auct.*

BELEMNITES ———.

Pl. 8, Fig. 9, and 9 *a*.

A FEW fragments of this fossil in the collection are sufficiently well preserved to leave no doubts in regard to its belonging to the genus *Belemnites*, though they present no reliable characters for specific identification. One of the specimens shows longitudinal and transverse sections of the anterior portion, with the conical cavity for the reception of the phragmocone filled with the same hard material as the matrix in which the fossil is embedded. Although somewhat altered by the metamorphic action to which it has been subjected, the substance of the guard retains its original fibrous structure. The sections across the anterior cavity for the reception of the phragmocone show that it wants the characteristic slit of the genus *Belemnitella*, and hence must be a true *Belemnite*, as that name is generally applied. Occurs associated with *Rhynchonella gnathophora*.

---

* It is probable that a strict compliance with the established laws of nomenclature may compel us to restrict the name *Belemnites* to the group D'Orbigny proposed to call *Belemnitella*, since Lamarck seems to have been the first regular binomial author who used it *in a binomial sense;* and his only example (Syst. An. 1801, 104) was his *B. paxillosus* (*B. mucronata*, Schlot.), the type of *Belemnitella*, D'Orbigny. If so, some one of the several names proposed by Montfort would have to be taken for the group to which authors most generally apply the name *Belemnites*.

PALÆONTOLOGY OF CALIFORNIA.

VOL. I.

SECTION IV.

DESCRIPTION OF THE CRETACEOUS FOSSILS.

BY W. M. GABB.

CRUSTACEA.

CALLIANASSA, Leach.

C. Stimpsonii, n. s.

Pl. 9, Fig. 1, *a*, *b*, *c*.

Hand subquadrate, flattened, equally convex on both sides, slightly twisted. Upper and lower edges acute; the lower one crenulate. Fixed finger (from cast) nearly as long as the hand, not toothed, very slightly curved on its inner edge. Movable finger unknown. Surface irregularly and minutely wrinkled, and marked along the upper edge by a row of about seven foramina, surrounded by a raised lip looking forwards, and over the rest of the surface by a number of pustules, which are largest and most closely placed on the upper half.

The figures are of natural size. Fig. *b* represents a hand from Chico Creek, collected by Mr. Rémond. Fig. *c*, another hand, found by myself at Clayton, Contra Costa County, in the sandstone above the coal. Fig. *a*, three segments of the abdomen, very imperfect, found in the same mass as the preceding specimen. Also found near Cañada de las Uvas. From both divisions of the California Cretaceous.

Compared with *C. Danai*, H. and M., from Nebraska, the hand of this species is proportionally shorter, broader, and apparently less robust. There are two species found in New Jersey, and as far south, in the Cretaceous, as Mississippi; but, as well as I can remember, the hands are in both cases narrower than in the present one. I placed specimens of both the above in the hands of my friend, Dr. Stimpson, for description; and take pleasure in dedicating the present species to him.

CEPHALOPODA.

BELEMNITES, Cuv.

B. impressus, n. s.

Pl. 9, Fig. 2, and 2 *a*.

Shell elongated, robust, subcylindrical, tapering convexly towards the point for about a fourth of its length; upper portion expanded, thin. Alveolus extending about half the length of the shaft; the cavity being divided by plates placed at short distances apart. On one side is a well-marked groove extending from the tip to near the top of the shaft; becoming nearly linear below and widening out above, until it loses itself in the general swell of the surface.

From north fork of Cottonwood Creek, southwest of Horsetown, Shasta County; collected by Messrs. Brewer and Rémond.

One fragment of an alveolus was discovered by myself at Mount Diablo in the gray limestone, associated with *Ammonites Rémondii* and *Inoceramus Piochii*. This is, I believe, the most southern locality of the species yet known. It is only found in the older division of the Cretaceous (Div. A.).

Figures, natural size. The section is taken from the point marked *a*, on the large figure.

NAUTILUS, Breyn., Auct.

N. Texanus? Shum.

Pl. 9, Fig. 3, *a*, *b*.

(*N. Texanus*, Shumard. Trans. Acad. of Sciences St. Louis, 1860, p. 590.)

Shell subglobose. Whorls increasing rapidly in size. Body whorl, sides convex, narrowing towards the dorsum, widest about a third of the distance from the ventral to the dorsal side; back rounded, sides sloping convexly and somewhat rapidly from the widest part towards the umbilicus. Umbilicus small, apparently not covered. Surface marked by a number of undulations, which arise at or near the umbilicus, pass straight to the middle of the whorl, whence they arch gracefully backwards, crossing the dorsum, where they are most strongly marked. Siphon nearly central, a little nearest the dorsal side. Septa gently undulated; and, at their widest part, placed about one-fourth the width of the whorl apart.

Figures, two-thirds of the natural size.

Three specimens were obtained at Alderson's Gulch, Shasta County; and one from near Mount Diablo, in Mr. Pioche's collection; the last was found by Mr. Clayton. (Div. A.)

The specimens from which Dr. Shumard described his species were all imperfect. I refer the present form provisionally to the Texas species, with which I am unacquainted, since it seems to agree very closely with Dr. Shumard's description.

ATURIA, Bronn.

Megasiphonia, D'Orb.

A. Mathewsonii, n. s.

Pl. 17, Fig. 31.

Shell subglobose, whorls increasing rapidly in size, deeply enveloping; sides sloping regularly towards the dorsum, somewhat flattened; dorsum regularly rounded, narrower than in the preceding species; umbilicus small, closed; surface of the shell sloping inwards for but a short distance. Distance between the septa on the dorsum equals about half the distance between the umbilicus and the dorsum.

Septa arching gently outwards and forwards for about half their length in a regular curve, which becomes more abrupt, and, suddenly bending backwards, forms a long tongue or lobe, the sides of which are nearly straight; from this lobe the septal margin proceeds directly to the dorsum in nearly a straight line. Surface smooth, or marked only by fine radiating lines. Siphon large.

Figure, natural size, from a Martiñez specimen.

Localities: Martiñez and Clayton (Div. A.), and Cañada de las Uvas (Div. B.).

Four specimens of this species have been found, of which two were collected by Mr. Mathewson. A very young, but perfectly characterized specimen, was found by myself at Alizos Creek, near Cañada de las Uvas; and, more recently, I was fortunate enough to procure a nearly perfect specimen, sixteen and a half inches in diameter, at Clayton, Contra Costa County. All of the specimens are unfortunately too much weathered on one or the other side to give a good transverse section. A perfect shell would probably present nearly the same outline as Fig. 3 *b*, except that it would be narrower on the dorsum and more regularly rounded.

AMMONITES, Brug.

A. SUBTRICARINATUS, D'Orb.

Pl. 10, Fig. 4, and 4 *a*.

(*A. subtricarinatus*, D'Orbigny. Prodrome; Vol. 2, p. 212, Étage 22. No. 9.)

(*A. tricarinatus*, D'Orb. (not Poitiez), Pal. Fr., p. 307, Pl. 91, Fig. 1, 2.)

SHELL discoidal; whorls many (number unknown) slightly embracing. Section of whorls subquadrate, narrowest towards the dorsum. Sides marked by a few large ribs, which rise at the margin of the umbilicus, sometimes by means of a small, flattened tubercle, pass obliquely forwards and outwards, and terminate in a large distinct tubercle.

Dorsum marked by three prominent angular ridges, the middle

one being the highest; between these ridges are broad, concave, shallow grooves.

Septum composed of a dorsal, two lateral and a ventral lobe. The dorsal saddle at its top is broader than the dorsal lobe, and is deeply divided in the middle. The superior lateral lobe is largest. Lateral saddle about as wide as the superior lateral lobe, and is not bifurcated. Further details unknown.

Figures, natural size.

Presented to the Geological Survey by a gentleman at Battle Creek, Tehama County, and said to have come from that vicinity.

This shell is of the style of *A. Leonensis*, Con., but can be distinguished by the proportionately narrower whorls and the presence of three well-marked ridges on the dorsum, instead of the single one of that species. It is one of the handsomest species in the State.

A. Newberryanus.

Pl. 10, Figs. 5, 6, and 6 *a*, *b*; also, Pl. 27, Fig. 199, *a*, *b*, *c*.

(*A. Newberryanus*, Meek. Trans. Albany Institute, vol. 4, p. 47.)

The specimens represented by Figures 5, 6 *a*, *b*, and *c*, correspond in the main with the form described by Mr. Meek from Vancouver Island, under the above name. The principal points of difference are in the ribs not being so definite as described by Meek, and in the absence of the umbilical row of nodes.

By a careful comparison of these specimens with one nearly seven inches in diameter, obtained by myself on Vancouver Island in the fall of 1863, I find no differences, except such as can be fully accounted for by the difference in age.

This specimen, much larger than the one originally described, also shows some other characters. It is figured on Pl. 27, Fig. 199, *a*, *b*, *c*. The whorls are thicker transversely, the umbilical margin is rounded, and the costæ are, proportionally, very much smaller, being barely more than a quarter as wide as the interspaces.

Another peculiar character, not heretofore mentioned, is a minute pustular roughening of the external surface, producing an appearance not unlike that caused by the spine tubercles of some of the *Spatangidæ*. These pustules are small, scattered, and the surface between them is somewhat roughened.

The periodical constrictions mentioned by Mr. Meek are not visible on all of the California specimens, and when they do occur, are not always regularly placed. On the large Vancouver Island specimen they are entirely wanting.

Figures, natural size. Fig. 6 *b*, is from a specimen but little over an inch in diameter.

Localities: Comax ("Koomooks" of Meek), Vancouver Island; north fork of

Cottonwood Creek, Shasta County; Martiñez and Clayton, and south of Mount Diablo, Contra Costa County. Some fragments from Vancouver Island, in the collection of the California Academy of Natural Sciences, indicate individuals of a foot in diameter.

A. Brewerii, n. s.

Pl. 10, Fig. 7.

Shell discoidal. Whorls four or five, sides slightly arched, curving inwards towards the umbilicus, on the margin of which it is angulated and abruptly truncated.

Dorsum rounded. Surface marked by numerous rounded or subangular flexuous ribs, which arise in the umbilicus, passing obliquely forwards, cross the angle of the umbilical margin, keeping nearly the same direction, then curving so as to cross the middle of the whorl transversely; after which they again curve forwards, usually becoming obsolete on the dorsum, although, in one specimen I have seen, they retain their size completely across the shell.

Septum unknown.

The figure is two-thirds of the natural size. The specimen before me, collected by Mr. Brewer, is six and a half inches in diameter.

Locality: North fork of Cottonwood Creek, Shasta County (Div. A.). The specimens are all fragmentary casts in a sandstone, and are so distorted as to render it impossible to ascertain the shape of a section of a whorl; or even to show the amount of enveloping of the whorls.

The character of the ribs indicates that this species is related to *A. Belknapii*, Marcou; also to *A. Peruvianus*, Von Buch, and remotely to *A. flaccidicosta*, Roemer. From the first two, it can be distinguished by the dorsum being distinctly rounded and not carinate; from the latter, by the more numerous and more distinctly curved ribs and the abrupt umbilical margin.

A. Haydenii, n. s.

Pl. 10, Fig. 8, and 8 *a*, *b*.

Shell compressed discoidal. Whorls about four, or more, deeply embracing, flattened on the sides, nearly flat on the dorsum, abruptly truncated in the umbilicus. Surface smooth, or marked by very faint undulations.

Septum: Dorsal lobe small, not more than a third as long as the superior lateral; divided for half its length into two bifurcated branches with a small spur above on each side. Dorsal saddle broad, oblique, divided into two unequal branches, each of which is again subdivided. Superior lateral lobe broader than the dorsal saddle, one large branch at the end with five alternating spurs; on the dorsal side of this there is a very large oblique branch with several smaller branchlets; the corresponding branch on the ventral side is much smaller, and has but three terminal spurs. Lateral saddle very oblique, smaller than the dorsal, and divided into three bifurcate branches. Inferior lateral lobe narrower than the superior lateral, with a terminal branch, and two large and two small alternating spurs on each side. The first supplementary lobe is not more than half the size of the preceding one. The rest, two more, decrease regularly in size.

Figures 8 and 8 *a*, are two-thirds of the natural size.

Locality: North fork of Cottonwood Creek, Shasta County. (Div. A.)

Named after Dr. F. V. Hayden, to whom we are indebted for so large a proportion of our knowledge of the geology of Nebraska and the neighboring Territories.

A. Peruvianus, De Buch?

Pl. 10, Fig. 9.

The fragment figured is referred with doubt to this species. It is the only specimen yet found, and was collected at Tuscan Springs, Tehama County, by Dr. J. A. Veatch. The ribs have almost exactly the character of those of the specimen figured by Marcou, Geol. of N. America, Pl. 5, Fig. 1 a.

A. Traskii, n. s.

Pl. 11, Fig. 10; Pl. 12, Fig. 11.

Shell robust. Whorls six or more, embracing about one-half; rounded on the sides and back. Umbilicus broad and deep, about a third of the diameter of the shell, sides abrupt, but uniting with the surface by a regular curve. Surface marked by numerous rounded dichotomous ribs, which arise in the umbilicus, and after crossing the margin, divide into from three to five branches, which cross the sides straight to the dorsum; crossing it, arched slightly forwards. Occasionally a single rib arises at the umbilical margin, and crosses the back without branching.

Septum: Dorsal lobe large, divided for half its length into two complex branches with a small tongue between them; above these branches are two large and one small side branch. (On the diagram, Fig. 11, the terminal branch is represented broader than usual, owing to the original being somewhat weathered at that point.) Dorsal saddle occupying half the width of the septum, deeply divided into four branches, one of which is simply notched at the end; two of the others are divided into three, and the remaining one into four smaller branches. Superior lateral lobe long and slender, divided above the middle into one long and one shorter oblique branch; the long branch is nearly straight, terminates in a long single tooth, and has four or five spurs; the short one is on the dorsal side of the lobe, terminates in two points, and has two spurs on each side; above the origin of these branches are two spurs on the dorsal, and one on the ventral side. Lateral saddle about as wide as the superior lateral lobe, divided into three branches at the end. Inferior lateral lobe, two-thirds the length of the preceding one, with four branches on each side and a terminal one. Two additional saddles are simply dentate, and the two lobes have merely four alternating branches.

Figure 10 is of the natural size.

From the collection of the California Academy of Natural Sciences, presented by Dr. J. B. Trask.

Locality: Arbuckle's Diggings, Shasta County. (Div. A.)

This species is well marked, especially by the character of its septum. Externally, it is likely to be confounded with one of the varieties of the Protean species, *A. Rémondii*, of this section. From Cottonwood Creek, I have seen specimens of that species, having identically the same septum as Fig. 14 *a*, but with ribs, only differing from those of Fig. 10, in being more narrow and isolated at the umbilical margin.

A. RAMOSUS.

Pl. 11, Fig. 12, and 12 *a*; Pl. 12, Fig. 12 *b*.

(*A. ramosus*, Meek. Trans. Albany Inst., Vol. 4, p. 45.)

ONLY two imperfect specimens of this species were found. They came from the lower division of the California Cretaceous, at Cottonwood Creek, Shasta County. Mr. Meek, to whom I sent a sketch, says that it "agrees with *A. ramosus*, except in some details of the septa, which are probably not specific."

A. HOFFMANNII, n. s.

Pl. 11, Fig. 13, and 13 *a*; Pl. 12, Fig. 13 *b*.

SHELL robust; whorls five or more, enveloping about one-half, abrupt, but rounded on the umbilical edge, somewhat flattened on the side, rounded on the dorsum. Umbilicus nearly half the diameter of the shell, shallow. Surface marked by slightly sinuous ribs, and by an indefinite number of constrictions. There are nine of these on the last volution of the specimen figured, while on another there are but six in the same space.

Septum: Dorsal lobe divided nearly half its length into two branches, each with a long and a short branch on the outer side; and with one long branch above on each side. Dorsal saddle twice as wide as the lobe; deeply bifurcate, each branch divided into two double spurs. Superior lateral lobe longer than the dorsal, with three spurs at the end and one above, on each side. Lateral saddle of the same pattern as the dorsal, but smaller. Inferior lateral lobe like the superior lateral, but not more than half as large. Three supplementary lobes, nearly plain, and with their saddles bifurcate.

Figure, two-thirds of natural size. One fragment before me must have belonged to an individual of at least ten inches in diameter.

Locality: Horsetown, Shasta County. (Div. A.)

The septum of this species is very much like that of *A. Newberryanus*, Fig. 6; but while it differs in some trifling details, the external forms of the shells are very distinct. *A. Newberryanus* is a very much flatter shell, at all ages, and the umbilicus is always small, compared with the width of the shell, while in this it is nearly half of the largest diameter.

A. Rémondii, n. s.

Pl. 12, Fig. 14, 14 *a*, and Fig. 15.

Shell robust, discoidal. Whorls six or seven; enveloping about one-third to two-fifths. Umbilicus about a third of the whole diameter, rather deep, sides rounded. Sides of the whorls somewhat flattened; dorsum broadly rounded.

Surface exceedingly variable. One form (Fig. 14) is ornamented by a few large, straight, or slightly sinuous ribs, which arise in or on the margin of the umbilicus, and pass over the sides and completely cross the dorsum. Between these are interpolated ribs, arising about the middle of the side, and crossing the dorsum like the others.

A second form has ribs, not more than half the width of the preceding, sometimes dichotomous, and with several series of nodes on the sides.

Another variety is almost identical externally with *A. Traskii*, Fig. 10, being ornamented by a series of ribs, which arise on the margin of the umbilicus, and afterwards divide into from two to five branches, which cross the dorsum. The septa are, however, markedly constant. Dorsal lobe broad above, narrower below, a well-marked tongue between the branches, two spurs on the outer side of each branch, and three above these. Dorsal saddle occupying a third of the septum, deep, and divided into two large and two smaller branches. Superior lateral lobe nearly as wide as the dorsal, terminated by a trifurcate branch, with four spurs above on the dorsal side and two on the ventral. Lateral saddle deeply divided into two parts, each of which is subdivided. Inferior lateral lobe very small, terminating in two dentate spurs, and with two on the dorsal side. Two very small supplementary lobes beyond these are merely dentate; the saddles being equally simple.

Fig. 14 is of the natural size. Fig. 15 is a part of a specimen, the outer whorl of which is fifteen inches in diameter.

Locality: North fork of Cottonwood Creek, Shasta County (Div. A.).

I should have hesitated in considering all of these forms as one species, had I not had a large series for study. In every case the septum is the same, and there are many specimens showing intermediate characters between those specially mentioned above.

A. Batesii.

Pl. 13, Fig. 16, and 16 *a*, *b*.

(*A. Batesii*, Trask. Proc. Cal. Acad. Nat. Sciences, 1855, vol. i, p. 40.)

Shell discoidal. Whorls eight or nine, not enveloping, merely in contact for about a third of the transverse width; section nearly circular, slightly sinuous on the ventral side; sometimes the dorso-ventral diameter being greatest; at others, especially in old shells, the transverse diameter is longest. Surface marked by numerous fine, rather sharp, elevated ribs, crossing from the interior of the umbilicus obliquely forwards over the dorsum. In some specimens the interspaces are marked by fine revolving lines. In others these lines are absent.

Septum composed of a dorsal lobe and three on the side. Dorsal lobe deeply divided, each branch bearing two lateral ones; above the origin of these are two others. Dorsal saddle divided into two bifurcate branches. Superior lateral lobe a third larger than the dorsal, bifurcate at the end, each branch divided into two smaller, and these again divided; above the origin of the large branches are a large and a small spur on each side. Superior lateral saddle like the dorsal. Lateral lobe of the same pattern as the superior lateral, but a third smaller. Inferior lateral saddle like the others, but smaller and a little less minutely divided. Inferior lateral lobe simply divided into three or four dentate spurs.

Figure, natural size of the specimen. One broken specimen, showing none of the body chamber, measures fifteen inches in diameter; and, when perfect, must have been at least twenty-two inches across. In this specimen the end of the whorl measures five and a half inches in height and seven and a half in transverse diameter. The width of the umbilicus, measured from the sutures, is seven inches. This measurement is not in proportion with the figure given; the whorls increasing more rapidly in size as the shell becomes larger.

Locality: The specimen figured, one of Dr. Trask's original specimens, is from Arbuckle's Diggings, Shasta County. This species has been found abundantly on the north fork of Cottonwood Creek, Shasta County, and the large specimen mentioned above is from Bald Hills, in the same county. It is also found at Benicia and at Curry's, south of Mount Diablo. It is one of the most characteristic species of the older beds in this State.

A. Chicoensis.

Pl. 13, Fig. 17, and 17 *a*, *b*.

(*A. Chicoensis,* Trask. Proc. Cal. Acad. Nat. Sci., 1856, vol. i, p. 85, Pl. 2, Fig. 1.)

Shell discoidal, flattened. Whorls five or more, enveloping about two-thirds. Sides nearly flat, slightly convex in the middle, truncated abruptly on the dorsal and umbilical margins. Sides marked by a series of dichotomous ribs, which originate on the margin of the umbilicus, usually from a series of flattened nodes, branch on or a little beyond the middle of the side, and terminate at the margin of the dorsum in another row of similar nodes. There are also on the ribs usually from one to four tubercles, distributed regularly along their length. Dorsum carinate in the middle. One small specimen shows the usual form, septum and dorsal carina, but the ribs and nodes on the sides and on the angle of the dorsum are absent.

Septum composed of a dorsal and three very unequal lateral lobes. Dorsal lobe small, confined entirely to the flat dorsum, divided by a shallow, rounded sinus, each branch terminating in three or four teeth, two small spurs above. Dorsal saddle broad, oblique, bifurcate. Superior lateral lobe terminating in a tridentate branch, with two large oblique spurs above. Lateral saddle divided into four rounded branches. Inferior lateral lobe with six small spurs. One supplementary lobe with two small terminal spurs, and on the umbilical aspect of the whorl is a single tongue-like process.

The young form of this species resembles closely the corresponding stage of *A. Delawarensis*, Morton, but in adult specimens of that species the whorls become very thick, the ribs decrease in number and carry large tubercles, and the difference of the septum is sufficiently marked to distinguish them.

Localities: Chico Creek, collected by Dr. Trask; Pençe's and Kelly's Ranchos, twelve miles north of Oroville, Butte County; Siskiyou Mountains, Siskiyou County; and I have found a single specimen on the Rancho de San Luis Gonzaga, Pacheco's Pass, Merced County (Div. A.).

A. COMPLEXUS ?

(*A. complexus*, H. and M. Trans. Amer. Acad. of Arts and Sciences, 2d series, vol. 5, p. 394, Pl. 4, Fig. 1.)

A SPECIMEN in the collection of the California Academy of Natural Sciences, from the debris of the Cretaceous at Folsom, probably belongs to this species. The external shape agrees with the specimen figured in the plate quoted above, as well as does the septum, as far as I have been able to trace it. It differs, however, in having distant, well-marked ribs, which arch forwards and cross the dorsum. There are fourteen of these on half a whorl, of a specimen originally about five inches in diameter. The ribs are most prominent on the latero-dorsal portion of the whorl, being nearly obsolete on the back itself. I can only refer it doubtfully to the above species, though I trust that I shall hereafter be able to settle the point; more particularly on account of the valuable link in the chain of evidence of the parallelism of the California Cretaceous with known beds on the eastern side of the continent. A variety of this species has been described by Mr. Meek from Vancouver Island, under the name of *A. complexus*, var. *Suciaensis*.

? A. COOPERII, n. s.

Pl. 14, Fig. 23, and 23 *a*.

I PROPOSE this name for a Cephalopod from near San Diego, of which I have only seen fragments, very much compressed. The surface is ornamented by two rows of nodes (on the side?) with ribs extending across, some passing through one, some through two of the nodes; while others originate in one and end in another. By the peculiar arrangement of the ribs, there are about a third more on the middle of the fragment than on the margins.

Septum: The fragment exhibits two lobes and one and a half saddles. The small lobe on the diagram is placed on the upper (dorsal?) side of the upper row of tubercles. Both lobes are of the same pattern, differing only in size, and consequently in complexity of their minuter details. They are bifurcate, each branch being divided into two or three spurs; above these branches are two spurs on each side, all being finely dentate. Saddle deeply divided for more than half its length, each branch bifurcate. This septum approaches that of *Ammonites Batesii*, but differs in many of its details; the smaller lobe being towards the dorsal margin, and apparently occupying the place of the superior lateral, is a well-marked character. The ornaments of the surface are also very peculiar.

The reference of this shell to the genus Ammonites may probably prove to be incorrect. Two or three specimens were collected, the best of which is figured. No whorls having been found in contact, it may prove to be a *Helicoceras*, or even *Hamites*. It is of particular interest from the fact that it is one of the oldest fossils found in the southern part of the State, being considerably below the newer Cretaceous fossils of San Diego.

Locality: From a shaft sunk in search of coal on the west side of Point Loma, opposite La Playa, San Diego, and presented by Mr. E. W. Morse to the Geological Survey.

HAMITES, Parkinson.

H. Vancouverensis, n. s.

Pl. 13, Fig. 18.

Shell large, section elliptical, longest diameter from dorsal to ventral side. Inner width of the curve less than the diameter of the smaller arm. Surface marked by numerous sharp ribs crossing the shell, inclined obliquely forwards; well marked, but diminished in size on the ventral side; largest laterally; each rib carrying a small flattened tubercle on the latero-dorsal angle; some ribs in the curve, on the ventral side, exhibit a tendency to tuberculation, but, the shell being broken off at that point, their presence cannot be certainly determined. Interspaces between the ribs broadly concave.

Septum unknown.

Figure, one-half natural size.

Locality: "Vancouver Island," associated with *Ammonites Newberryanus* and another Ammonite, species undetermined; and a Baculite, figured on pl. 9, fig. 28 *a*, and pl. 6, fig. 28, *b*.

Closely allied, in form and ornamentation, to *H. Fremontii*, Marcou, Geol. N. America, p. 36, pl. 1, fig. 3. It differs in the ribs continuing completely across the ventral face, and in each rib carrying a node, instead of every third rib, as in Marcou's species.

HELICOCERAS, D'Orb.

? H. VERMICULARIS, n. s.

Pl. 13, Fig. 19, and 19 *a*, *b*.

SHELL small, subcompressed. Section elliptical. Curve broad, regular. Surface marked by numerous small rounded ribs, regular in size, and extending completely around the shell, being slightly oblique and less distinct on the ventral side.

Septum composed of a dorsal, ventral, and on each side two lateral lobes. Dorsal lobe divided into two bifurcate branches, with three rounded spurs above. Dorsal saddle wider than the lobe, bifurcate, each branch being divided into two. Superior lateral lobe about as long but wider than the dorsal; the pattern is the same. Lateral saddle shorter than the dorsal, and of the same pattern. Inferior lateral lobe two-thirds as large as the superior lateral, and more simple. Ventral saddle small, divided into two unequal bifurcate branches. Ventral lobe half as long as the preceding; trifid at the extremity, and with two or three teeth above on the sides.

Figure, twice natural size.

This species has only been found at one locality, namely, on a hill southwest of Martiñez, in Contra Costa County, in the lower division. It appears to be allied to *H. Mortonii*, Hall and Meek, sp., Mem. Amer. Acad. Arts and Sciences, 2d ser., vol. 5, p. 396, pl. 4, fig. 3, but differs in being much smaller, having proportionately smaller ribs, no nodes, and in details of the septum. It is not rare at the locality mentioned above, but has never been reported from elsewhere. It is the smallest Cephalopod in the Cretaceous formation of California, so far as is yet known.

H. Brewerii, n. s.

Pl. 14, Fig. 22, and 22, *a*, *b*.

Shell small, whorls slightly compressed. Surface marked by small oblique ribs, encircling the whorls, faintest on the ventral side. At intervals of every four or five ribs there occurs a much larger one, faint on the ventral surface, but prominent on the sides and back. These ribs bear a small tubercle on each side of the dorsum.

Septum unequal on the upper and lower side. Dorsal lobe larger than the others, rather slender, bifurcate; each branch with a lateral spur externally and two smaller ones above. Dorsal saddles nearly equal, bilobate at the extremities. Superior lateral lobes shorter than the dorsal. The one on the lower side is broad, with the sides nearly parallel; the other is of the same shape as the dorsal, except that the terminal branch on the dorsal side is longer than the other. Lateral saddles of the same pattern as the dorsal, the upper one being broadest. Inferior lateral lobes of the same pattern as the dorsal, the lower one being largest. Ventral saddles very small, equal and simply notched. Ventral lobe not as large as one of the branches of the dorsal; trifid at the extremity, and with one small tooth above on each side.

Length of the fragment, .85 inch.

This species is founded on a single specimen, found by Prof. Brewer at Pence's Ranch, twelve miles north of Oroville, Butte County, associated with *Ammonites Chicoensis*, *A. Rémondii*, and many other species of Division A.

H. DECLIVE, n. s.

Pl. 28, Fig. 200, and 200 *a*.

I PROPOSE this name for a fragment of a small species, forming about three-fifths of a whorl from the non-septate portion of the shell. It is sinistral; the umbilicus is about equal in diameter to the greatest width of the largest portion of the whorl; the whorls appear to be nearly their own width apart. The surface is ornamented by numerous uniform, oblique ribs, nearly obsolete on the ventral side, prominent on the dorsum. Section elliptical.

Figures, natural size.

Locality: Pence's Ranch, Butte County (Div. A.).

This shell resembles, in size and general appearance, *H. Brewerii*, *supra*, but differs in being more oblique, in the greatest diameter of the whorl being vertical, instead of transverse, and in the absence of the occasional large ribs.

TURRILITES, Lam.

T. (sp. indet.)

Pl. 20, Fig. 201.

A FRAGMENT, showing the outer and part of the under surface of about a fourth of a whorl. The outer surface is marked by a series of regular, oblique, and slightly curved ribs, nearly obsolete in the middle, and each bearing four nodes, two above and two below. Under surface plain.

Figure, natural size.

Locality: From a brown sandstone (Div. A.), near Jacksonville, Oregon. Collection of Prof. Whitney.

PTYCHOCERAS, D'Orb.

P. ÆQUICOSTATUS, n. s.

Pl. 13, Fig. 20.

SHELL robust, section subcircular, slightly flattened on the ventral side. Surface ornamented by a series of rounded ribs with regularly concave interspaces. These ribs appear to differ in size only in proportion to the growth of the shell; they pass entirely around the shell, obliquely backwards from the ventral to the dorsal side, being somewhat faint on the ventral surface. There is no sign of bifurcation of these ribs on any of the specimens I have seen. From one imperfect impression, showing twenty-six ribs, it seems that on a single rib there have been two tubercles or spines; one near the dorsal and the other near the ventral side. This is on the small branch. I can detect no trace of this character on any of the other specimens.

Figure, natural size.

Localities: North fork of Cottonwood Creek, Alderson's Gulch, and Eagle Creek, Shasta County (Div. A.).

P. (? HAMITES) QUADRATUS, n. s.

Pl. 15, Fig. 21; Pl. 14, Fig. 21 *a*.

SHELL small, section subquadrate, angles rounded, sides nearly flat, dorso-ventral diameter about a third more than the transverse. Surface marked by very small rounded ribs, which cross at right angles with the length, and become linear and slightly arched forwards on the ventral side. Besides these ribs are periodical constrictions, placed about the width of the shell apart, and which are deepest on the sides and back.

Septum: Dorsal lobe slender, divided into two bifurcate branches, and with three regularly diminishing spurs above. Saddles all of the same pattern, but differing in size. Dorsal wider than the lobe, deeply bifurcate, each branch divided into two smaller ones, notched at the ends. Superior lateral lobe bifurcate; each branch divided into two processes at the end and a lateral one above; above the origin of these branches are a large and a small spur on each side. Lateral saddle like the dorsal, except that it is wider at the top and narrower at the bottom. Inferior lateral lobe like the superior, but smaller. Ventral saddle smallest of the three. Ventral lobe deeply trifurcate at the tip with two lateral spurs.

Figures, natural size.

Locality: A single specimen from the lower division (A.), at Pence's Ranch, Butte County.

CRIOCERAS, Lev., D'Orb.

C. (ANCYLOCERAS?) RÉMONDI, n. s.

Pl. 14, Fig. 24, and 24 *a*.

DISCOIDAL; whorls increasing rapidly in size, flattened on the sides; dorsal surface narrow, convex; ventral, flat or very slightly concave. Transverse diameter less than half the dorso-ventral. Space between contiguous whorls narrow, but well marked. Surface marked by numerous small flexuous ribs, of about equal size, which arise on the ventral margin of the whorls and pass entirely across the back; these ribs are often dichotomous, and occasionally, though rarely, anastomose near the dorsum. In one case, remains of a few small dorsal spines were observed. These were placed in two rows, one on each side of the back. The ventral surface is finely striate transversely, the striæ arching forwards. Of the septum, I have only been able to see the dorsal and superior lateral lobes and their corresponding saddles. I have not been able to detect any difference other than that of size and consequent complexity between this and the one figured on pl. 15, fig. 30 *a;* except that the dorsal lobe is somewhat shorter relatively in the present specimens.

Locality: North fork of Cottonwood Creek, Div. A. Named in honor of Mr. Rémond, who collected all the specimens I have seen.

Figure, natural size. There are specimens which show about a third of a volution in addition to the size figured.

C. LATUS, n. s.

Pl. 15, Fig. 25, and 25 *a;* and Pl. 14, Fig. 25 *b*.

SHELL broadly spiral; section of whorls nearly as broad as high, narrowest towards the dorsum. Surface ornamented by alternate large and small ribs; of the former, there are twenty-six or twenty-seven on the last whorl, with sometimes three, sometimes four of the small ones between each pair. These ribs commence on the ventral margin and cross towards the back, either directly or curving slightly backwards, and then bend slightly forwards in crossing the dorsum. The ventral surface is marked by very small ribs, which arch strongly forwards. Each large rib bears on its dorsal front two spines, which are represented by tubercles on the cast. Besides these, there are two others on each side, one on the ventral margin, and one about midway between this and the one on the dorsum.

Septum composed of a dorsal and ventral lobes, and two lateral ones on each side. Dorsal lobe divided for about half its length with a small bilobate tongue in the middle; each branch carries two lateral projections; above the origin of these branches are two smaller spurs, the upper one smallest. Dorsal saddle bilobate; each branch divided into three or four smaller ones. Superior lateral lobe longer than the dorsal, divided at the middle into three enormous branches, the middle one of which is straight, trifurcate at the end, and with two small spurs above on each side; lateral branches long, curving downwards; that on the dorsal side longest, and both with several side spurs. Above the origin of these branches the lobe has on each side a couple of spurs, the longest being below. Lateral saddle of the same pattern as the dorsal, but smaller. Inferior lateral lobe not more than half as long as the superior lateral, more simple, but of the same pattern. Ventral saddle half the size of the dorsal, divided in nearly the same manner. Ventral lobe as long, nearly as broad, and of almost the same pattern as the superior lateral, being slightly more complex.

Figure, four-fifths of natural size.

This species is very closely allied to *C. Duvalii*, Lev.; but there are several strong points of difference. The section of the whorls, in the present species, is nearly twice as broad as in the figure given by D'Orbigny, Pal. Fr., vol. 1, pl. 113, or that by Bayle and Coquand, Mem. Geol. Soc. France, 2 ser., vol. 4, pl. 3. The whorls are smaller in diameter when young, and increase more rapidly in size than in the figure given by D'Orbigny. The spaces between the whorls are also larger in proportion to the size of the shells, and the number of large ribs to a volution is nearly twice as great as given by D'Orbigny. There are also several points of difference in the septum. The lobes are all more slender, and the inferior lateral lobe is much smaller in proportion than in D'Orbigny's figure. The ventral lobe, however, shows the greatest difference. In *C. Duvalii* it is small; in this species it is as long as the superior lateral and more complex.

Locality: Near Weaverville, in the Trinity River, Trinity County; from a boulder.

C. PERCOSTATUS, n. s.

Pl. 16, Fig. 26; and Pl. 17, Fig. 26 *a*.

SHELL large; section of whorls rounded, subquadrate, as broad as high, somewhat narrowed towards the dorsum; sides flattened; back flat, or but slightly convex; ventral surface usually a little concave, sometimes plain. Surface marked by plain ribs, small and numerous on the younger whorls, but which become fewer and larger as the shell increases in size, until in the adult state they are large, prominent, isolated by broad interspaces, and sometimes forming a sixth of the whole height of the whorl. These ribs commence at the ventral margin, curve backwards slightly, and then pass directly to and across the back; they are often dichotomous in the young shells, but never so in the adult.

Interspace between the volutions very small, being scarcely greater than the thickness of the shell substance.

Septum almost exactly like the succeeding. I have not been able to see all of the parts, but such portions as I have been able to study do not seem to differ in any details; although probably perfect specimens would show some points of difference.

Figures, half natural size.

Locality: Found in Div. A, of the Cretaceous, abundantly on the north fork of Cottonwood Creek; also at Arbuckle's Diggings, Shasta County; and a specimen was picked up by Mr. Rémond on the shore of the Straits of Carquines, west of Martiñez.

In the square dorsum and the mode of costation, this shell is not unlike some of the forms of *Ammonites Rêmondii* (supra); but it can be at once distinguished by the separation of the whorls.

ANCYLOCERAS, D'Orb.

A. (sp. indet.)

Pl. 15, Fig. 30, and 30 *a.*

Four specimens of this fossil have been discovered, two at Cottonwood Creek, and two at Arbuckle's Diggings, Shasta County. They all agree in being nearly cylindrical, the section being elliptical. They taper very gradually from one end to the other, and are all of nearly the same size. They differ, however, somewhat in the surface-markings, the ribs being more or less distinct, and in the angle which these ribs take with the axis of the shell. In one specimen, the ribs are well marked, curved, and occasionally dichotomous; in another they are much more oblique, more numerous, and vary very much in size.

The septum is composed of a dorsal and ventral lobes, and two lateral ones on each side. Dorsal lobe divided for half its length, each branch bearing four or five external lateral spurs, and three or four smaller internal ones; between these branches are two small, distant, tongue-like spurs; above the origin of the terminal branches are two large lateral ones, the upper one being the smaller. Dorsal saddle broad, deeply divided into two lobes, each of which is divided into two smaller ones, which are in turn subdivided. Superior lateral lobe placed in the middle of the septum; longer than the dorsal lobe, with the body more slender; divided at the middle into three very large branches, the middle one nearly straight, and almost an exact miniature of the whole lobe, each branch being similarly placed, but not so complex; the lateral branches send off numerous spurs above and below, some of which are again divided. Above these three main branches are three smaller ones on each side, increasing in size from above downwards. Lateral saddle like the dorsal, but a third smaller. Inferior lateral lobe half the size of the superior lateral, with nearly the same pattern. Ventral saddle a little smaller than the lateral. Ventral lobe as long as the dorsal, and differing from the superior lateral only in some small details of the smaller branches.

Figure 30, two-thirds of natural size.

After a careful study of these specimens, and comparison with all the forms with similar septa, it seems to me more than probable that they should be associated with *C.* (*Ancyloceras?*) *Rêmondii.* The reasons are as follows: No part of the septum, of either form, would militate against such a union; the surface ornamentations of the two are not more unlike than are often found in the same species; and, lastly, the two groups of specimens are of just the proper size to fit each other, the smallest of the present specimens having a long diameter of 1.9 inch, while the largest of the spiral specimens measures 1.7 inch across.

The remarkable resemblance between the details of the septa of so many forms, widely distinct in external characters, cannot fail to strike the least acute observer. Here we have *Crioceras percostatus*, *C. latus*, *C. Duvalii*, and *C.* (*Ancyloceras?*) *Rêmondii*, with septa differing from the present form much less than is often observed among individuals of the same species; and only differing from *Ammonites Newberryanus* in the number of lobes and saddles; but without any important variation in the pattern of the dorsal, or next two succeeding lobes and their saddles; and yet it would be preposterous to call them all by the same specific name. It will thus be seen, that while the septum is one of the most important aids in determining the species of Cephalopods, it cannot always be relied on, even so far as to prove that specimens belong to the same genus. At the same time, however, when taken in connection with other characters, it is undoubtedly of great value.

BACULITES, Lam.

B. Chicoensis.

Pl. 17, Fig. 27, and 27 *a*; Pl. 14, Fig. 27, *b*, and 29, and 29 *a*.

(*Bac. Chicoensis*, Trask. Proc. Cal. A. N. S., 1856, p. 85, Pl. 2, Fig. 2.)

Shell elongated, very slightly tapering, section varying from subelliptical or ovoid to subtriangular; dorsal side narrowest, sometimes marked by a narrow, square carina. Sides smooth, or ornamented by broad, slightly prominent, curved ribs, which have their convexity downwards and the longest limb on the dorsal side. Mouth (restored from lines of growth) deeply emarginate on the sides, with a long lip on the dorsal side, and a shorter one, not more than half as high, on the ventral side. Septum on the same plan as in *B. anceps*. Dorsal lobe broad, with a small tongue-like projection in the middle and a minute spur on each side; terminal branches forming nearly half the length of the lobe, bifid at the end, with a short side branch at the base, one small spur above. Dorsal saddle deeply divided into two double branches. Superior lateral lobe a fourth longer than the dorsal, terminating in two narrow parallel branches, each ending in three spurs with a tooth above on each side; above these branches the lobe suddenly widens, and bears on each side an oblique, robust branch, with a shorter one above it, and sometimes a small spur above this. Lateral saddle larger than the dorsal, and a little more minutely divided. Inferior lateral lobe a little shorter and slightly broader than the superior lateral, divided for a third of its length into two double branches, each one ending in two unequal spurs; between these, the excavation is either simple or bears a single minute tooth; above these, on the dorsal side, are three small spurs, and on the ventral side two larger ones. Ventral saddle minute and simply notched. Ventral lobe not more than a third as long as the preceding, ending in three spurs, with two or three above.

Figures, natural size.

Localities: Chico Creek; Pence's Ranch, Butte County; Cottonwood Creek, Shasta County; Orestimba Cañon, Stanislaus County; in debris at Point Loma, near San Diego (?); and near Martiñez (Mathewson). Only found in Div. A.

The most common form is that found in the above localities, in the northern part of the State, having few or no ribs, and with an outline more or less approaching an ellipse (Fig. 27). The costate form (Fig. 29), in which the dorsum is more or less acute, is connected by imperceptible gradations with the other, and differs from it in that, while every branch and spur of the septum agrees with the diagram (Fig. 27 *b*), still the lobes are all somewhat more slender. The specimen illustrated by Fig. 29 is from near Martiñez, and is one of the best examples of this form.

B. (sp. indet.)

Pl. 17, Fig. 28, 28 *a;* Pl. 14, Fig. 28 *b*.

This form, labelled "Vancouver Island," in the collection of the California Academy of Natural Sciences, is figured, in the hope that it may throw some light on the determination of this truly difficult group of fossils. Externally, it cannot be distinguished from the preceding, unless by its usually greater size, some specimens being two inches in their dorso-ventral diameter. The lines of growth appear to indicate somewhat shorter lips to the aperture. The differences in the septum can be better understood by a comparison of the figures on pl. 14, than by any description. In place of the tongue, in the middle of the dorsal lobe, there is always a minute emargination. The relative sizes of the dorsal and lateral saddles are well marked, as well as the proportionate size and general form of all the lobes. The terminal branches of the superior lateral lobe are markedly different; and the two large and two smaller teeth in the middle of the inferior lateral lobe of the present form cannot fail at once to distinguish it. A careful comparison of a large number of specimens of both the forms has failed to detect any important variation in any of these details.

GASTEROPODA.

TYPHIS, Montf.

T. antiquus, n. s.

Pl. 18, Fig. 31.

Shell small, spire high, whorls five (or six?) angular, subcarinate on the shoulder, and marked by several varices, number unknown. Varices small, obtusely angular, and not very elevated; one, or perhaps two, elongated tubercles between each pair of varices; tubuli short, open. Last tube broad, short, circular at its end. Mouth pyriform, acute below, rounded above. Outer lip thickened, canal closed, anterior extremity unknown. Surface marked only by lines of growth.

Length, about .6 inch.

Locality: Two imperfect specimens have been found by Mr. Mathewson at Bull's Head Point, northeast of Martiñez (Div. B.). They are both very much mutilated, the upper whorls being entirely denuded of shell and the anterior end of the canal broken. The species is, however, interesting, as being the oldest known species of the genus.

FUSUS, Lam.

F. Martinez, n. s.

Pl. 18, Fig. 32.

Shell fusiform, elongated; whorls six, very convex, suture distinct, spire high. Canal straight, aperture unknown. Surface marked by large longitudinal ribs, which commence a little below the suture and merge into the surface below the point of greatest convexity of the whorl; these are crossed by a few small, but distinct, revolving ribs. Where the longitudinal ribs approach the perpendicular, they show, in one or two cases on the specimen, a tendency to form an obtuse angle. Between these ribs the surface is broadly and regularly concave, the interspaces being a little wider than the ribs themselves.

Figure, natural size.

Locality: A single specimen found by myself at Bull's Head Point, northeast of Martiñez.

F. MATHEWSONII, n. s.

Pl. 18, Fig. 33.

SHELL fusiform, spire turreted; whorls seven, angular. Aperture about as long as the spire, narrow; inner lip slightly incrusted, outer lip simple. Body whorl biangular; the upper angle acute and more prominent than the lower, which is obtuse. Surface marked by alternating ribs, some of which are linear, while others are quite broad.

Figure, natural size of the largest specimen.

Locality: Martiñez (Div. A.), collected by Mr. Mathewson, to whom the Survey is indebted for a number of fine specimens. I have also found it at Clayton, in a stratum of brown sandstone, overlying the coal; and at Cochran's, six miles east of Mount Diablo, in Div. B. Imperfect specimens from Curry's, south side of Mount Diablo.

F. AVERILLII, n. s.

Pl. 18, Fig. 34.

SHELL slender, fusiform, spire high, acute; whorls seven, sloping on the upper surface, rounded on the side, except the body whorl, which is obtusely angulated. Lower part of the body whorl unknown. Suture impressed, distinct. Surface marked by slightly oblique, rounded ribs, which commence just below the suture, and, after crossing the shoulder of the whorl, pass about an equal distance below it. These are crossed by a few revolving lines, which are somewhat enlarged on the crest of the ribs, forming small tubercles. Two of these lines, just below the suture, form distinct ribs above the origin of the longitudinal ones.

Figure, about two-fifths magnified.

Locality: Tuscan Springs, Tehama County (Div. A.). Named after Mr. Averill, one of the members of the Survey.

F. Diaboli, n. s.

Pl. 18, Fig. 35.

Shell elongated, fusiform, slender, spire acuminate, a little longer than the aperture, sides flattened. Whorls seven, very slightly convex. Aperture narrow; columellar lip apparently incrusted by a very thin layer of enamel; outer lip simple. Surface marked by longitudinal ribs, about a dozen on the body whorl; these ribs extend, on the last volution, for about half its length, gradually blending into the surface. Across these are numerous fine, impressed lines; although in some of the specimens they appear to be faint, or perhaps entirely absent.

The figure is somewhat magnified.

Locality: From the strata above the coal at Cochran's, east of Mount Diablo; and some casts, probably of this species, from near Clayton, in the same position. (All in Div. B.)

F. aratus, n. s.

Pl. 28, Fig. 202.

Shell robust, fusiform, spire rapidly tapering; whorls six, or six and a half, rounded on the side, abruptly truncated above, and strongly channelled below the suture. Aperture rounded, acute behind, columella not incrusted, anterior portion unknown. Surface marked by lines of growth, and anteriorly by a few revolving lines.

Figure, about two and a half times the natural size.

Locality: A single specimen, marked, "near Martiñez," in the collection of Mr. Rémond.

F. FLEXUOSUS, n. s.

Plate 21, Fig. 109.

SHELL elongated, slender, fusiform; aperture slightly longer than the spire. Whorls seven or eight, rounded; suture impressed. Surface marked by numerous small longitudinal ribs, crossed by small revolving lines. Mouth long, narrow, broadest above; canal long, curved.

Figure, slightly magnified.

Locality: Division A., near Martiñez.

This shell differs from *F. Diaboli* in the shorter and more robust spire, the less strongly marked longitudinal ribs, and the long, crooked canal.

F. KINGII, n. s.

Pl. 28, Fig. 204.

SHELL long, slender, fusiform; spire high; number of whorls unknown. Mouth long and narrow, canal straight. Surface unknown; from the cast, it seems to be ornamented by at least two, if not three revolving rows of tubercles, and by a series of elevated revolving lines.

Figure, natural size.

Locality: A single cast from Division A., from Cottonwood Creek, Siskiyou County, north of Yreka. Named after Mr. Clarence R. King, who, with Prof. Brewer, collected all the fossils brought from this locality.

F. CALIFORNICUS.

Pl. 28, Fig. 205, and 205 *a*.

(*? Clavatula Californica*, Con. P. R. R. Report, vol. 5, p. 322, pl. 2, fig. 11.)

SHELL fusiform, ventricose; spire barely as long as the mouth; whorls seven, rounded, the upper ones longitudinally ribbed; these ribs becoming obsolete with age, and entirely absent on the last whorl. Suture impressed. Mouth narrow in advance; canal slightly curved. Surface, in addition to the longitudinal ribs, crossed by numerous fine revolving ribs, sometimes showing a tendency to alternation in size, especially on the anterior part of the shell.

This shell does not appear ever to attain so large a size as either of the preceding species.

Figures, natural size, and magnified.

Localities: Clayton; Cochran's, near Mount Diablo; and Alizos Creek, near Fort Téjon.

SUBGEN. HEMIFUSUS, Swains.

F. (H.) HORNII, n. s.

Pl. 28, Fig. 206, and 206 *a*.

SHELL unequally fusiform; spire low, tapering concavely. Whorls six, the last bi- or tricarinate; the others with one rounded carina, except the one or two forming the extreme apex, which are rounded, smooth, and without markings. Mouth biangular above, gradually narrowing below; canal straight. Surface marked by two or three series of prominent tubercles, connected longitudinally by acute ribs, which are prolonged above to the suture, and below to irregular distances, becoming gradually obsolete.

Between these are numerous linear, revolving ribs, which rarely cross the longitudinal ribs. In addition to these are numerous fine lines of growth.

The upper whorls are merely cancellated.

Figures, natural size and magnified.

Locality: Near Fort Téjon.

Named after Dr. Geo. H. Horn, who collected all the specimens I have seen of this, the prettiest species of California Cretaceous Fusus.

F. (H.) COOPERII, n. s.

Pl. 28, Fig. 207.

SHELL of nearly the same outline as the preceding, except that the spire is a little higher, and tapers convexly; whorls six, in a shell of nearly twice the size of the former. Surface marked by three rows of large, rounded tubercles, one on the extreme upper edge, two below. These tubercles are not always placed directly opposite each other, and could not have been connected by the rib of the former species. Details of surface-marking unknown.

Figure, natural size.

Localities: San Diego, and Cochran's, east of Mount Diablo.

In all of the specimens the surface is so much decayed that, while the coarser ornaments are still discernible, the fine markings are obliterated. Better specimens will probably show revolving lines, since traces of that character seem to be retained by one specimen.

F. (H.) Rémondii, n. s.

Pl. 18, Fig. 36.

Shell fusiform, spire low; whorls five, rounded or subangular. Aperture long, moderately wide. Inner lip simple; outer lip thin, acute; canal long, straight. Body whorl rounded, or in some specimens marked by three faint angles on the widest part, the lower two placed nearer than the middle and upper ones. Surface closely cancellated by numerous fine, linear ribs, sharply defined, the included spaces being flat.

The low spire and regular form of the last whorl will serve to distinguish this pretty species, even in fragments.

Localities: Collected at Cochran's, east of Mount Diablo, by Mr. Rémond, and afterwards found by Mr. Mathewson and myself at Bull's Head Point, north-east of Martiñez (Div. B.). Of the specimens found at Cochran's none were more than an inch in length; while few of the Martiñez shells were smaller than the figure. Also found at Alizos Creek, near Fort Téjon.

NEPTUNEA, Bolt.

N. CURVIROSTRIS, n. s.

Pl. 18, Fig. 37.

SMALL, robust. Spire low; whorls six, rounded. Aperture moderate, inner lip simple, outer lip acute, crenulated internally. Canal long, broadly recurved. Suture distinct. Surface marked by numerous revolving, impressed lines, finer above, becoming more distinct below. One of these lines, immediately below the suture, is much broader and deeper than the rest. Across these lines are numerous, somewhat irregular, curved lines of growth.

Usual length, about .8 inch, although one fragment before me must have belonged to a specimen about 1.2 inch in length.

Locality: Cow Creek, Shasta County (Div. A.). Collected by Messrs. Brewer and Rémond.

N. PONDEROSA, n. s.

Pl. 18, Fig. 38.

THICK, robust, spire high, whorls plane or slightly convex; four or five in number; suture linear, more distinct as the shell increases in size; undulated. Surface marked by a few large ribs, varying in number and size on different specimens. These ribs are crossed by numerous revolving lines, all of the same size, on young specimens, but alternating irregularly on the larger whorls. Aperture broad, rounded subquadrate; columella slightly curved, outer lip straight, crenulate internally. Canal short, having at the extremity an oblique groove, indicating a rudimentary umbilicus, but entirely closed and very shallow.

The figure is of about average size. The largest specimen I have seen is broken; but, were it perfect, it would have been about 1.8 inch in length.

Localities: Tuscan Springs ("Lick Springs"), collected by Dr. Veatch; and Pence's Ranch, above Oroville, Butte County (Div. A.), collected by Prof. Brewer.

N. PERFORATA, n. s.

Pl. 18, Fig. 39.

SMALL, robust; whorls five, very convex, suture deep; first two whorls smooth or finely cancellate, remainder ornamented by large, oblique ribs, nearly as high as wide, starting at the suture, and extending nearly the whole width of the whorl, becoming obsolete at their lower ends. These are crossed by numerous sharply defined, linear, revolving ribs, which cover the whole surface, and occasionally, though rarely, alternate in size. Aperture wide, rounded. Outer lip acute on the edge, inner surface smooth (? judging from the cast); columella incrusted, pierced anteriorly by a minute, shallow, umbilical depression; no trace of a sinus anteriorly.

The usual size of the specimens is about .4 inch; the largest is .55 inch.

Locality: North fork of Cottonwood Creek (Div. A.); not rare.

? N. SUPRAPLICATA, n. s.

Pl. 18, Fig. 40.

SHELL small, fusiform; whorls five or more, regularly convex; suture well marked; spine nearly as long as the mouth. Surface marked by a number of small longitudinal folds on the upper half of the whorls, commencing at the suture; remainder of the body volution covered by distinct revolving ribs of about equal size throughout. Canal slightly curved. Aperture unknown.

Length, about .55 inch.

This shell is of about the same size, and nearly the shape of *Nassa cretacea;* but, even in fragments, it can be distinguished by the higher and more slender spire, and the peculiarity of the surface-markings.

Localities: San Diego, collected by Dr. Cooper; and (?) Clayton, Contra Costa County (casts).

N. Hoffmannii, n. s.

Pl. 18, Fig. 41.

Short, robust, shell thick; whorls five or six, convex; suture linear, marked below by a slight carina on the upper edge of the succeeding whorl. Surface ornamented by oblique, slightly sinuous ribs, which do not extend to the suture above, and become obsolete just below the line of greatest convexity of the whorl. These are crossed by a few revolving ribs, which disappear on the lower third of the whorl. Besides these, there are irregular, and, in some cases, prominent lines of growth. Aperture wide; columellar lip slightly incrusted; canal short, not emarginate anteriorly.

Figure, natural size.

Locality: North fork of Cottonwood Creek (Div. A.). Named in honor of Mr. Hoffmann, the topographer of the Geological Survey.

N. gracilis, n. s.

Pl. 18, Fig. 42.

Slender, fusiform; shell very thick; spire small, slender, not as long as the mouth; whorls convex. Aperture narrow, rounded posteriorly; canal somewhat elongated, slightly curved. Surface marked by small, regular, angular, revolving ribs, crossed by longitudinal undulations.

The only specimen I have seen is injured by the external layer of the shell having been broken off with the matrix, leaving only undulations in the place of the ribs. The internal surfaces of the shell in the aperture seem to exhibit the same ribs as the surface, although the substance of the shell itself is unusually thick.

Length of the fragment (having lost the upper one or two whorls), .8 inch.

Locality: Bull's Head Point, northeast of Martiñez (Div. B.). Collected by Mr. Mathewson.

PERISSOLAX, Gabb.

P. BREVIROSTRIS, n. s.

Pl. 19, Fig. 43.

SHELL short, robust, thick; spire of moderate height; whorls five, enveloped in such a manner that only the upper surface of the preceding whorls is visible. Suture distinct, bordered below by a carina, or sometimes a mere swelling of the upper edge of the whorl. Apical angle variable, sometimes uniform from the apex to the angle of the last whorl; in other specimens it is irregularly convex, from each whorl making the angle more acute. In one specimen the first two whorls are very acute, and the rest unusually obtuse. Surface biangular, sometimes with a smaller ridge below; marked on each angle by a row of large blunt tubercles, usually placed opposite each other, and each series connected by a low, rounded rib. These, as well as the rest of the shell, except the canal, are crossed by numerous variable revolving ribs, which are largest in the deep excavation just below the lower carination. Mouth simple, wide above, suddenly narrowed into the long, slender canal in advance. Columella slightly incrusted and faintly undulated in the middle.

Figure, natural size.

Localities: Tuscan Springs, Martiñez, Pence's Ranch, &c.; very characteristic of Division A.

The only marked variation in this species is in the somewhat irregular manner in which the spire is enveloped by each successive whorl. A slight difference may be found in the presence or absence of the third (lowest) row of tubercles. It is rare to find them entirely absent.

I place this shell in the genus Perissolax, *nobis*, although the canal is unusually short; a character which approaches that group to the true Fusus, and of which it may probably be considered only a subgenus.

P. Blakei.

Pl. 21, Fig. 110.

(*Busycon ? Blakei*, Con. Pacific R. R. Report, vol. 5, p. 322, Pl. 2, Fig. 13.)

Shell elongate; spire moderately elevated; whorls six to six and a half, angular; suture small, faintly channelled. Body whorl ornamented by two prominent, nodose carinæ, with a concave surface between them; the upper one only visible on the upper whorls; upper surface of the whorls inclined, plain or gently concave; surface marked by faint revolving lines. On one specimen there is a distinct, non-tuberculate rib between the two constant ones, and a faint angulation below the lower one.

Aperture elongated, broad above; below, rapidly narrowing into the long, slender canal. The aperture and canal are more than two and a half times as long as the height of the spire, measured from the posterior angle of the mouth. Canal slender, very slightly curved.

Figure, natural size.

Localities: From Division B., near Martiñez, where the only perfect specimen has been found. I have found it abundantly near the coal-mines at Clayton, in the same strata at Cochran's, east of Mount Diablo, and near the Cañada de las Uvas, Los Angeles County, where it is abundant.

TURRIS, Bolt., 1798.

Pleurotoma, Lam., 1799.

T. Claytonensis, n. s.

Pl. 18, Fig. 46.

Elongated, fusiform; spire slender, high. Aperture narrow, straight, widest posteriorly, about as long as the spire. Sinus deep, narrow, rounded, commencing a little below the suture, and situated entirely above the nodose angle of the whorl; outer lip acute, rounded, most prominent about half-way between the angle and the anterior extremity. Surface ornamented by a row of oblique nodes on the angle of the whorls, and by small ribs above and below; a single one, larger than the rest, bordering the upper edge of the whorl, just below the suture; the ribs above the angle are linear, those below are larger, subnodose, and diminish in size anteriorly. The lines of growth are faint.

Length of the specimen, less the upper whorls, .5 inch; probable total length, .58 or .60 inch.

A single specimen, found by myself, in an excavation above the "Clark" or upper coal-vein, near Clayton, Contra Costa County (in Division B.).

T. (S. G. Drillia) varicostata, n. s.

Pl. 18, Fig. 47.

Shell elongated, fusiform, spire high, whorls eight, subangular, suture indistinct; surface marked by a few large, rounded, oblique ribs, most prominent on the angle of the whorl, slightly extended below, and becoming suddenly obsolete above; these are crossed by numerous linear ribs, largest on the most prominent part of the whorl. Aperture elongated, widest above, and rapidly narrowing below. Sinus broad, rounded, commencing at the suture.

Length, .6 inch.

Locality: Same bed as the above, but in an adjoining hill.

CORDIERA, Rouault.

C. microptygma, n. s.

Pl. 28, Fig. 203.

Small, slender, fusiform; spire high, composed of eight slightly convex whorls; suture sharply impressed. Aperture elongated, subacute behind, prolonged below; canal unknown; inner lip heavily incrusted; columella curved, bearing four or five small, rounded, oblique folds, placed close together; outer lip with the sinus broad, rounded, and shallow. Surface marked by small, curved, longitudinal ribs, running parallel with the outline of the outer lip, most prominent a little below the suture, obsolete in advance, and placed close together; there are about from thirteen to fifteen of these ribs to a volution, and they are crossed by fine, revolving striæ.

Figure, slightly magnified.

Locality: Near Fort Téjon; Dr. Horn.

The discovery of this shell in the Cretaceous Formation is interesting, inasmuch as it carries the origin of the genus one formation lower than was heretofore known. As might be expected in the oldest known species, the generic characters are not as strongly marked as they are in the Tertiary forms. The folds on the columella are small, very oblique, broad, and not prominent; showing an approach to the plain columella of the true *Turris*.

TRITONIUM, Link.

Triton, Montf.

T. Hornii, n. s.

Pl. 28, Fig. 208.

Shell robust, fusiform; spire high, whorls seven, angular, and sloping above. Aperture elongated, broad, and biangular above; columella but slightly incrusted; canal gently curved. Surface marked by an irregular number of rows of tubercles; sometimes there is but a single row on the upper angle of the whorl; in other specimens there are three rows, more or less distinctly connected by longitudinal ribs; these are crossed by prominent revolving lines. Varices prominent, not numerous. The elevated apex and angular form, as well as the prominent tubercles, will at once distinguish this from either of the following species.

Fig. 208, magnified to about twice the size of the specimen. Some fragments before me, however, indicate that the species sometimes attains a size even greater than the figure.

Localities: Not rare at Alizos Creek, near Fort Téjon; and a single specimen was found at Cochran's, near Mount Diablo (Division B.).

T. Diegoensis, n. s.

Pl. 18, Fig. 44.

Shell fusiform, robust; whorls five or six, convex; spire about as long as the aperture. Surface ornamented by sinuous, rounded, longitudinal ribs, which extend almost entirely across the body volution, and by fine, revolving, linear ribs, which cover the whole surface. Aperture rounded, wide; columella slightly curved; lip but slightly emarginated anteriorly. The varices are few and small.

Length, .55 inch.

In shape and markings this species resembles *Neptunea perforata;* but the spire is higher, the whorls less prominently convex, the longitudinal ribs much longer, less prominent and sinuous; while in that species they are nearly straight and much more oblique. In this species the columella is thicker and curved, instead of straight as in *N. perforata,* and the umbilical depression is absent.

Locality: San Diego (Division B.). Collected by Dr. Cooper.

T. paucivaricatum, n. s.

Pl. 28, Fig. 209, and 209 *a*.

Shell short, robust; spire elevated, whorls six, convex, convexly truncated above; mouth broad, outer lip crenulated internally; inner lip incrusted, recurved, and dentate anteriorly. Suture deep. Surface marked by numerous small, longitudinal ribs, very oblique above, more transverse below; these are crossed by numerous, alternating, revolving lines.

Varices large, but few.

Length, .6 inch.

This shell is of nearly the same size and shape as *Neptunea perforata.* It can be distinguished, however, even in weathered specimens, by the more numerous and finer ribs, the presence of varices, and the curved columella. From *T. Diegoensis* it is sufficiently separated by the smaller and more numerous ribs, the more convex whorls, and the deeper suture.

Locality: Alizos Creek, near Fort Téjon (Division B.)

T. Whitneyi, n. s.

Pl. 28, Fig. 210, and 210 *a*.

Shell fusiform, turreted; spire high, whorls seven or eight, subangular; suture small, but distinct. Mouth wide above, narrowed in advance; canal slightly curved anteriorly. Surface marked by prominent nodes on the angles of the whorls, prolonged slightly above and below; these are crossed by numerous, well-marked, revolving lines, sometimes alternating in size.

Figures, natural size, and magnified to show the peculiarities of the surface markings.

Localities: Alizos Creek, near Fort Têjon, and a single cast from San Diego.

BUCCINUM, Linn.

B. liratum, n. s.

Pl. 28, Fig. 211.

Shell ovoid, robust, test thick; spire low, whorls four and a half to five, convex. Aperture elongate, deeply notched in advance; outer lip simple; inner lip lightly incrusted, more heavily below than above; umbilicus distinct, but imperforate. Surface marked by numerous rounded, longitudinal ribs, with intermediate spaces somewhat smaller than the ribs themselves; these run somewhat obliquely, especially at the top, where they curve slightly from behind forwards. The lower third to half of the shell is marked by numerous small, revolving, impressed lines.

Figure, natural size.

Localities: Not rare at Martiñez, Clayton, and Marsh's Ranch, in Contra Costa County (Division B.).

Except for the absence of the deep revolving groove on the middle of the body whorl, this shell might be placed in the genus *Pseudoliva*.

NASSA, Lam.

N. CRETACEA, n. s.

Pl. 18, Fig. 49.

SHORT, fusiform, spire rather elevated; whorls five, rounded, suture distinct. Surface ornamented by small longitudinal ribs, commencing at the suture and passing nearly across the whorl; these are crossed by fine revolving lines. Canal not very strongly recurved; sinus small, distinct (represented somewhat too small in the figure). Aperture acuminate posteriorly; columella but slightly incrusted.

Length, usually about half an inch.

Locality: Not rare at Bull's Head Point, near Martiñez (Div. B.).

N. ANTIQUATA, n. s.

Pl. 18, Fig. 50.

SHELL thin, proportionally broader than the preceding species; whorls five, rounded, suture impressed. Surface ornamented by fine longitudinal ribs, almost linear and numerous, crossed by revolving impressed lines, closely placed above, more distant below. Aperture ovate, very narrowly rounded posteriorly; columella very slightly incrusted, broad; canal but slightly recurved. Length of the specimen, .7 inch; probable length when perfect, .8 inch.

This species is founded on a single specimen, found by Mr. Mathewson at Bull's Head Point, near Martiñez. It is larger than any of the specimens of the preceding species that I have seen. The form is proportionally shorter and broader, and the sculpturing of the surface is markedly different. The shell appears to be minutely cancellate to the naked eye, and the cast, where denuded, exhibits no traces of ribs, while in the other species the cast is distinctly undulated.

HAYDENIA, N. Gen.

SHELL massive, allied, in general form, to *Oliva*, spire low. Outer lip simple, not thickened nor crenulate; inner lip incrusted, callus most marked posteriorly, without teeth or folds; canal slightly recurved; anterior extremity of the mouth notched, and a small sinus at the posterior extremity of the aperture, where the outer lip unites with the body whorl. Surface ornamented as in some of the Buccinidæ.

This curious form is probably a link between *Buccinum* and the genus *Volutharpa*, Fischer. It differs from the latter in the thick shell, the presence of the posterior sinus, the strongly recurved canal, and the sculpturing of the surface. The irregular, rough surface at once separates it from *Oliva;* since, in the present form, the mantle of the animal, evidently, never enveloped the shell.

Named in honor of Dr. F. V. Hayden, of Washington.

H. IMPRESSA, n. s.

Pl. 18, Fig. 51.

SHORT, robust, shell thick, spire low; whorls four, almost entirely enveloped; body whorl expanded. Aperture broad, columella curved, coated by a callus varying in size slightly, in different individuals, extending posteriorly above the suture. Canal slightly recurved; anterior sinus broad, posterior sinus small, as deep as wide, rounded. Surface marked by a groove parallel with the suture and immediately below the sinus and on the anterior half of the shell, by seven or eight distinct, impressed, revolving lines. These are crossed by numerous strong, irregular lines of growth.

Figure, natural size.

Localities: Tuscan Springs, Tehama County (Division A.), collected by Dr. Veatch ("Lick Springs" of Dr. Veatch); and Pence's Ranch, Butte County.

PSEUDOLIVA, Swains.

P. LINEATA, n. s.

Pl. 18, Fig. 52.

SHELL nearly conical; whorls four, spire low, suture excavated, bordered by a rounded rim on the succeeding whorl; body whorl terminating above in a rounded or somewhat flattened border, below which is a narrow, concave depression; below this the whorl attains its greatest width, and then gradually narrows, sometimes a little convexly, to the anterior end. Sides of the aperture nearly parallel; incrustation of the columella small, thin, and not extending posteriorly beyond the aperture; anterior sinus broad, shallow; posterior sinus placed entirely in the upper surface of the whorl, next the suture, twice as wide as deep. Canal but slightly recurved. Surface ornamented by numerous linear, revolving ribs, and by a single, deep impressed line, about the middle of the whorl.

Figure, average size.

Locality: Northeast of Martiñez, in Division B.; collected by Mr. Mathewson.

P. VOLUTÆFORMIS, n. s.

Pl. 28, Fig. 212.

SHELL thick, robust, resembling in shape the subgenus *Athleta* of the Volutes. Spire elevated, acute; whorls five and a half, sloping; suture irregular; body whorl sloping inwards convexly. Aperture long, rather narrow, biangular above, deeply notched below; outer lip simple, acute; inner lip heavily incrusted; columella slightly twisted in advance. Surface ornamented by a row of prominent, compressed tubercles on the angle of the body whorl, and below this by a series of revolving, impressed lines, faint above the median groove, more distinct below.

Figure, natural size.

Locality: But two specimens of this beautiful but aberrant form have been found; they are from near Fort Téjon, and were collected by Dr. Horn.

OLIVELLA, Swainson.

O. Mathewsonii, n. s.

Pl. 18, Fig. 53.

Small, fusiform, spire somewhat elevated; whorls five, suture deeply channelled and margined above by a slightly raised rib. Surface smooth. Anterior end, with two or three plications. Aperture acute behind, broad in front, and deeply notched.

Length, .8 inch.

Localities: Northeast of Martiñez; collected by Mr. Mathewson. Also found abundantly at Alizos Creek, near Fort Téjon.

ANCILLARIA, Lam.

A. elongata, n. s.

Pl. 18, Fig. 54.

Shell small, slender, elongated; spire high, whorls six, sides flattened, suture obliterated (from an impression in the matrix). Aperture narrow, acuminate posteriorly, columella folded in advance. Surface smooth.

Length, .4 inch; width of body whorl, .14 inch.

Two specimens were collected by Dr. Cooper from the most recent Cretaceous, near San Diego. The shell in both cases is very soft and much injured, but the impressions in the matrix still exhibit the surface characters. The long slender form will serve to distinguish this shell from the preceding, even in casts.

Localities: Near San Diego; Cochran's, east of Mount Diablo; and Clayton, (Division B.)

FASCIOLARIA, Lam.

? F. læviuscula, n. s.

Pl. 18, Fig. 55.

Fusiform, shell thick, spire elevated, whorls? Body whorl convex, smooth, except on the canal, where it is faintly marked by a few indistinct, oblique, revolving lines. Upper part of columella and aperture unknown; lower portion of the columella tortuous.

Figure, natural size. The outline is in part restored from another fragment. The species is founded on the fragment figured, and another, still more imperfect, of the body and preceding volution. I describe it here, because it is one of the few species found in the strata immediately below the coal in the Mount Diablo district, and may be important in identifying the same beds elsewhere. It is associated with several species found also at San Diego and Martiñez (Bull's Head Point), in Division B. From a hill, southeast of "Mine Hill," near Clayton, from a formation below the coal-bearing strata.

F. SINUATA, n. s.

Pl. 28, Fig. 213 *a*.

SHELL robust, fusiform; spire high, whorls six to six and a half, rounded; suture linear, impressed. Mouth rounded on the sides, acute above, narrowed below. Columellar lip very slightly incrusted; canal curved. Surface marked by about eight sinuous ribs on each volution, most prominent on the angle. These are crossed by numerous revolving, elevated lines, usually alternating very regularly in size.

Figures, natural size and magnified.

Localities: Alizos Creek, near Fort Téjon; and San Diego (in Division B.).

? F. Io, n. s.

Pl. 28, Fig. 214.

SHELL turreted, spire high, whorls seven and a half, angulated, flat or slightly concave above, and nearly straight below; marked on the angle by a series of prominent, flattened tubercles. Mouth biangular above, rapidly narrowing in advance; outer lip simple; inner lip very faintly incrusted; columella abruptly bent in advance; extremity of the canal unknown. Surface marked by numerous revolving lines, crossed by lines of growth.

Figure, natural size.

Locality: A single specimen found by Dr. Geo. H. Horn, near Fort Téjon.

I have not been able to expose sufficient of the inner lip to ascertain satisfactorily whether there are the requisite folds to place this shell in the genus *Fasciolaria*. Until more material shall have been obtained, the determination will therefore have to remain doubtful. The species is named from its resemblance to the fresh-water genus Io.

VOLUTILITHES, Swainson.

V. Navarroensis, Shum. ?

Pl. 19, Fig. 56.

Large, fusiform, thin, tapering nearly equally from the middle towards both extremities. Spire conical; whorls six to seven; those of the spire sometimes flattened, sometimes convex below, and flattened or slightly concave near the suture; body whorl flattened near the suture, gently swelling in the middle, and tapering or broadly and regularly concave below. Mouth long, narrow, acute behind, and with the sides nearly parallel in advance; outer lip acute; columella with three thin, linear, oblique folds on the middle. Suture distinct, impressed. Surface marked by longitudinal ribs, faintly sinuous, sometimes distinct and prominent, at others nearly obsolete; commencing a short distance below the suture, and losing themselves about or just below the middle of the whorl. When they are well marked, there are about fourteen or fifteen on the body whorl; but, as they become less distinct, they are more numerous. These are crossed by sixteen or seventeen revolving ribs; the first three (sometimes four) of which are small, plain, and placed above the origin of the longitudinal ribs; the next five or six are represented by a tubercle on each longitudinal rib, but are obsolete in the interspaces, the rest being plain, or more or less nodose. Three of the tubercular ribs are visible on the upper whorls.

Figure, natural size of the largest specimen.

Locality: Tuscan Springs, abundant; collected by Dr. Veatch. Also found at Pence's Ranch, above Oroville, Butte County; Jacksonville, Oregon; Siskiyou Mountains; Chico Creek, Butte County; and Cow Creek, Shasta County (in Division A.).

This species agrees so closely with Dr. Shumard's description of *V. Navarroensis* (Proc. Boston Soc. of Nat. Hist., Sept., 1861), that I have called it by his name. One specimen of the same length as his, 3.72 inches, is .2 inch wider in the body whorl, and with a length of aperture .2 inch greater. This slight variation would of course not separate it. There is a very slight discrepancy in the surface-markings, but not more than might be expected. The plain ribs at the top of the whorl are always more numerous than in his description, and I have not been able to find on any specimen more than seventeen of the revolving ribs in all. The greater number of volutions can easily be accounted for by the larger size of the specimen figured.

Should my determination of this species be correct, it will be an interesting link between the Cretaceous deposits on the two sides of the continent, associated, as it is, in Texas, with many species, the position of which, in the formation, has been satisfactorily determined east of the Mississippi.

MITRA, Lam.

M. CRETACEA, n. s.

Pl. 28, Fig. 215.

SHELL small, elongated, subfusiform; spire high; whorls seven and a half or eight, angulated, sloping on the upper margin, slightly sinuous below. Aperture long, rather narrow; columella with four (or five?) oblique folds. Surface marked by very fine revolving lines and indistinct lines of growth. Anterior extremity of the shell unknown.

Figure, three times natural size.
Locality: A single specimen from Martiñez; Mr. Mathewson.

WHITNEYA, N. Gen.

SHELL pyriform, spire low, suture channelled. Mouth with a well-marked notch posteriorly; outer lip simple, canal twisted and emarginate at the extremity; columellar lip incrusted, and with two or more very oblique folds below, like those of *Fasciolaria*.

This genus resembles in most of its characters *Fasciolaria*, although its *tout ensemble* is different from any species of that genus with which I am acquainted.

The low spire, the channelling of the suture, the posterior notch, the heavy incrustation of the inner lip, and the absence of crenulation on the inner surface of the outer lip, distinguish it sufficiently.

Named in honor of Prof. J. D. Whitney.

W. ficus, n. s.

Pl. 28, Fig. 216.

Shell pyriform or fig-shaped; spire low, whorls four and a half; suture channelled or impressed. Mouth elongate, narrowed in front; outer lip simple, inner lip covered by a rather heavy callus; canal twisted, and with two oblique folds below, the lower of which is the most prominent, placed at the base of the columella, and extending to the end of the canal. Surface marked by fine revolving lines, least prominent on the middle of the whorl; upper whorls longitudinally plicated.

Figure, slightly magnified.

Locality: Abundant near Fort Téjon. (Division B.)

MORIO, Montf.

Subgen. SCONSIA, Gray.

M. tuberculatus, n. s.

Pl. 19, Fig. 57.

Shell short, robust, thin; whorls seven, spire low. Surface marked by two, rarely three, rows of small tubercles; two bounding the widest portion of the volution, with a plane or slightly concave surface between them; the third, which occurs rarely, is placed below the others: besides these, the whole surface is ornamented by fine revolving striæ. Aperture broad; outer lip thick, longitudinally striate externally, inner surface crenulate; columellar lip covered by a broad plate, plicate or crenulate anteriorly. Canal strongly recurved. A distinct varix, nearly as large as the outer lip, occurs on the body whorl, and sometimes there is a smaller one on the penultimate volution. I have not always been able to detect the latter.

Figures, natural size. The view of the aperture is a restoration, based on several fragments showing different portions of that aspect of the shell.

Localities: Bull's Head Point, Martiñez; Clayton, Contra Costa County, in strata overlying the coal (in Division B.); and some specimens were collected near San Diego, by Dr. Cooper.

FICUS, Klein.

Sycotypus, Brown.

? F. CYPRÆOIDES, n. s.

Pl. 19, Fig. 58.

SHELL subconical, resembling a young *Cypræa;* spire very low; whorls four, barely exsert; body whorl large, broadly rounded above, sides nearly straight and approaching anteriorly; suture faint. Surface marked by rather distinct lines of growth, and anteriorly by a few obsolete, oblique, revolving lines. Aperture simple; columella very slightly curved in the middle.

Figure, natural size.

Locality: Tuscan Springs, Tehama County; collected by Dr. Veatch.

The remarkable resemblance of this shell to a young, imperfect *Cypræa*, has suggested its specific name. That this is its adult, perfect form, cannot be doubted, since I have seen half a dozen good specimens. It is probable that the generic reference given above will have to be changed; but I know of no described genus more suitable than the one to which it is referred, and do not feel warranted, with the material before me, in instituting a new genus to receive the shell.

LUNATIA, Lam.

L. AVELLANA, n. s.

Pl. 19, Fig. 60.

SUBGLOBOSE, spire somewhat elevated; whorls five, convex; suture impressed. Aperture subelliptical, narrow behind, rounded; a little produced anteriorly. Columella incrusted by a moderate callus of uniform thickness throughout its whole length; merging into the lip anteriorly. Umbilicus minute, barely visible. Surface marked by somewhat irregular lines of growth. There is no opercular scar on the columellar callus.

Length, .75 inch.

Locality: Cottonwood Creek, north fork (Division A.).

L. Shumardiana, n. s.

Pl. 19, Fig. 61.

Subglobose; spire not prominent; whorls four to four and a half, convex; suture impressed. Surface marked by pretty distinct and somewhat irregular lines of growth, most strongly marked in the larger specimens. Aperture ovate, broadly rounded in front, subacute posteriorly. Columellar callus distinct, somewhat thickened, abruptly contracted just above the umbilicus, and then continued, much narrower, to the anterior end of the mouth. Umbilicus small, but distinctly perforate. No opercular impression on the columella.

Figure, natural size.

This species is closely allied to *L. concinna*, M. and H., but is considerably larger and more oblique; the callus is heavier and more suddenly truncated at the umbilicus; it wants the opercular impression on the callus found in that species, and has one more volution. The latter character might be accounted for, however, by the difference in size.

Locality: Hills, southwest of Martiñez (Division B.); abundant. Named in honor of Dr. B. F. Shumard, of St. Louis, Mo.

L. Hornii, n. s.

Pl. 29, Fig. 217.

Shell subglobose; spire small, acute, not prominent; whorls five, almost entirely enveloped, except the newer portions of the penultimate volution. Aperture semilunar, rounded below; outer lip acute, nearly straight; columellar lip with a moderately large callus, thickened above, smaller and flat below, continuing as a thickened lip almost to the anterior end of the mouth. Umbilicus small, partially covered. Surface marked by irregular lines of growth.

Figure, natural size.

Locality: Alizos Creek, near Fort Téjon. All of the specimens of this species were collected by Dr. Geo. H. Horn.

L. NUCIFORMIS, n. s.

Pl. 28, Fig. 218.

SHELL small, subglobose; spire moderately high; whorls not enveloped to such an extent as in the preceding species, five to six in number; the extreme apical whorl very minute. Mouth wide, broadly rounded in advance. Outer lip nearly straight, or slightly more prominent near the suture; inner lip simple, or but slightly thickened. Umbilicus open, deeply perforated. Surface marked only by lines of growth.

Figure, natural size.

Locality: Alizos Creek, near Fort Téjon; and near Clayton (Division B.). A number of specimens, apparently belonging to this species, were collected by Dr. Cooper at San Diego; but they are not in a sufficiently good state of preservation to decide the point positively.

? L. (GYRODES ?) CONRADIANA, n. s.

Pl. 29, Fig. 219.

SHELL large, compressed-subglobose; spire somewhat prominent; whorls five, rounded; suture linear. Aperture elongated, terminating about equally at its upper and lower extremity. Outer lip sinuous, most prominent near the suture, and retreating below in a broad curve; inner lip simple. Umbilicus broadly open, perspective, forming about half of the diameter of the lower aspect of the shell; margin subangular. Surface, externally and in the umbilicus, marked by fine lines of growth.

Figure, natural size.

Locality: Two specimens, from Division A., on the San Luis Gonzaga Ranch, at the east end of Pacheco's Pass.

I have hesitated about placing this shell positively in either of the above genera; since, except for the patulous umbilicus, it would be undoubtedly a *Lunatia;* while this character is hardly conclusive, without the confirmatory one of the flattened or canaliculate upper portion of the whorl.

Named in honor of my friend, Mr. T. A. Conrad, one of the pioneers of American Cretaceous Palæontology.

GYRODES, Con.

G. EXPANSA, n. s.

Pl. 19, Fig. 62, *a, b, c.*

SHELL flattened; spire low; whorls four; apical channel slightly concave, or, more usually, flat, angulated, or rounded on the margin, but never carinate; whorls marked by a faint depression below the angle, most marked in old specimens. Mouth oblique, expanded laterally; lips simple. Umbilicus patulous, margin rounded, both on the shell and cast.

Figures, natural size. Figures *a* and *b* illustrate the adult form, showing the remarkable expansion of the body whorl. Fig. *c* is from a younger specimen.

This species is probably most nearly allied to *G. alveata,* Con.; but the whorls are less numerous, and the shell is more expanded. This character will also distinguish it from *G. abyssinis, Natica id.,* Morton.

Localities: Hills southwest of Martiñez; Pence's Ranch, above Oroville, Butte County; north fork of Cottonwood Creek; Tuscan Springs; and Texas Flat, Placer County (Division A.). Also in the Siskiyou Mountains, Siskiyou County; and at Jacksonville, Oregon, where I found a few distorted casts only.

NEVERITA, Risso.

N. SECTA, n. s.

Pl. 29, Fig. 220, and 220 *a.*

SHELL obliquely subglobose; spire moderately elevated; whorls five, almost entirely enveloped; apex acute; suture linear. Mouth acute behind, broadly rounded in advance; outer lip broadly rounded, acute; inner lip nearly straight, with a moderately heavy callus, a portion of which is developed into a large triangular mass, which nearly fills the umbilicus; across this and below the middle is a well-marked transverse groove. Umbilicus broad, but nearly closed. Surface marked by lines of growth.

Figures, natural size.

Locality: Alizos Creek, near Fort Téjon.

This species closely resembles *Lunatia Hornii* in its upper aspect, so much so that the differences would hardly appear of specific value. It differs, however, in being more oblique above, less regularly globose, and in the callus, which at once separates it from the genus *Lunatia*.

NATICINA, Gray.

N. OBLIQUA, n. s.

Pl. 21, Fig. 112.

SHELL small, oblique; spire slightly prominent; whorls four, rapidly increasing in size; suture faintly canaliculate. Surface marked by numerous compound revolving lines, minutely waved laterally, and showing a tendency to an alternation of larger and smaller ones; these are crossed by irregular lines of growth, which completely encircle the whorls, and are most distinct and crowded in the umbilicus. Aperture patulous, acute behind. Inner lip slightly thickened, and forming a small incrustation on the preceding whorl. Umbilicus moderate in size.

Figure, nearly twice natural size, linear.

Locality: Northeast of Martiñez (Division B.); also from Cañada de las Uvas and vicinity.

AMAUROPSIS, Mörch.

A. OVIFORMIS, n. s.

Pl. 19, Fig. 63.

SHELL ovoid; spire rather elevated; whorls six, rounded; suture slightly channelled. Aperture moderate, acute posteriorly, expanded in advance; columella faintly incrusted; umbilicus imperforate. Surface marked by irregular and sometimes very distinct lines of growth.

Figure, natural size.

Locality: Tuscan Springs, Tehama County (Div. A.).

A. ALVEATA.

Pl. 19, Fig. 59; and Pl. 21, Fig. 111.

(*Natica alveata,* Con., Pacific R. R. Report, vol. 5, p. 321, pl. 2, fig. 8, and 8 *a.*)

SHELL subglobose, elongated; spire high; whorls six and a half to seven, rounded on the sides, truncated horizontally, or a little obliquely above, and angulated, or sometimes slightly rounded on the edge. Suture linear, usually bordered by a slightly raised margin on the succeeding whorl. Aperture suboval, regularly rounded in advance, biangulate posteriorly; outer lip simple; inner lip thinly incrusted. Umbilicus small, perforate. Surface smooth, or closely striate by fine revolving lines; smooth specimens sometimes show fine lines of growth.

Figures, natural size. Fig. 59 is from San Diego; collected by Dr. Cooper. Fig. 111 is from northeast of Martiñez.

This species appears to attain the largest size of any American Cretaceous species in the family, one broken specimen from San Diego having been, at least, two inches high.

Localities: Found in Division B., at San Diego; Martiñez; Clayton; and at Cañada de los Alizos, near Fort Téjon (*Eocene* of Conrad); and in Division A., at Curry's, south of Mount Diablo, associated with numerous species of that group.

The San Diego specimens show none of the revolving lines; while in every case, at the other localities, I have found these lines on, at least, a part of the surface. They are usually most prominent on the upper part of the body whorl, sometimes being visible only on the truncated portion.

CINULIA, Gray.

Avellana, D'Orb.

C. OBLIQUA, n. s.

Pl. 19, Fig. 64, and 64 *a*, *b*, *c*.

SHELL subglobose, obliquely truncated below; whorls four, rounded; suture distinct. Surface ornamented by numerous fine revolving ribs, with deep interspaces, which are divided into minute, square compartments by cross-bars, which do not rise to the level of the ribs. Outer lip heavy, smooth, a little notched, or sinuous anteriorly. Columella coated by a heavy callus, which unites at both ends with the lip, and bears a large fold anteriorly, with a slight intumescence in advance of it.

Figure 64, and 64 *a*, are from the largest specimen I have seen; Fig. *b* is of about the average size; Fig. *c* shows the ornamentation of the surface.

Localities: Tuscan Springs, Martiñez; Pence's Ranch, above Oroville; Chico Creek; and Texas Flat, Placer County (Division A.). Also, at Cottonwood Creek, and in the Siskiyou Mountains, Siskiyou County.

C. MATHEWSONII, n. s.

Pl. 19, Fig. 65.

SHELL ovoid; spire moderate; whorls four and a half, convex, last one expanded; suture impressed. Surface marked by rows of minute punctations, with broader, somewhat elevated, flat ribs between them. Outer lip broad, heavy, slightly sinuous, longitudinally striate and slightly indented in advance, on the oral aspect. Columellar incrustation heavy, continuous above and below with the outer lip, and with three narrow, prominent, equal folds. Length, .47 inch.

Locality: From a compact, dark-green or gray limestone at Bull's Head Point, Martiñez (Division B.); collected by Mr. Mathewson. Also, from Orestimba Cañon, Stanislaus County.

C. pinguis, n. s.

Pl. 29, Fig. 221, and 221 *a*, *b*.

Shell robust, subglobose when young, ovoid when adult; spire moderately high; whorls probably as many as seven or eight, very convex; suture strongly marked. Aperture rounded, rapidly narrowed above; mature outer lip unknown; inner lip heavily incrusted, bearing an obtuse, angular prominence above, and two strongly marked, acute folds below, the lower of which is prolonged downwards, and becomes continuous with the anterior margin of the mouth. Surface marked by a series of square, revolving ribs, with interspaces larger than the ribs themselves; these are crossed by crowded and prominent lines of growth.

Figures of the shells magnified, the larger to a little over twice natural size; that of the immature shell, three diameters. Figure of the surface to show the details of ornamentation.

Locality: A very few specimens of this species have been found by Mr. Mathewson in the Bluffs, a mile west of Martiñez (in Division A.?).

A few specimens have been found at Martiñez and at Tuscan Springs, which may belong to this genus, or to *Ringicula;* but, on account of their imperfect condition, I am not yet able to make out with any certainty either their generic or specific relations. They seem to indicate two or even three species.

RINGICULA, Desh.

R. varia, n. s.

Pl. 29, Fig. 222 *a*, *b*.

Shell small, elongate-ovoid; spire high; whorls six, slightly convex; suture well-marked; body whorl broadly and regularly convex. Aperture wide, acute behind, narrowed in front, and with a deep, oblique notch. Outer lip nearly simple, the margin being not twice as thick as the shell behind it, and very narrow; inner lip covered with a small, circumscribed callus, bearing two small acute folds anteriorly. Surface variable, sometimes almost perfectly smooth and polished; at other times ornamented by sharp, impressed lines; and in still other specimens having square ribs of variable width, with the lines of growth strongly developed in the interspaces, and represented on the surface of the ribs by shallow undulations.

Figure *a*, twice natural size; Fig. *b*, a magnified view of the surface of the most highly ornamented variety.

Locality: Cow Creek, Shasta County, east of Shasta City.

NERINEA, Defr.

N. DISPAR, n. s.

Pl. 19, Fig. 66, and 66 *a*.

SHELL slender, elongated; whorls numerous, very oblique; apical angle very small; suture impressed. Surface ornamented by small, longitudinal ribs, which commence below the suture, and end some distance above the lower edge of the whorl; between the ends of these ribs and the next suture is a large, rounded fold. These are all crossed by fine, revolving lines, and by longitudinal lines of growth. Internally there are no ribs nor folds. The drawing and description of the external surface are taken from a very imperfect impression in the matrix.

Figures, natural size.

Locality: North fork of Cottonwood Creek, Shasta County, rare (Division B.).

The long, slender form, convex whorls, with the large fold at the base, and the entire absence of internal ribs, will at once distinguish this peculiar species.

ACTEONINA, D'Orb.

? A. PUPOIDES, n. s.

Pl. 19, Fig. 67.

SHELL small, ovoid; spire elevated, outline convex; whorls six or seven; suture faint. Surface ornamented only by lines of growth. Aperture unknown.

The anterior end of the figure is restored from the back of a cast. The first two or three whorls are very small, and the angle of the surface is much greater than that of the subsequent volutions.

Figure, natural size.

Locality: Three specimens were found on the north fork of Cottonwood Creek, Shasta County, by Mr. Rémond.

A. Californica, n. s.

Pl. 19, Fig. 68.

Shell large, ovate; spire elevated; whorls six or seven, rounded, somewhat flattened in the middle; suture distinct. Aperture moderate, acute behind, rounded in advance. Surface smooth, marked by faint, sinuous lines of growth, which show that the outer lip retreated gradually above, and was most prominent in the middle.

Figure, a restoration; about natural size.

Half a dozen specimens have been found northeast of Martiñez (in Division A.), and in beds of the same age, about two miles north of Benicia, and a single specimen was found eight miles north of Yreka. The substance of the shell is thick, and in all the specimens is so crystalline that not a specimen has been found sufficiently perfect to be drawn.

GLOBICONCHA, D'Orb.

G. (Phasianella ?) Rémondii, n. s.

Pl. 19, Fig. 69.

Shell subglobose, spire elevated, conical; whorls about five or six, convex. Aperture broad, acute behind, rapidly widening, and regularly rounded in advance. Surface?

Figure, natural size. A restoration from a cast, showing crystalline fragments of the shell, but none of the surface.

Locality: About two miles north of Benicia (in Division A.). A single specimen, found by Mr. Rémond.

CYLINDRITES, Morris and Lycett.

C. BREVIS, n. s.

Pl. 29, Fig. 223.

SHELL short, robust, ovoid; spire low; whorls four, rounded on the upper margin; suture deep. Aperture broad, produced and rounded in advance; outer lip simple; inner lip incrusted; the incrustation forming a large fold in advance. Sides of the body volution subflattened, approaching anteriorly. Surface marked only by a few indistinct lines of growth.

Figure, nearly three times natural size.

Locality: A few specimens have been found by Mr. Mathewson in the vicinity of Martiñez.

This shell is remarkable for its very short, robust form, making an outline different from any other species of the genus with which I am acquainted. As far as I am aware, this is the first species discovered in the Cretaceous formation.

CHEMNITZIA, D'Orb.

C. SPILLMANI, Con. ?

Pl. 19, Fig. 70.

(*C. Spillmani*, Con. Jour. Academy of Nat. Sciences Philadelphia, 2 ser., vol. 4, p. 287, pl. 46, fig. 48.)

SHELL elongated, slender; whorls flattened on the sides; suture impressed. Surface marked by slightly curved, obtuse, longitudinal ribs, crossed by four or five impressed lines; under surface smooth. Columellar lip thickened.

Except the difference in size—and this is in all probability a young specimen—I cannot find a single character on which to separate this shell from Mr. Conrad's species. The difference in the apical angle is not so great as would seem, from a comparison of the figures. The sides, in Mr. Conrad's specimen, are much more nearly parallel than he has represented them.

Locality: Pence's Ranch, north of Oroville, Butte County (Division A.); collected by Mr. Brewer.

NISO, Risso.

N. POLITA, n. s.

Pl. 21, Fig. 113.

SHELL small, slender, conical; whorls many (about ten or eleven ?), flattened on the sides; upper edge minutely truncated. Surface polished. Aperture imperfect in all the specimens. Umbilicus open, forming about a fifth of the lower surface.

Figure, a little more than three times natural size.

Locality: Four specimens from northeast of Martiñez (in Division B.).

CERITHIOPSIS, Forbes and Hanley.

C. ALTERNATA, n. s.

Pl. 21, Fig. 114, and 114 *a*.

SHELL long, slender; spire high; whorls about twelve or thirteen, convex; suture impressed. Surface marked by longitudinal ribs, crossed by numerous revolving ribs, alternating, pretty regularly, in size; the larger ones form small tubercles on crossing the longitudinal ribs, and occasionally, one of the latter is larger than the rest, presenting the appearance of a varix. Aperture broken; columella strongly curved, and lightly incrusted.

Figures, natural size and magnified.

Locality: Northeast of Martiñez and Cochran's, east of Mount Diablo (Division B.)

ARCHITECTONICA, Bolt.

(*Solarium*, Lam.)

A. VEATCHII, n. s.

Pl. 19, Fig. 71.

SHELL small; spire high; whorls biangular, number unknown. Surface marked by a number of small tubercular ribs; three on the upper surface of the whorls have their tubercles much larger than the others, and so arranged as to present a cancellated appearance; those on the side are small, and the tubercles are mere elevated points. Under surface convex, and minutely cancellated. Umbilicus marked internally by numerous, rather large lines. Margin unknown.

Figure, natural size.

Locality: Found at Tuscan Springs, Tehama County, by Dr. J. A. Veatch. Rare. (Division A.)

A. COGNATA, n. s.

Pl. 20, Fig. 72, and 72 *a, b, c, d, e.*

SHELL, low conical; whorls six to six and a half, flat or slightly convex and sloping above, acutely carinate on the margin. Mouth quadrangular, oblique. Surface marked by oblique lines of growth and faint revolving lines, sometimes obsolete. Near the margin, on the upper surface, is a prominent isolated rib. Under surface convex in the middle, and concave near the outer margin; in this concavity is another rib, somewhat larger than the one above. The rest of this side of the shell is like the upper surface. Margin of the umbilicus coarsely crenulated.

This species is very closely allied to the Eocene form, described by Mr. Conrad as *Solarium alveatum*, and by Mr. Lea as *S. bilineatum*. In that species (Fig. *e*) there are two impressed lines, near the margin, above, and two parallel linear ribs below; instead of the single large rib of the present species (Fig. *d*).

Figures, natural size. I have seen one specimen with a diameter of one and a third inches.

Localities: Seven miles south of Martiñez; and near Clayton, above the coal (in Division B.). It is most abundant at Bull's Head Point, near Martiñez, where Mr. Mathewson has collected numerous fine specimens, and where I found the individual figured.

A. HORNII, n. s.

Pl. 29, Fig. 224, and 224 *a, b.*

SHELL flattened; spire very low, slightly convex; whorls six and a half; suture distinct, impressed; outer margin of the body whorl bearing three ribs, one at the extreme edge, one above, and the third below. Mouth rounded, subtriangular. Umbilicus broad, margin strongly crenulated. Upper surface marked only by lines of growth; lower surface grooved by extension of the crenulation of the umbilical margin, and by variable revolving lines.

Figures, about three times natural size; Fig. 224 *b*, is from the under surface of the body whorl.

Locality: Three specimens were collected by Dr. Horn near Fort Téjon. (Div. B.)

This species differs from *A. cognata* in the lower spire, convex upper surface, less acute angle, the position of the marginal ribs, and much smaller size.

A. INORNATA, n. s.

Pl. 20, Fig. 73.

SHELL robust, conical; spire elevated; whorls five, flattened on the sides, compressed or channelled above, subangular on the margin; suture impressed. Surface usually only marked by lines of growth. Body whorl channelled above, angulated on the margin, with sometimes a slight depression below the angle. Lower margin rounded. Under surface slightly convex. Umbilicus narrow, but open the whole length of the spire; internally striate. Mouth rounded, subquadrate.

Figure, natural size.

Localities: Abundant in the hills southwest of Martiñez. A single specimen was found at Tuscan Springs, Tehama County, by Dr. Veatch. Only found in Division A.

One specimen from Martiñez shows faint revolving lines on the outside of the whorls.

MARGARITELLA, Meek and Hayden.

M. CRENULATA, n. s.

Pl. 20, Fig. 74.

SHELL minute, turbinate; spire proportionally not so elevated as in the preceding species; whorls five; suture channelled.

Surface marked by fine imbricating lines of growth, which arise at the suture, pass obliquely backwards around the whorl to the umbilicus, presenting a finely crenulated appearance on the upper angle of the whorl. Umbilical margin very coarsely crenulated. Aperture rounded, subquadrate. Body whorl flat, or sharply rounded and channelled above, nearly flat on the side, sloping outwards and convex below.

Height, .15 inch; width, .19 inch.

Locality: Three specimens were collected by Dr. Cooper, near San Diego.

M. GLOBOSA, n. s.

Pl. 29, Fig. 225.

SHELL very small, subglobose; spire moderately high; whorls five to five and a half, rounded, except the body whorl, which is sometimes obliquely flattened on the sides. Mouth subcircular, acute behind; lips simple. Umbilicus perspective, crenulated on the margin. Surface polished, marked by very fine lines of growth.

Figure, highly magnified.

Locality: Near Benicia (in Division A.). Collection of Mr. Rémond.

This shell is easily distinguished from *M. crenulata* by its larger size, more globose form, and its higher spire. Unlike that species, it is not truncated on the upper margin of the whorls, and it only occurs in the lower member of the formation; while *M. crenulata* is, so far as our information goes, peculiar to the upper member.

DISCOHELIX, Dunker.

(*Orbis*, Lea, *not Schröt, nor Lacep.*)

D. LEANA, n. s.

Pl. 20, Fig. 75.

SHELL discoidal, flat; spire none; whorls five, in contact, but not enveloping; section circular; the first whorl slightly more prominent on the upper than on the lower side. Surface smooth. Aperture simple, circular.

Diameter, .22 inch; width of body whorl, .05 inch.

Locality: Texas Flat, Placer County (Division A.). Collection of the Academy of Natural Sciences of California.

This shell, named in honor of Mr. Lea, President of the Philadelphia Academy of Natural Sciences, is almost a perfect miniature of *Ammonites Batesii.* The margin differs from *O. rotella,* Lea, of the Alabama Eocene, in being round, instead of bicarinate; and it can be distinguished from *D. foliacea,* Philippi, (recent) by the whorls being circular, instead of flattened.

STRAPAROLLUS, Montf.

(*Euomphalus*, Sow.)

S. PAUCIVOLVUS, n. s.

Pl. 20, Fig. 76.

SHELL flattened; spire low; whorls few, number unknown, increasing rapidly in size, rounded, subovate in section, most convex below; suture impressed. Umbilicus rather wide. Surface smooth, or marked only by lines of growth.

Diameter, .26 inch; width of aperture, .10 inch; height of aperture, .09 inch.

Locality: With the preceding.

S. LENS, n. s.

Pl. 20, Fig. 77, *a*, *b*, *c*, and *d*.

SHELL minute, lenticular; spire low, slightly convex; whorls seven, rounded above, subangular on the margin, sloping convexly inwards to the margin of the umbilicus. Umbilicus between a third and a quarter of the diameter. Mouth narrow, subquadrate, and sloping inwards. Surface smooth or striate by delicate lines of growth.

Diameter, .3 inch; height, about .14 inch; width of mouth, .04 inch.

Locality: With the preceding.

Associated with this is another shell. having all of the essential characters of this species, except that the tops of the whorls, instead of being convex, are sharply angulated a short distance from the suture, with a plain surface, sloping from the angle to the suture. To the outside of this angle, the side is more convex than in the specimen figured. With but one specimen, and that somewhat mutilated, I do not feel warranted in describing it as distinct, although a series will probably prove it to be so. Figures *c* and *d* illustrate the relative outlines.

ANGARIA, Bolt.

(*Delphinula*, Lam.)

A. ORNATISSIMA, n. s.

Pl. 20, Fig. 78.

SHELL turbinate; spire high; whorls six, sloping and subangular above; sides flat, under-surface convex; suture impressed, linear, bordered by a slightly raised rim on the succeeding whorl. Surface minutely cancellate by fine, thread-like, revolving and oblique longitudinal lines, smaller than the interspaces; the longitudinal lines commence at the suture and pass obliquely backwards and downwards, crossing the whole whorl and running up into the umbilicus; the revolving lines are equally placed over the whole surface, except in the umbilicus, where there are but five of them. Mouth simple; columellar lip faintly thickened.

Diameter, .45 inch; height, .43 inch; height of mouth, .26 inch.

Locality: With the preceding; abundant. Also found at Tuscan Springs.

CONUS, Linn.

C. Rémondii.

Pl. 20, Fig. 79.

(*Volutilithes Californica*, Con. Pacific R. R. Report, vol. 5, p. 322, Pl. 2, Fig. 9.)

Shell biconical; spire nearly a third of the total length; whorls six, sloping above, crenulated on the angle; sides straight, regularly conical. Aperture linear, biangular behind, a little narrowed in advance. Surface marked by numerous revolving, impressed lines, and by fainter lines of growth.

Length, usually about 1 inch.

Localities: Found by Mr. Rémond at Cochran's, east of Mount Diablo, and since found at Bull's Head Point, northeast of Martiñez; at Clayton, above the coal; and at San Diego (Division B.). Also near Cañada, or "Cajon de las Uvas," Los Angeles County, whence it was described by Mr. Conrad under the above name.

This shell resembles *C. Rouaultii*, d'Arc., of the French Eocene: see Mem. Soc. Geol. de France, 2 ser., tom. 3, pl. 13, fig. 22. It tapers more regularly anteriorly, and the surface-markings are less distinct; it is also more robust. The specific name *Californicus* having been used by Hinds for a recent species, I propose the above name in honor of Mr. Rémond, who discovered the specimens from which I became acquainted with the species.

C. Hornii, n. s.

Pl. 29, Fig. 226.

Shell very unequally biconical; spire low; whorls seven and a half or eight, concave above, acute on the angle, with a very fine thread-like groove just inside of the margin. Mouth long, narrow, straight; outer lip curved, most prominent above; sides of the body whorl straight. Surface marked by a few oblique, revolving bands below, and sometimes by one or two on the top of the whorl.

Figure, natural size.

Locality: Alizos Creek, near Fort Tĕjon. (Division B.) Collected by Dr. Horn.

This shell is of the same size as *C. Rémondii*, but can be at once distinguished by its low spire, the absence of tubercles on the whorls, and the acute, channelled angle. I have not seen it from any other locality than the one above quoted, where it does not appear to be very rare.

C. SINUATUS, n. s.

Pl. 29, Fig. 227.

SHELL moderate in size, subfusiform; spire elevated, turreted; whorls five or more, angular, concave above, and strongly sinuated below; suture channelled, the upper margin of the whorl bearing a fine thread-like groove, similar to that on the angle of the whorl of the preceding species; upper surface of the whorls finely striate, the angle minutely crenulated or plain; anterior portion of body whorl (as much as is known) marked by a few pretty distinct revolving lines.

Figure, natural size.

Locality: A single, imperfect specimen was found by Dr. Horn, near Fort Téjon. The anterior fourth of the shell is gone, and the lines of growth are too indistinct to ascertain the exact shape of the missing portion. The curved whorl and the elevated, turreted spire will distinguish this very peculiar species.

ROSTELLARIA, Lam. *Gladius*, Klein.

SUBGEN. RIMELLA, Agas.

R. CANALIFERA, n. s.

Pl. 29, Fig. 228.

SHELL small, unequally fusiform; spire elevated, longer than the mouth; whorls six or seven, convex; suture deep. Aperture long, rather narrow, oblique, acute behind, and broadly and obliquely emarginate in front; the posterior angle of the mouth is continued in a deep, narrow canal, slightly curved, along the spire to the apex; anterior canal broad, strongly curved upwards; outer lip thickened along its whole extent, but most strongly so above; inner lip incrusted by a callus, which extends posteriorly, so as to unite with the posterior canal. Surface marked by prominent longitudinal ribs, crossed by distinct revolving linear ribs, very uniform in size, and with interspaces of about the same size as the ribs.

Figure, slightly magnified.

Localities: Martiñez, and near Fort Téjon.

In 1861, in my "Synopsis of the Mollusca of the Cretaceous Formation," I used Klein's name, in preference to that of Lamarck's, for this genus. Since then, in common with the majority of American conchologists and palæontologists, I have determined to ignore all pre-Linnæan names, unless first adopted under the binomial system by some subsequent author, on account of the confusion which must inevitably arise, unless we have some settled starting-point for our nomenclature.

R. (RIMELLA) SIMPLEX, n. s.

Pl. 20, Fig. 80.

SHELL elongated, robust; spire high; whorls about seven, rounded; suture distinct. Surface marked by numerous longitudinal ribs, small on the upper volutions, becoming larger, more distant, oblique, and proportionally shorter, as the shell increases in size; these are crossed by small, regular, revolving lines. Outer lip suddenly expanded; posterior canal continued along the surface of the penultimate whorl; anterior canal suddenly recurved. Aperture unknown.

Figure, natural size.

Locality: Collected by Dr. Cooper, at San Diego; and I have found a single specimen at Clayton, in the strata above the coal (Division B.).

Larger than the preceding species, and easily distinguished by its large, longitudinal ribs.

PUGNELLUS, Con.

P. HAMULUS, n. s.

Pl. 20, Fig. 81, and Pl. 18, Fig. 48.

SHELL robust; spire moderately high; whorls six, angular, sloping above and crenulated on the carina. In the immature state, suture impressed, linear, angle of body whorl crenulated; surface marked by numerous fine, revolving lines; lip thin, broadly rounded, most prominent in the middle. In the adult shell, the surface-markings and suture are obliterated by a heavy incrustation, which covers the spire and body volution. Aperture broad behind, narrowed in advance; outer lip provided on the margin with a broad, heavy callus above and a smaller one below, with a narrow, subangular sinus between them; between the upper callus and the body whorl there is a broad, deep emargination; below, the margin rapidly retreats towards the canal, which is strongly curved forwards in the form of a blunt hook. Viewed from the back, the upper margin of the lip presents a thick, rounded callus, commencing at the club-shaped extremity, and which, curving upwards, merges into the general contour of the shell, on the upper surface of the body whorl.

Figures, natural size.

Locality: In the hills southwest of Martiñez (Division A.). The strong hook-like canal, and the notch in the outer lip, will at once distinguish this from the other four known species of the genus.

P. MANUBRIATUS, n. s.

Pl. 29, Fig. 229.

SHELL small, rather thin; spire moderately high; whorls six, rounded; suture distinct. Mouth long, narrow, very acute posteriorly; canal wide, straight, not very deeply notched; outer lip with a square callus, prolonged above into a long, slightly curved hook; the notches above and below the origin of the callus are well marked, the lower one being somewhat variable; the margin of the lip is thickened along its whole length; inner lip heavily incrusted, the layer being prolonged so as to cover the whole ventral face of the shell to the apex. Surface marked by numerous sinuous ribs, extending from the suture about two-thirds of the distance towards the anterior end.

Figures, natural size.

Locality: Cottonwood Creek, Siskiyou County.

This is the first species of this genus in which the callus of the lip has been found to assume a falcate form. This peculiar character seems to ally the genus to *Aporrhais;* but the constant thickness of the callus and the strombiform shape of the shell will serve sufficiently to distinguish the two genera.

TESSAROLAX, N. Gen.

SHELL fusiform, spire and aperture about equal; spire incrusted by a thin deposit, so as to obliterate the sutures. Body whorl bearing two (or more) varix-like processes. Aperture broad above, continued below in a long, curved canal; a posterior canal continues for some distance up the spire. Columella incrusted, but without folds or teeth. Outer lip produced into two long spine-like canals.

This very curious genus seems to combine the characters of several genera in the family of the *Strombidæ.* It has the dactylate lip of *Pteroceras,* the clavate tubercles or varices of some of the species of true *Strombus,* the anterior and posterior canals of *Rostellaria,* and the enveloped spire of *Calyptraphorus.*

T. DISTORTA, n. s.

Pl. 20, Fig. 82, and 82 *a, b.*

SHELL elongated; spire high; whorls five or six (from casts), slightly convex in the middle, so as to produce a faint undulation on the smooth surface of the spire. Apex usually flattened and somewhat twisted; at other times bluntly rounded. Surface of body bicarinate, bearing on the upper carina, at a point about a third of the circumference from the mouth, a short, clavate process, abruptly truncated at the end and flattened on the sides. On the lower carina is another process, flattened above and below, prominent and angular at the extremity. This is placed about half-way between the first and the outer lip. Aperture small, broad above, rapidly narrowed and prolonged below into a canal, which curves obliquely forwards and to the left. Above, the mouth is continued into a canal, which runs beside the spire for about two-thirds of its height, and then curves off obliquely backwards and to the right. The outer lip is prolonged into two long, slender, channelled spines, continuations of the carinæ on the whorl, which diverge rapidly, and which are not in the same plane, the lower one being directed much in advance of the upper.

Figures, natural size.

Abundant at Tuscan Springs, Tehama County. Collected by Dr. Veatch (Division A.).

APORRHAIS, Petiver, Dacosta.

A. FALCIFORMIS, n. s.

Pl. 20, Fig. 83.

SHELL elongated, slender; spire very high; whorls usually eleven, sometimes twelve; suture distinct; surface ornamented by about fourteen rounded, longitudinal ribs, slightly curved and narrower than the interspaces; these are crossed by from seven to nine rather large revolving ribs on the upper whorls. Body volution somewhat uniangular near the lip; the ribs dwindle to mere broad, oblique tubercles, and the revolving lines extend down to the canal. Mouth biangular above, rapidly narrowing to the canal, which, from casts, appears to form nearly a third of the total length of the shell. Lip long, falcate, sometimes almost as high as the spire, usually ending about two-thirds of an inch below the apex; inner margin diverging at a small angle from the spire; outer margin nearly perpendicular and very slightly convex, ending in an angle; lower margin concave, with a small tubercle at its inner end. The shape of this side of the lip is variable; sometimes the angle is replaced by a broadly rounded process. The inner face of this lip is angularly concave; back carinate. Columella incrusted by a large callus, forming a tubercular projection immediately on the oblique lower surface of the body whorl.

Figure, natural size.

Localities: Tuscan Springs, Dr. Veatch; Chico Creek, Mr. Brewer; Pence's

Ranch, Butte County; and Texas Flat, Placer County. One of the most abundant fossils in the State, and very characteristic of the lower group of Cretaceous strata.

A. ANGULATA, n. s.

Pl. 20, Fig. 84.

SHELL elongated; spire high; whorls numerous, number unknown; upper whorls convex, widest a little below the middle; last whorl sharply and acutely angulated, sloping and gently concave above and below the angle; suture impressed. Surface ornamented by fine, thread-like, revolving lines, and by sinuous lines of growth. Canal long, narrow, straight. Outer lip curved, unicarinate, exact form unknown.

Figure, natural size.

Locality: In a single stratum of greenish-gray limestone, at Bull's Head Point, near Martiñez. Very rare. (Div. B.)

I am indebted to Mr. Mathewson for the chance of describing this species. The specimen figured is the only one I have seen showing the body whorl, and in this case entirely denuded of its shell. Another specimen, consisting of three whorls of the spire, is in the collection of the Survey. Mr. Brewer collected three specimens at Huling Creek, near the Cottonwood Creek locality, resembling this species in surface ornamentation and in the shape of the upper whorls, but in which the last whorl was distinctly bicarinate. None of the specimens show either lip or canal, and the lower carina is less prominent and less acute than the upper. They are probably a variety of the present species.

A. CALIFORNICA, n. s.

Pl. 29, Fig. 230 *a*, *b*.

SHELL small; spire high; whorls eight, convex; suture deep. Mouth long, prolonged below into a moderate, straight canal; outer lip prominent, somewhat variable in shape, usually regularly concave above, rounded on the external margin and angular below, prolonged above, on its outer edge, into a long falciform process, which extends almost as high as the spire; inner lip but slightly incrusted. Body whorl nearly plain, with an angle above bearing a few tubercles; this angle is prolonged on the lip to the base of the superior process; upper whorls marked by fine longitudinal ribs, crossed by a few fine, impressed lines, most distinct above.

Figure *a*, natural size; Fig. *b*, magnified view of a young specimen, showing the sculpture.

Localities: Orestimba Cañon; Martiñez; Puerto Cañon, Stanislaus County; Siskiyou Mountains.

A. EXILIS, n. s.

Pl. 29, Fig. 231.

SHELL minute; spire high; whorls six, upper whorl convex, the apex blunt; body whorl biangular, the upper angle very prominent; canal produced, straight; lip unknown. Upper whorls ornamented by curved ribs placed somewhat obliquely; on the body whorl these ribs incline forward to the upper angle of the whorl, and then downwards and backwards, becoming obsolete anteriorly; below the lower angle, they are crossed by smaller revolving lines, producing a somewhat cancellated appearance.

Figure, two and a half times natural size.

Locality: A single, imperfect specimen, collected by Mr. Mathewson at Martiñez.

CYPRÆA, Linn.

? C. BAYERQUEI, n. s.

SHELL ovoid, convex, widest towards the upper end, gradually tapering below; under surface flattened. Spire hidden. Mouth narrow, linear; outer lip rather broad. Surface unknown. A cast.

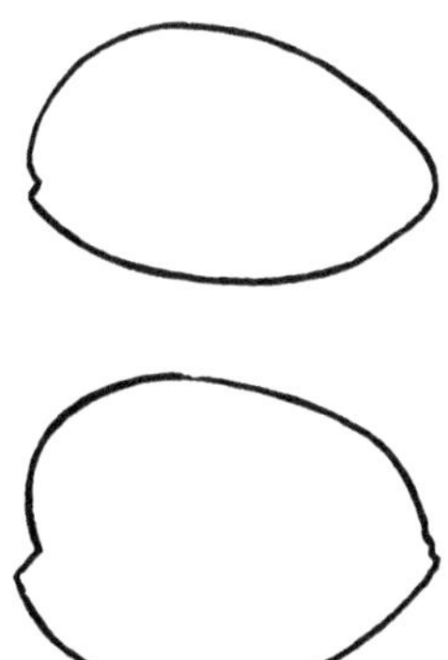

Locality: Clayton, Contra Costa County. Collection of Mr. Bayerque.

This species, of which I have only seen a

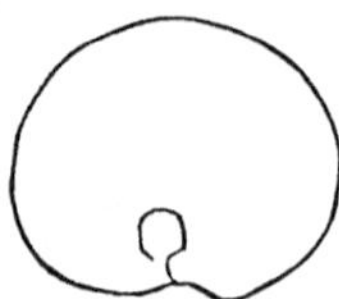

single cast, will probably be found to belong to the subgenus *Luponia*. From the narrowness of the aperture, the shell appears to have been thin. The accompanying outlines illustrate the form better than would be possible in a description.

POTAMIDES, Brongn.

P. DIADEMA, n. s.

Pl. 20, Fig. 85.

SHELL turriculated; spire high; whorls eight, concave, and sloping above, carinate, and strongly undulated on the angle by sharp, flattened tubercles; suture impressed, linear. Surface marked by numerous, fine, somewhat irregular, revolving lines, larger below the carina, and by fine lines of growth. Aperture broad above, rapidly narrowing below. Outer lip acute, retreating from the suture to the carina, sinuous below. Columella lightly incrusted. Canal short, nearly straight, not emarginate in front.

Figure, natural size.
Locality: Abundant on the north fork of Cottonwood Creek. (Div. A.)

P. TENUIS, n. s.

Pl. 20, Fig. 86.

SHELL elongated, slender; spire high; whorls increasing gradually in size, seven to seven and a half. Upper two-thirds sloping almost perpendicularly; lower third sloping rapidly inwards towards the suture, which is narrowly channelled. Angle of whorls marked by pretty distinct, elongated tubercles, which, on the body whorl, sometimes take the form of elongated sinuous ribs; at other times the surface of this whorl is smooth. Aperture elongated, acute behind, widest in the middle, contracted in advance. Outer lip acute, sinuous; inner lip thinly incrusted. Canal gently curved.

Length, .75 inch; width of body whorl, .25 inch.

Locality: Common at Pence's Ranch, twelve miles north of Oroville, Butte County. (Div. A.)

LITTORINA, Férussac.

? L. COMPACTA, n. s.

Pl. 20, Fig. 89.

SHELL small, subglobose, thick; spire moderately high; whorls five, convex; suture minutely impressed. Surface marked by numerous, fine, rounded, revolving ribs, crossed occasionally by minute, oblique lines of growth. Sometimes these latter lines are entirely absent; but they can usually be detected where the surface is in the least weathered. Mouth nearly circular; outer lip acute on the margin, rapidly thickening behind; inner lip thickened, bordered externally by a ridge, a continuation of the outer edge of the mouth; slightly excavated inside of this ridge.

Height, .35 inch; width of body whorl, .3 inch.

Locality: Texas Flat, Placer County; not rare. I have not observed this shell at any other locality.

TURRITELLA, Lam.

T. INFRALINEATA, n. s.

Pl. 20, Fig. 87.

SHELL elongated; whorls increasing very gradually in size, sides nearly parallel, convexly excavated below; suture impressed, placed at the base of an angular channel. Surface marked by three principal square ribs, one placed at the upper angle of the whorl, one at the lower angle, and the third nearest the lower one; between the third and the upper one are two smaller ribs, the lower of which is largest, the upper being linear, and in the younger whorls obsolete. Between the highest rib and the suture, on the shoulder of the whorl, is another linear rib; and below the one on the lower angle, and on the inferior surface, are two or three smaller ribs and numerous (about twenty) fine elevated lines. These are all crossed by lines of growth which, on the sides, are only visible between the ribs, where they form fine connecting bars. These lines show that the lip was broadly emarginate on the outer side and sinuous below, being most prominent on the columellar side of the middle.

Figures, natural size, and a magnified view of one volution.

Locality: North fork of Cottonwood Creek, Shasta County, and Orestimba Cañon, Stanislaus County.

T. SERIATIM-GRANULATA, Roem.

Pl. 20, Fig. 88.

(? *T. planilateris*, Con.; Emory's Rep. Mexican Boundary, p. 158, pl. 14, fig. 1.)
(? *T. irrorata*, Con.; Proc. Acad. Nat. Sci. Phila., 1855, p. 268.)
(*T. seriatim-granulata*, Roem.; Kreide von Texas, p. 39, pl. 4, fig. 12.)

SHELL elongated; whorls numerous, sides flattened, upper and lower margins very slightly bevelled, the lower most strongly so. Mouth subquadrate. Surface marked by a variable number of crenulate, or finely tuberculate, ribs; between these ribs are fine, elevated lines, some of the largest of which are faintly undulated.

Figures, natural size and magnified.

Localities: Three specimens from Tuscan Springs, collected by Dr. Veatch; also found at Cottonwood Creek, Shasta County, and in the Siskiyou Mountains, Siskiyou County.

No two of the specimens are ornamented exactly alike. The large ribs are four and five in number, with from three to no intermediate ones. The number of the latter varies on different whorls of the same specimen, and their arrangement appears to follow no definite rule.

These specimens being so variable, it is more than probable that the forms described from Texas by Roemer and Conrad, which are, at least, very closely allied, and which only differ by the presence or absence of one or two ribs, and in no essential specific detail, are identical, not only among themselves, but with the present one. This view of the case is rendered still more plausible from the fact that I have seen *Turritellas* from Texas having the crenulated and alternating ribs of these forms, but which differed from all of the descriptions in their exact number and arrangement.

If these views are correct, Dr. Roemer's name, being the oldest, will have to stand, all of the others becoming synonyms; unless, indeed, farther examination should prove that the species is the same as *T. Uchauxiana*, D'Orb., with which he compares it as follows: "Diese art lässt sich am nächsten mit *Turritella Uchauxiana*, D'Orbigny, Pal. Fr., pl. 151, fig. 21–23, vergleichen, jedoch hat diese französische Art nur 4 Reihen gekörnter spiraler Streifen auf jedem Umgange während die texanische deren 5 hat." With this species I am unacquainted, and have not, at present, access to any figure or description of it.

T. Veatchii, n. s.

Pl. 20, Fig. 90.

Shell elongated; whorls increasing very slowly in size; sides flat, or nearly so; suture impressed, rather distinct. Surface marked by numerous small, longitudinal ribs, crossed by rather variable revolving ribs, sometimes so closely placed that the interspaces are merely impressed lines. Lower surface of body whorl convex, marked by revolving ribs similar to those on the side. Aperture ovoid, broadly rounded below; columellar side most oblique. Outer lip simple; inner lip heavily incrusted and sometimes faintly striate.

Length of specimen figured, .75 inch.

Locality: Tuscan Springs, Tehama County. Collected by Dr. Veatch.

T. Chicoensis, n. s.

Pl. 21, Fig. 91.

Shell moderate in size, elongate; whorls numerous (about fourteen, by combining fragments), flattened on the sides, or gently convex; sometimes concave above and convex below; bevelled underneath. Suture impressed, bordered by a rim on the whorl below, and sometimes by one above. Surface marked by three prominent revolving ribs, besides the one at the top of the whorl and one on the lower margin, on the border of the inferior excavation. There is sometimes an additional one interpolated. Between these ribs are minute revolving lines, sometimes obsolete, and very closely placed; four or five between each pair of ribs. These are all crossed by fine lines of growth, regularly and broadly curved; retreating from the suture to about the middle of the whorl, and then descending nearly straight to the base. Under-surface of body whorl slightly convex, and marked by fine revolving lines and striæ of growth, or perfectly smooth.

Length, restored, about 2.5 inches; width of body whorl, .6 inch.

Locality: Chico Creek, Butte County (Div. A.).

T. Uvasana.

Pl. 21, Fig. 92.

(*T. Uvasana*, Con.; Pacific R. R. Report, vol. 5, p. 321, pl. 2, fig. 12.)

Shell moderate in side, very elongated and slender; whorls numerous (about seventeen or eighteen, probably), increasing very gradually in size, convex; suture impressed. Surface marked by from six to ten distinct, nearly equal, and rather prominent, revolving ribs. No lines of growth, nor intermediate lines were observed, although better specimens may show them.

Figure, natural size.

Localities: Along the hills from Bull's Head Point to Clayton, Contra Costa County, and east of the mouth of the Cañada de las Uvas, Los Angeles County (Division B.).

Near Martiñez, the specimens are embedded in sandstone, and they all appear to have been more or less eroded before fossilization. The species is very common, some strata being almost composed of this one shell.

T. SAFFORDII, Gabb.

Pl. 21, Fig. 93.

(*T. Saffordii*, G.; Journ. Acad. Nat. Sci. Phila. 2 ser., vol. 4, p. 392, pl. 68, fig. 12 (11 in text, per err.)

SHELL elongated, many-whorled (about fourteen in the largest specimen); whorls increasing very gradually in size, flattened or concave on the side, and bevelled above and below; suture impressed. Whorls marked by a variable number of small revolving lines, which are sometimes obsolete on a part, and sometimes on the whole surface; besides these, there are sinuous lines of growth. Mouth subquadrate, rounded on the angles.

Figure, natural size.

Localities: Six miles northeast of Suisun, Solano County; south of Clear Lake, Lake County. The latter collected by Dr. Veatch. Also near Martiñez (Division A.).

This species is the largest Cretaceous *Turritella* of California, and can be readily recognized, even in casts, by its size. The surface-markings are somewhat variable. In the Tennessee form there were distinct lines on the under side of the whorl, when those on the sides were obsolete. In the Suisun specimen the whole surface is strongly marked; while in the older specimens from Clear Lake the revolving striæ are entirely wanting, but are found on the younger whorls. In this case, too, there are well-marked undulations parallel with the lines of growth, which are most prominent on the angles of bevelment.

T. ROBUSTA, n. s.

Pl. 21, Fig. 94.

SHELL conical, robust; whorls increasing rather rapidly in size, convex; suture linear. Surface marked by four rather prominent, revolving ribs, with concave interspaces; the upper one is placed some distance from the top of the whorl, with a broadly concave space between; the others are placed at about equal distances, the lower one being on the under side of the whorl; of these, only two are visible on the upper whorls. Aperture, unknown.

Figure, natural size.

Locality: Tuscan Springs, Tehama County (Division A.), collection of the California Academy of Natural Sciences.

This shell approaches in shape *T. Leonensis*, Con.; but the ribs are plain, without an intermediate line, and with the interspaces deeper. The distance of the upper rib from the top of the whorl is also a strong distinguishing character.

GALERUS, Humph.

G. EXCENTRICUS, n. s.

Pl. 20, Fig. 95, and Pl. 29, Fig. 232 *a*.

SHELL rounded, irregular; spire low, excentric; volutions two to two and a half. Body whorl irregularly rounded, sometimes slightly flattened above. Suture obliterated. Surface marked by very oblique striæ of growth.

Figures, natural size.

Localities: Northeast of Martiñez; Clayton, above and below the coal; in an isolated mass of Cretaceous rocks, seven miles south of Martiñez; also at San Diego; not rare near Fort Téjon (Division B.).

CRYPTA, Humph.

Crepidula, Lam.

SUBGEN. SPIROCRYPTA, Gabb.

SHELL oval, convex above, concave below, summit posterior, lateral and submarginal, spiral. Internal plate attached to the margin on the lower or outer side, curving upwards and inwards, and uniting with the opposite side at a considerable distance from the margin.

This form approaches the subgenus *Crepipatella* of Lesson, but differs in the more markedly spiral character of the apex, and in the very oblique position of the internal plate. This plate presents a subspiral character, forming the strongest link yet discovered between the genera *Crypta* on one side, and *Trochita* and *Galerus* on the other.

C. PILEUM, n. s.

Pl. 29, Fig. 233, and 233 *a*, *b*.

SHELL deep, usually more or less oblique; whorls about one and a half, increasing very rapidly in size. Surface marked only by very fine lines of growth. Margin of the internal plate concave at the sides, convex in the middle, surface concave; the upper or right hand edge curved downwards abruptly, and uniting with the side at an acute angle; the posterior portion of the plate running up spirally into the apex.

Figures, magnified. The largest specimen is about .6 inch in length.
Locality: Not uncommon near Fort Téjon, in Division B.

NERITA, Linn.

N. DEFORMIS, n. s.

Pl. 21, Fig. 96.

SHELL thick, robust, oblique; spire rather elevated; whorls not distinguishable; body whorl flattened above, rounded on the angle, pretty regularly convex below. Surface smooth, sutures obliterated. Aperture irregularly quadrate; inner lip incrusted, not (?) crenulate.

Figure, natural size.
Locality: North fork of Cottonwood Creek (Division A.).
This peculiar shell is the most irregular of all the species with which I am acquainted in the genus. In fact, except its distorted outline, it has almost no tangible specific characters.

N. CUNEATA, n. s.

Pl. 21, Fig. 97.

SHELL flattened, cuneate; outline elliptical, or sometimes narrower at one end than the other; apex nearly terminal, blunt;

spire not visible. Surface marked only by irregular, concentric lines and undulations. Aperture semi-elliptical; outer lip thickened internally, and finely crenulate; inner lip thickly incrusted, curving downwards towards the mouth, straight and crenulated on the edge.

Figures, natural size.

Locality: Three specimens were collected by Dr. J. A. Veatch at Tuscan Springs, Tehama County. The line from the apex to the outer lip varies in all the specimens; in one it is straight, in another quite convex.

LYSIS, N. Gen.

General form like *Stomatia*. Shell subspiral, very oblique; spire moderately prominent; whorls costate. Aperture narrow, oblique; outer lip simple; columellar lip straight, and rather heavily incrusted. Umbilicus broad, but entirely closed by a concave expansion of the incrusting layer of the inner lip.

L. duplicosta, n. s.

Pl. 21, Fig. 98.

Shell oblique; spire not very prominent; whorls three, rapidly increasing in size; suture impressed. Surface marked by from five to seven prominent ribs, each grooved along its whole length by a sharp, deep channel; the interspaces are broad, regularly and rather deeply concave, and marked by a few fine revolving lines. Mouth very oblique, rounded posteriorly, and subacute in advance; outer lip simple; inner lip straight when viewed from the front; seen laterally, it is very slightly concave. Umbilical region broad, concave, especially above and towards the outer margin; covered by an expansion of the incrusting substance on the inner lip; umbilical margin sharply carinated.

Figures *a* and *b*, natural size. Fig. *c*, a magnified section across the ribs, to show the groove.

Locality: Texas Flat, Placer County (Division A.).

DENTALIUM, Linn.

D. (Ditrupa ?) pusillum, n. s.

Pl. 21, Fig. 99.

Shell small, gently curved. Section circular. Slightly widest near the mouth; the sides, from the widened portion, running nearly parallel to the aperture, or very slightly approaching. Surface polished.

Length, .38 inch; greatest width, .05 inch.

Locality: Several specimens found northeast of Martiñez (Division B.); one at Alizos Creek, near Fort Téjon; and one, striated longitudinally, from Tuscan Springs. I am not certain that the last may not be distinct; but, with the present material, shall not venture to separate it.

D. Cooperii, n. s.

Pl. 21, Fig. 100.

Shell growing to a large size; very slightly curved. Angle of divergence of the sides, about 4.5°. Section usually circular, sometimes slightly elliptical. Surface polished, in ordinary sized specimens; marked by faint longitudinal impressed lines, in the largest. Substance of the shell thin, except in the largest specimens, where it becomes unusually thick.

Figures, natural size.

Localities: Numerous specimens found by Dr. Cooper at San Diego. Not rare northeast of Martiñez, and a few specimens were collected near Fort Téjon (Div. B.); and in Division A. it has been collected at Curry's, south of Mount Diablo, and in the Siskiyou Mountains.

D. stramineum, n. s.

Pl. 21, Fig. 101.

Shell moderate in size, slightly curved. Section varying from circular to elliptical. Surface marked by about thirty small, regular, rounded ribs, with sometimes finer ones interpolated.

Figure, slightly magnified.

Locality: Northeast of Martiñez; San Diego (Div. B.); and Curry's, south of Mount Diablo (Div. A.).

EMARGINULA, Lam.

E. RADIATA, n. s.

Pl. 21, Fig. 102, and 102 *a*.

SHELL subelliptical, moderately elevated; apex a little in advance of the middle, slightly curved. Surface marked by about eighteen rather large radiating ribs, with occasional small intermediate ones; these are crossed by a few irregular, concentric lines. Emargination narrow and rather deep; the corresponding ridge sharply defined and nearly square.

Length, .3 inch; width, .18 inch; height, .12 inch.

Locality: Texas Flat, Placer County.

I have seen but a single specimen of this rare and beautiful little shell. It is in the collection of the California Academy of Natural Sciences.

PATELLA, Linn.

P. TRASKII, n. s.

Pl. 21, Fig. 103.

SHELL depressed, subelliptical; apex subcentral; height variable. Surface marked by from twelve to fourteen radiating ribs with intermediate lines, from one to three in number; these are crossed by irregular lines of growth. Margin gently undulated, the ends of the ribs being more prominent than the interspaces. Muscular impression horseshoe-shaped; ends connected by a sharp impressed line.

Figures, natural size.

Locality: Texas Flat, Placer County (Division A.).

HELCION, Montf.

? H. circularis, n. s.

Pl. 29, Fig. 234, and 234 *a*.

Shell minute, subcircular, elevated, height about half the length; apex subcentral, in advance of the middle, slightly inclined forwards; sides sloping, concavely in front, convexly behind, nearly straight on the sides. Surface marked by concentric undulations and lines of growth, and by numerous dichotomous ribs, irregular in size.

Length, .15 inch.

Figures, magnified to the same scale.

Locality: Near Martiñez (Division A.); collected by Mr. Mathewson.

I have seen but a single very perfect specimen of this species, and suspect that it may be young. It closely resembles *Anisomyon;* but I have been unable to detect any perforation of the apex, under a lens of high power, and the muscular scar being hidden, it is, as yet, impossible to settle definitely its generic relations.

H. dichotoma, n. s.

Pl. 21, Fig. 104.

Shell subelliptical, obliquely conical; apex blunt, anterior, nearly terminal. Surface marked by irregular concentric lines, and small dichotomous ribs, obsolete towards the apex.

Figures, natural size, and magnified.

The higher and more anterior apex, and the small, very numerous, dichotomous ribs, will distinguish this species from the preceding one. In *P. Traskii*, the specimens, when eroded, show no trace of the external ribs; and small specimens of that species are liable to be confounded with the present one, except for the somewhat more central position of the apex.

Locality: Texas Flat, Placer County. (Div. A.)

ANISOMYON, Meek and Hayden.

A. Meekii, n. s.

Pl. 21, Fig. 105.

Shell elliptical, very thin; the width and length are about as 5 to 6; apex moderately elevated, small, nearly central; sides sloping nearly straight in all directions to the base. Surface (of cast) marked by numerous irregular concentric undulations, which do not always continue entirely around the shell; there are also marks which probably indicate a few faint, radiating lines.

Figures, natural size.

Locality: North fork of Cottonwood Creek. (Division A.)

This shell appears to be most nearly related to *A. alveolus*, M. and H.; but Mr. Meek, to whom I sent a sketch, assured me that it was distinct. The fragments of shell, preserved on the only specimen I have seen, are only large enough to show that its substance was very thin.

ACTÆON, Montf.

(*Tornatella*, Lam.)

A. impressus, n. s.

Pl. 21, Fig. 106.

Shell subovoid, elongated; spire moderately high; whorls six, slightly convex; suture channelled. Upper third of body whorl, and all of the preceding whorls, smooth; lower two thirds marked by from twelve to fifteen regular impressed grooves; the interspaces are square and flat; those above plain, or with a slight depression in the centre, which becomes deeper anteriorly, until these are as large as the first set of grooves. Aperture narrow; outer lip simple; inner lip incrusted with a thin plate. Columella truncated abruptly in advance, and not reaching the anterior end of the mouth; at the extremity is a prominent fold, and a short distance above it another one, somewhat larger and sharper.

Length, .53 inch; width, .28 inch.

Locality: Common on the north fork of Cottonwood Creek. Collected by Messrs. Brewer and Rémond.

BULLA, Klein, Brug.

B. Hornii, n. s.

Pl. 29, Fig. 235.

Shell moderate in size, thin, ovoid, most prominent about one-third of the length from the upper end, the sides gradually curving downwards and approaching to near the anterior end, when they curve rapidly inwards; summit umbilicated. Mouth broad, the upper end projecting a short distance above the preceding whorl, and regularly rounded; anterior end broad, produced; outer lip simple, thin; inner lip unknown, apparently not incrusted, covered in such a manner by the matrix, especially in advance, as to hide the characters. Surface marked by numerous, very fine, impressed, revolving lines.

Figure, slightly magnified.

Locality: A single specimen was found by Dr. Horn, near Fort Téjon.

The shorter and more convex outline will serve to distinguish this species from *Cylichna costata*, which is also found at the same locality. A further difference is to be found in the sculpture, the lines, in this species, being much further apart than in the other; the shell is also much thinner.

I take great pleasure in dedicating this species to the discoverer, to whom I am indebted for many fine specimens, not a small portion of which were new to me.

CYLICHNA, Lovén.

C. costata, n. s.

Pl. 21, Fig. 107.

Shell elongated, subcylindrical, widest anteriorly; spire hidden; whorls (from casts) three or four. Surface marked by very numerous, flattened, revolving ribs, with narrow interspaces. Aperture linear; inner lip incrusted. A single small fold in advance, on the columella.

Figure, natural size. Usually found smaller.

Localities: Martiñez; Texas Flat, Placer County; Clayton; Cochran's, east of Mount Diablo; San Diego; and Alizos Creek, near Fort Téjon.

This is one of the most common Cretaceous fossils in the State, and is one of the few species that range through both divisions of the formation represented here. Through an inadvertence, the lithographer has deprivëd the summit of its proper pit-like character.

MEGISTOSTOMA, N. Gen.

SHELL shaped like *Philine*, thin, slightly enrolled; body volution very much expanded, produced above. Aperture occupying nearly all of the front surface. Columellar lip thickened, flat, rather heavily incrusted.

The peculiar character on which this shell is separated from the genus *Philine* (*Bullæa*, Lam.), is the flat, thickened, and incrusted columella, that genus having no columella, and the oral surface of the penultimate whorl being regularly rounded.

M. STRIATA, n. s.

Pl. 21, Fig. 108, and 108 *a*, *b*.

SHELL flattened, involute, oval; body whorl composing nearly the whole bulk of the shell. Mouth broadly expanded; outer lip produced posteriorly in a broad, rounded process; inner lip flattened, and heavily incrusted by a longitudinally striate layer of shell. Surface marked by numerous square, thread-like and slightly elevated striæ, which are usually grooved in the middle; these are crossed by lines of growth.

Figures, natural size, and a magnified view of the surface.

Locality: All of the specimens I have seen were collected by Mr. Mathewson, about a mile northeast of Martiñez, in Division B.

CONCHIFERA.

MARTESIA, Leech

M. CLAUSA, n. s.

Pl. 22, Fig. 115.

SHELL elongate, cuneate; beaks anterior, incurved, approaching. Posterior cardinal margin sloping regularly towards the extremity of the shell, which is narrow and rounded; basal margin nearly straight. Anterior opening moderate in size, angular, closed. Umbonal groove double, widening rather rapidly below. Surface marked by regular lines, concentric on the posterior part of the shell, and which, after crossing the umbonal groove, run nearly parallel with the margin of the anterior opening.

Figure, slightly magnified.

Localities: Pence's Ranch, Butte County; Texas Flat, Placer County; and Tuscan Springs, Tehama County (Division A.).

TURNUS, N. Gen.

SHELL thin, pholadiform; bearing internally a rib which rises in the apex, and passes downwards and backwards to the basal margin, in the same manner as, and posterior to, the umbonal groove. Accessory plates unknown. Tube simple, thin.

This genus appears to occupy a position in subfamily Teredininæ, and to form, as it were, a link with the Pholadinæ. With the shell of the latter, it seems to inhabit a long calcareous tube, like the former. At least, there are numerous fragments of tube associated with all the specimens I have seen. The strong internal rib, as large or larger than the rib produced by the umbonal groove, is a character which will at once distinguish it.

T. PLENUS, n. s.

Pl. 22, Fig. 116.

SHELL thin, broad; apex a third of the distance from the anterior end; beaks strongly incurved. Anterior sinus broad, extending almost to the cardinal margin, and gracefully rounded. Umbonal groove deep; internal rib larger than that produced by the groove. Surface marked by irregular, concentric ribs, which, on crossing the umbonal groove, become linear, and parallel with the curved margin of the anterior sinus.

Figure, natural size.

Locality: North fork of Cottonwood Creek (Division A.).

Imperfect casts have been discovered on the Rancho de San Luis Gonzaga, at the eastern end of Pacheco's Pass, Merced County. These contain shells of about the same shape and size as the above, but in too imperfect a condition for satisfactory determination. The tubes are over an inch in diameter; and fragments, eight or nine inches long, showing but little diminution in size, are common. These are always found in fossil wood.

SOLEN, Linn.

S. PARALLELUS, n. s.

Pl. 22, Fig. 117.

SHELL elongated, slender, thin; sides parallel, ends rounded; anterior end somewhat more abruptly truncated than the posterior, and slightly reflected. Surface marked by a few irregular lines of growth.

Figure, natural size.

Locality: Not rare in Division B., at Bull's Head Point, near Martiñez. Also found at Marsh's, east of Mount Diablo; and at Alizos Creek, near Fort Téjon.

PHARELLA, Gray.

P. ALTA, n. s.

Pl. 22, Fig. 118.

SHELL elongated, narrow; beaks about a third of the distance from the anterior end, high, acute. Cardinal margins sloping slightly concavely from the beak; basal margin nearly straight. Ends rounded; the posterior the narrowest, and slightly expanded. Surface marked by a few indistinct lines of growth.

Figure, twice natural size.

Locality: In most of the hills west of Martiñez (in Division A.).

This shell is smaller than *P. Dakotensis*, Meek and Hayden, and differs in the beaks being higher and placed nearer the anterior end.

SILIQUA, Mühlf.

Leguminaria, Schum.

S. OREGONENSIS, n. s.

Pl. 29, Fig. 237.

SHELL subelliptical, slightly convex; beaks placed about a third of the length from the anterior extremity. Cardinal margin nearly straight; basal broadly curved. Anterior end regularly rounded; posterior obliquely truncated above. Internal ribs small, narrow, and oblique. Surface unknown.

Figure, natural size.

Locality: Two casts, with the shell entirely decomposed; from the north side of the Siskiyou Mountains, Oregon, near the Toll House, on the stage road. Collection of Prof. Whitney.

PANOPÆA, Ménard.

P. CONCENTRICA, n. s.

Pl. 22, Fig. 119.

SHELL subquadrate, about a third longer than wide; beaks small, about a third of the length from the anterior end. Posterior cardinal line very slightly sloping; basal margin usually regularly curved, sometimes nearly straight. Ends gaping; posterior end widest. Surface marked by rather large, irregular, concentric ribs.

Figure, natural size. Sometimes the species attains twice this size; and one specimen in the collection of the California Academy of Natural Sciences, from Tuscan Springs, which probably belongs to this species, has a length of four and a half inches.

Locality: Cottonwood Creek and Martiñez (Division A.).

CORBULA, Brug.

? C. PRIMORSA, n. s.

Pl. 22, Fig. 120, and 120 *a*.

SHELL small, thin, abruptly truncated posteriorly; beaks nearly central, small; anterior end produced, broadly rounded, excavated below the beaks; a well-marked angulation extending from the umbones to the posterior basal angle. Surface marked by numerous fine, radiating lines, and by coarser, irregular lines of growth.

Length, .37 inch; width, .25 inch.

Figure 120 *a* is from the posterior end.

Locality: South side of Corral Hollow, Alameda County. Probably Cretaceous. I have not been able to uncover the hinge of the only specimen I have seen, and therefore refer this species to the genus *Corbula* with some doubt.

C. Traskii, n. s.

Pl. 22, Fig. 121, and 121 *a*.

Shell small, convex; beaks large, strongly incurved. Left valve most convex; anterior end produced, slightly curved; posterior end obliquely truncated; surface closely marked by small but regular and well-marked concentric ribs. Right valve flatter; anterior end not so produced; surface not so strongly striate.

Length, .27 inch; width, .19 inch.

Localities: Texas Flat, Placer County; Tuscan Springs, Tehama County; and Pence's Ranch, Butte County (Division A.).

C. cultriformis, n. s.

Pl. 22, Fig. 122.

Shell elongated, narrow; beaks moderate, nearly central. Valves nearly equal. Left valve broadly excavated in advance of the beaks, convex posteriorly; anterior end produced, rounded narrowly; basal margin broadly and regularly convex. Right valve more deeply and abruptly excavated in front of the beaks, not so convex as the left valve. Surface plain, or marked only by a few faint lines of growth.

Length, .4 inch; width, .23 inch.

Locality: Abundant west of Martiñez (in Division A.).

C. Hornii, n. s.

Pl. 29, Fig. 238.

Shell rather large, broad, narrow and very convex; beaks central; anterior end produced and regularly rounded; posterior end obliquely truncated; cardinal margins sloping equally; basal broadly and regularly convex. On the left valve a sharp, angular ridge passes from the beaks to the posterior basal margin, behind which the surface is concave. The right valve has nearly the same form as the left; is perhaps a little more convex, and wants entirely the posterior umbonal ridge, the surface being rounded instead of angular. Surface unknown.

Figure 238, a left valve, natural size. The right valve is too imperfect for illustration.

A cast of a single left valve and a broken right valve, from near Fort Téjon. Collected by Dr. Horn.

C. PARILIS, n. s.

Pl. 29, Fig. 239, and 239 *a*.

SHELL nearly equivalve, small, somewhat inequilateral; beaks prominent, broad, strongly incurved, and inclined slightly forward. Anterior end sloping downwards abruptly, and regularly rounded below; posterior obliquely truncated and biangular; a distinct umbonal ridge passes from the beaks to the posterior angle in both valves, most acute on the left. Basal margin of the right valve regularly and broadly convex, straighter on the left. Surface marked by prominent, concentric ribs, crossed by fine, radiating lines.

Figures, about twice natural size.

Localities: Martiñez to Marsh's, east of Mount Diablo; and at San Diego (Division B.).

ANATINA, Lam.

A. TRYONIANA, n. s.

Pl. 29, Fig. 240.

SHELL thin, compressed, long, narrow, and nearly equilateral, twice as long as wide; beaks central; cardinal margin concave, and slightly sloping in advance, nearly straight behind; anterior extremity rounded above, sloping convexly inwards below; posterior end narrow and regularly convex; basal margin broadly and regularly rounded. Surface polished and marked by fine, concentric lines.

Figure, natural size.

Locality: Two specimens, collected by Mr. Mathewson, at Martiñez.

Named after my friend, Mr. George W. Tryon, of Philadelphia.

A. INEQUILATERALIS, n. s.

Pl. 29, Fig. 241.

I PROPOSE this name for an imperfect cast, which I discovered in Division A., on the north side of the Siskiyou Mountains, Oregon, near the stage road. The beaks are about a third of the length from the posterior end; the cardinal and basal margins are subparallel; and, judging from undulations on the cast, the two ends of the shell are nearly of the same shape and size. Surface unknown.

Figure, natural size.

Collection of Prof. Whitney.

? A. LATA, n. s.

Pl. 22, Fig. 126.

SHELL broad, thin, lenticular; valves very much flattened; beaks small, inclined backwards, placed posterior to the middle of the shell. Anterior cardinal margin sloping convexly from the beak; posterior excavated. Posterior end truncated. Surface marked by minute, irregular lines of growth.

Figure, natural size.

Locality: A single specimen from Pence's Ranch, Butte County (Division A.).

I have not been able to expose the hinge of this specimen; but, judging from the general form, think there can be little doubt of the correctness of the generic reference. It can be distinguished from *A. elliptica*, nobis, from New Jersey, by its being shorter and broader, by the beak being more posterior, and by the entire absence of any ridge.

PHOLADOMYA, Sow.

P. BREWERII, n. s.

Pl. 22, Fig. 123.

SHELL ovate or subquadrate, compressed; beaks anterior, moderate in size; buccal end unknown; anal extremity rounded, subtruncate; cardinal border nearly straight behind the beaks, gently sloping; base very slightly convex. Surface marked by twenty-four or twenty-five fine, linear ribs, which radiate regularly from the beaks, covering all the surface, except a narrow portion posteriorly, near the cardinal margin, about as wide as two or three ribs; besides these, the surface is covered by fine, irregular lines of growth.

Figure, natural size.

Locality: A single specimen found by Prof. Brewer, at Pence's Ranch, Butte County (Division A.).

This species approaches *P. subelongata,* Meek, from Vancouver Island; but, besides the difference in form, the marked difference in the number of ribs will at once serve to distinguish them; the latter species having but sixteen ribs.

P. NASUTA, n. s.

Pl. 30, Fig. 124.

SHELL oblique, convex; beaks high, anterior, incurved, nearly touching; umbones prominent. Buccal end obliquely truncated inwards towards the base, nearly straight; posterior end produced, rounded, gaping; base and anterior end closed. Surface marked by from twelve to sixteen small, radiating ribs, which cover about two-fifths of the surface, leaving a small portion of the anterior end and the posterior third uncovered; besides these, the whole surface is covered by prominent, irregular, concentric ribs.

Figure, natural size.

Locality: On the shore of the Straits of Carquines, two miles west of Martiñez. Collected by Mr. Mathewson (from Division A.).

NEÆRA, Gray.

N. DOLABRÆFORMIS, n. s.

Pl. 22, Fig. 125.

SHELL small, convex; beaks central, strongly incurved, nearly touching; anterior end suddenly narrowed, produced; extremity unknown; posterior end narrowly rounded; base broadly sinuated. Surface marked, except on the anterior end, by moderately large, rounded ribs, somewhat variable in size and closely placed.

Length, .45 inch; width, .33 inch.

Locality: East of Martiñez (Division B.).

MACTRA, Linn., Lam.

M. ASHBURNERII, n. s.

Pl. 22, Fig. 127.

SHELL moderate in size, subtrigonal; base broadly and regularly convex; beaks central, slightly inclined forwards; posterior cardinal margin sloping, straight, or slightly convex; anterior faintly excavated; some specimens show an umbonal angle well marked, while in others it is nearly or entirely obsolete. Surface variable; specimens from some localities showing a large number of regular, nearly uniform, rounded, concentric ribs; while those found at other places have these ribs few, entirely absent, or only represented by fine lines of growth.

Figure, average size. Some few specimens have been found a third larger.

Localities: Pence's Ranch, Butte County, Mr. Ashburner; Chico Creek; Texas Flat, Placer County; near Martiñez; Tuscan Springs, Tehama County; Orestimba Cañon, Stanislaus County; Benicia; San Luis Gonzaga Ranch, Pacheco's Pass, in Division A.; and in Division B., at Martiñez; Marsh's, southeast of Mount Diablo; Alizos Creek, near Fort Téjon, &c.

This is one of the most common fossils in the State.

LUTRARIA, Lam.

L. TRUNCATA, n. s.

Pl. 22, Fig. 128.

SHELL thin, compressed, somewhat elongated, length compares with the breadth as about four to three; beaks nearly central, prominent, small, acute and slightly inclined forwards; anterior cardinal margin slightly sinuous, posterior convex, nearly straight; anterior end rounded; posterior obliquely truncated, gaping. Surface marked by faint, irregular lines of growth.

Figure, natural size.

Localities: Pence's Ranch, Butte County, collected by Mr. Ashburner. Also at Chico Creek (from Division A.).

ASAPHIS, Modeer.

A. UNDULATA, n. s.

Pl. 22, Fig. 129.

SHELL minute, oval, convex, very thin; beaks small, nearly central, and prominent; posterior cardinal line regularly convex, anterior slightly excavated; extremities round and equal; basal margin broadly and regularly convex. Surface marked by minute, equal, concentric lines (about 5 or 6 in .01 inch); and at the two ends by a few large radiating ribs or undulations; these are most marked on the posterior end, and are entirely absent on the middle half of the surface. Hinge small, the bifid tooth of the left valve being only represented by two minute tubercles.

Figure, magnified a little more than three times.

Locality: From the lower beds, Texas Flat, Placer County; collection of the California Academy of Natural Sciences.

GARI, Schum.

Psammobia, Lam.

? G. TEXTA, n. s.

Pl. 22, Fig. 130.

SHELL equivalve, nearly equilateral, subcompressed, about twice as long as wide; beaks broad, not prominent, a little in advance of the middle; anterior extremity narrowest, produced and regularly rounded, sloping below towards the basal margin, posterior extremity subtruncate obliquely backwards; basal margin most prominent posterior to the beaks; a broad, not well-defined ridge passes from the beaks to the posterior basal angle, behind which the surface is slightly concave. Surface marked by very small radiating and concentric lines, producing a woven appearance.

The internal surface of the shell being slightly undulated, I have been unable to detect any pallial impression on any of the casts I have seen.

Figure, natural size.

Locality: From Division B., in the neighborhood of Martiñez; collected by Mr. Mathewson.

All of the specimens of this shell that I have seen are embedded in a very hard calcareous sandstone, in which it was impossible to expose the hinge. I have, therefore, referred it doubtfully to the above genus.

TELLINA, Linn.

T. LONGA, n. s.

Pl. 22, Fig. 131.

SHELL elongate, slender, compressed; beaks small, sharp, rather prominent, nearly central; anterior cardinal margin sloping, nearly straight; posterior slightly excavated; posterior end rostrate, subbiangular; anterior end rounded; basal margin convex, most prominent anteriorly, and sloping upwards to the posterior end nearly straight; shell a little more than twice as long as wide. Surface marked by numerous microscopic, concentric lines, generally somewhat irregular. Muscular scars deep; pallial sinus broad, shallow.

Figure, natural size.

Localities: In Division B., near Martiñez; and abundant at Marsh's, fifteen miles east of Mount Diablo. A single specimen was found at Alizos Creek, near Fort Téjon.

T. Rémondii, n. s.

Pl. 22, Fig. 132.

Shell broad, thin, compressed, about a third longer than wide; anterior end broadly rounded; posterior rostrate, narrow, and truncated obliquely outwards and downwards; beaks small, central, prominent; base broadly rounded, slightly sinuous near the posterior extremity; a well-marked ridge passes from the beak to the posterior basal angle; cardinal margin convex in front, concave behind the beaks, and sloping downwards concavely towards the truncated posterior end. Surface ornamented by numerous small, regular, concentric ribs, and by smaller, radiating, interstitial lines.

Figure, natural size.

Locality: Two specimens from Cochran's, six miles east of Mount Diablo, collection of Mr. Rémond; one from near Fort Téjon.

T. Hoffmanniana, n. s.

Pl. 22, Fig. 133, and 133 *a*.

Shell moderate in size, compressed, a little longer than wide; beaks nearly central, somewhat variable, prominent; cardinal margin sloping each way, nearly straight, most abrupt posteriorly; anterior end broadly rounded, posterior produced, narrow, rounded or subtruncate, and sometimes slightly reflected laterally; basal margin convex, most prominent directly under the beaks, sloping upwards, and sometimes nearly straight posteriorly. Surface plain, or marked only by lines of growth. Muscular scars rather faint; pallial sinus deep, narrow.

Figures, natural size.

Locality: Abundant in Division A., west of Martiñez; also found at Pence's Ranch, Butte County.

This species sometimes attains a size twice as large as Figure 133 *a*, but can always be distinguished by its straight or slightly convex cardinal margins.

T. monilifera, n. s.

Pl. 22, Fig. 134, and 134 *a*.

Shell small, subelliptical, equilateral; beaks central, prominent, with the cardinal margins sloping symmetrically on each side, straight, or a little convex; extremities regularly rounded, equal; basal margin broadly convex, most prominent in the middle. Surface marked by fine, regular, concentric ribs, with narrow impressed lines between them, except on the posterior fifth or sixth, where they become faint, and are replaced by a series of rather coarser, moniliform, radiating ribs. Hinge composed of one small, simple, and a larger bifid primary tooth, and two prominent lateral teeth. Pallial line very faint.

Figure 134, natural size; Fig. 134 *a*, magnified view of the posterior half.

Locality: From Division A., Texas Flat, Placer County; collection of the California Academy of Natural Sciences, presented by Dr. Trask.

This shell is of the same size and shape as *Nucula perequalis*, Con., of the Alabama "Ripley Group," but can be distinguished by the peculiar external ornamentation.

T. ooides, n. s.

Pl. 22, Fig. 135, and 135 *a*.

Shell large, oval, compressed, a fifth longer than wide; beaks small, anterior, subcentral; cardinal margin sloping regularly and convexly on both sides; extremities regularly rounded, the anterior broadest; basal margin convex, most prominent in the centre. Surface marked only by rather distinct, irregular lines of growth.

Figures, natural size.

Localities: Fig. 135 is of a specimen found west of Martiñez; 135 *a*, from Pence's Ranch, Butte County (Division A.).

T. Mathewsonii, n. s.

Pl. 23, Fig. 136.

Shell equilateral, compressed; beaks broad, prominent, central; extremities equal, or nearly so, broadly rounded; basal margin regularly convex. Surface marked only by irregular lines of growth.

Figure, natural size.

Locality: In Division A., in the neighborhood of Martiñez. The finest specimens are from an outcrop about a mile north of the village of Pacheco, southeast of Martiñez.

I am indebted to Mr. Mathewson for the discovery of this species, and for the specimens now in the collection of the Survey.

T. decurtata, n. s.

Pl. 23, Fig. 137.

Shell moderate in size, compressed, very inequilateral; beaks anterior; cardinal margin sloping posteriorly gently, very slightly convex; anterior end abruptly truncated; posterior end narrow, rounded; base broadly and gently convex. Surface unknown. Muscular impressions slight; pallial sinus oblique, shallow and round at the base. Primary teeth narrow, the anterior the largest; lateral teeth small, almost obsolete.

Figure, natural size.

Locality: I found but a single specimen of this peculiarly shaped shell; this was obtained at Pence's Ranch, twelve miles north of Oroville, Butte County (Division A.).

Although I have but a single imperfect cast of this species, I do not hesitate in describing it, in the confidence that its remarkable shape will not fail in distinguishing it from all known species.

It approaches most nearly to *T. ooides* (supra); but, in addition to its more abrupt anterior end, in the latter species the pallial sinus lies more nearly parallel with the base of the shell. It is narrower and somewhat angular at the base of the notch.

? T. QUADRATA, n. s.

Pl. 23, Fig. 138.

SHELL inequilateral, subquadrate, about two-fifths longer than wide; beaks prominent, subcentral, nearest the anterior end, which is obliquely subtruncate; posterior end a little the narrowest and regularly rounded; basal margin nearly straight. Surface marked by numerous, closely placed, irregular lines of growth. Muscular scars and pallial sinus almost invisible on the cast.

Figure, natural size.

Locality: A single specimen, from Tuscan Springs, Division A., collection of the Academy of Natural Sciences of California; collected by Dr. Veatch.

I have only seen a portion of the hinge of this shell, but believe it to belong to the genus *Tellina*.

T. ASHBURNERII, n. s.

Pl. 23, Fig. 139.

SHELL moderate in size, subequilateral, compressed, nearly twice as long as broad; beaks central, small; cardinal margins sloping nearly equally on both sides; ends symmetrically rounded, nearly equal; base broad, regularly convex. Surface marked only by lines of growth. Hinge small; lateral teeth, if any, unknown.

Figure, natural size.

Locality: Pence's Ranch, north of Oroville, Butte County (in Division A.).

Named after Mr. Ashburner, who first made known this prolific locality.

This species is not unlike *T. Mathewsonii* (supra), but can be distinguished from young specimens of that by being narrower at all ages. It is slightly more convex, and the beaks are not so prominent.

T. (? Sanguinolaria) Whitneyi, n. s.

Pl. 30, Fig. 242.

Shell large, thin, compressed, subelliptical; beaks a little in advance of the centre, small; cardinal margins subequal, the posterior side sloping downwards more obliquely than the anterior; basal margin convex, most prominent a little behind the beaks, sloping upwards in advance towards the anterior end. Surface marked by fine, concentric lines.

Figure, natural size.

Locality: Jacksonville, Oregon, associated with many species of the lower division of the California Cretaceous. Collection of Professor Whitney.

I have not seen the hinge of this shell, and cannot therefore be positive in the generic determination. In its compressed, inequilateral form, it resembles some of the modern *Sanguinolarias*, and may possibly belong to that group.

T. parilis, n. s.

Pl. 30, Fig. 243.

Shell small, robust, nearly equilateral; beaks central, or nearly so, elevated, with the margins sloping rapidly, nearly straight, towards either end; basal margin broadly and regularly convex; anterior end narrow and regularly rounded; posterior a little broader and faintly subtruncated obliquely upwards and inwards. Surface polished and ornamented by a few faint lines of growth.

Figure, a little larger than natural size.

Locality: A few specimens collected by Mr. Mathewson, near Martiñez.

This species approaches most nearly to *T. Ashburnerii;* but it is thicker, shorter, more regularly equilateral, and the beaks are much more prominent.

T. Hornii, n. s.

Pl. 30, Fig. 244.

Shell long, narrow, subequilateral; beaks small, subcentral; cardinal margins sloping slightly towards the ends; anterior extremity regular, slightly broader than the posterior, which is a little more prominent below than above; basal margin nearly straight. Surface marked only by faint lines of growth.

Figure, natural size.

Localities: In Division B., near Fort Téjon, where it is abundant, many fine specimens having been collected by Dr. Horn. I have found a single small specimen at Clayton, near the coal-mines.

T. Californica, n. s.

Pl. 30, Fig. 245.

Shell small, very inequilateral; beaks prominent, a little behind the middle of the shell; posterior margin abruptly truncated obliquely from the beaks to the base; anterior end very prominent and rounded; base slightly sinuous. Surface slightly convex and marked by very fine lines of growth.

Figure, slightly magnified.

Localities: Marsh's, east of Mount Diablo. Also near Fort Téjon (Division B.).

VENUS, Linn.

V. (Mercenaria?) varians, n. s.

Pl. 23, Fig. 140, 140 *a*, and 141.

Shell thick, robust, inflated, variable in outline, subtriangular; length and breadth sometimes nearly equal, in other specimens, length a fifth greater than width; beaks anterior, nearly terminal; cardinal margin prominently convex, and sloping rapidly downwards; in advance of the beaks, the margin of the shell is rather deeply excavated; anterior end broadly rounded, posterior narrower; basal margin broadly and regularly convex. Surface marked by coarse, irregular lines of growth. Lunule variable, small, sometimes deep, sometimes nearly obsolete.

Figures, natural size.

Localities: Widely distributed in Division A.; most abundant near Martiñez, and Pence's Ranch, Butte County.

The two figures, 140 and 140 *a*, are from specimens found near Martiñez.

These two forms are the most common, and I have before me every possible gradation between them. The form, figure 141, is more rare, and seems to be confined to the northern portions of the State. Specimens from Pence's and from Tuscan Springs, Tehama County, usually approach it more or less closely. Although the shell represented in figure 141 appears to be widely distinct in outline, shape of the umbones, &c., from the others, still, after studying a series of not less than a hundred specimens, I can find no good grounds on which to separate it.

On account of the nature of the matrix, I have been unable to examine all the details of the hinge, and the generic determination must therefore remain, to a certain extent, in doubt, for the present.

V. Veatchii, n. s.

Pl. 23, Fig. 142.

Shell small, subquadrate; beaks large, anterior, nearly terminal; cardinal margin sloping slightly convexly to the posterior end, which is rounded-subtruncate; anterior slightly concave above, narrow-convex below; basal margin nearly straight; a broad, rounded ridge passes from the beaks to the posterior basal angle, in the rear of which the surface is nearly flat.

Surface marked by moderately large, regular, concentric ribs.

Figure, magnified from three to four times.

Locality: Abundant in Division A., at Tuscan Springs; collected by Dr. Veatch.

V. lenticularis, n. s.

Pl. 30, Fig. 246.

Shell thick, subtriangular, compressed; beaks high, a little in advance of the centre; posterior cardinal margin sloping very abruptly, slightly convex; anterior side broadly excavated under the beaks, convex below; base broadly and regularly convex. Lunule small, rather distinct. Internal margin not crenulated. Surface marked by regular, rounded, concentric ribs.

Figure, natural size.

Locality: Benicia; collection of Mr. Rêmond.

V. TETRAHEDRA, n. s.

Pl. 30, Fig. 247.

SHELL small, thin, subquadrate; beaks small; anterior end broadly rounded below, excavated under the beaks; cardinal margin sloping posteriorly, nearly straight; posterior end obliquely truncated; basal margin convex. Surface polished, divided by a broad, rounded, umbonal ridge, into two planes, so that when the two valves are in apposition they present four well-marked curved faces.

Figure, a little more than twice natural size.

Locality: Not rare in the vicinity of Martiñez (Div. A.).

MERETRIX, Lam.

M. UVASANA, Con.

Pl. 30, Fig. 248.

(*M. Uvasana*, Con. P. R. R. Report, vol. 5, p. 320, pl. 2, fig. 3.)

SHELL thick, oval, robust, a fourth longer than wide, very inequilateral; beaks large, strongly incurved, placed less than a third of the length from the anterior end; buccal margin prominently rounded below, deeply excavated under the beaks; cardinal margin sloping very convexly towards the posterior end, which is subtruncated. Surface marked by small lamelliform ribs, separated by spaces about equal to four times the thickness of the ribs themselves; the interspaces are sometimes plain, sometimes striated. Inner margin plain.

Figure, natural size.

Localities: Abundant near Fort Téjon, whence it was described by Mr. Conrad; also found, not rarely, near Martiñez, and nearly everywhere in Division B.

This is the largest species of the genus, and one of the commonest fossils in California. The figure given in the Pacific Railroad Report is from a fragmentary specimen, and conveys a very incorrect idea of the outline of the shell. There can be no doubt of the identity of the present form with Mr. Conrad's species, since I collected numerous specimens myself, at the original locality; and this is the only species with the peculiar surface ornamentation, mentioned by Mr. Conrad, that has been found in California.

M. LENS, n. s.

Pl. 23, Fig. 143.

SHELL compressed, lenticular; outline variable, subelliptical; beaks small, placed about two-fifths from the anterior end, which is broadly convex; posterior end narrower; cardinal margin curved, gradually sloping; basal regularly convex. Surface marked by a few irregular lines of growth.

Figure, natural size. The species sometimes grows a third larger.

Locality: Chico Creek, Butte County (Division A.).

The outline of this shell is rather more variable than is usual in the genus. The specimen figured is 1.15 inch long and .9 inch wide; another is 1.2 inch long and 1.1 wide. The convexity also is not constant, old specimens being proportionally deeper than young ones, and often specimens of the same size will vary. The average depth of a single adult valve is about .2 inch.

M. HORNII, n. s.

Pl. 23, Fig. 144.

SHELL subtrigonal, cuneate; beaks anterior, with the cardinal margin sloping convexly to the posterior end, which is narrow; anterior end prominent above, and curving inwards rapidly below towards the base. Lunule small, very narrow, acute below and impressed. Surface marked by prominent, large, concentric ribs, with interspaces of about the same width.

Figure, natural size, from a small specimen.

The species grows to about one-third larger than the figure. The artist has, to some extent, misrepresented the characters of this shell. It should be more acute posteriorly, the anterior end should be higher above and more oblique below, and the concentric markings are at least a third too numerous. Judging from the figure, there would seem to be little if any difference between this shell and *M. arata*, fig. 250; but the triangular form, much larger size and distinct surface-characters cannot fail to distinguish them.

Locality: Near Fort Téjon. Dr. Horn.

M. NITIDA, n. s.

Pl. 23, Figs. 145 and 146.

SHELL moderate in size, inequilateral; beaks small, prominent, anterior, about a third of the length from the anterior end; buccal extremity deeply excavated under the beaks, prominently convex below; cardinal margin sloping convexly and rapidly towards the anal extremity; basal margin broadly rounded. Surface polished and marked by a few smooth, irregular lines of growth. Lunule moderately large and bordered by a deep, impressed line.

Figures, natural size.

Locality: Near Martiñez, in loose blocks on the shores of the Straits of Carquines; Orestimba Cañon; Chico and Cow Creeks (Division A.).

This shell changes its shape materially in passing from the young to the adult. The young form is shorter and proportionally more convex than is ever seen in full-grown individuals. In general shape there is a great resemblance between the present species and *Venus varians* (supra), but the smaller size, polished surface, fewer and less distinct lines of growth, and the presence of the deeply impressed line bordering the lunule will at once distinguish it. I am indebted to Mr. Mathewson for the specimens described and figured.

M. LONGA, n. s.

Pl. 23, Fig. 147.

SHELL elongate, nearly equilateral; beaks small, broad, not prominent; buccal ends broadly rounded, sloping inwards below more rapidly than above; posterior end faintly subtruncated; base broadly convex, most prominent below, or a little in advance of the beaks. Surface marked by faint, irregular lines of growth, and towards the beaks by minute, radiating lines, which become obsolete as the shell increases in size. Lunule long, narrow, and deeply impressed.

Figure, natural size.

Locality: From Division A., found in a mass of rock having the lithological characters and the same grouping of species as is found at Texas Flat, Placer County, but labelled "Shasta." From Dr. Behrens.

M. ARATA, n. s.

Pl. 30, Fig. 250.

SHELL thick, rounded-subtriangular, nearly as high as long; beaks large, prominent, a third of the length from the anterior end, which is narrowly excavated above, rounded below, and broader than the posterior extremity; base regularly convex; cardinal margin curving regularly to the anal end. Lunule small. Surface ornamented by regular, concentric, acute, impressed lines.

Figure, natural size.

Localities: Cottonwood Creek, Shasta County; Siskiyou Mountains; and Orestimba Cañon, Stanislaus County.

Allied to *M. nitida* in form, but is less produced in advance, more prominent behind, and is easily distinguished by the well-marked surface ornamentation.

M. OVALIS, n. s.

Pl. 30, Fig. 251.

SHELL oval, convex, rather thick; beaks small, acute, subcentral; anterior margin broadly convex, produced, most prominent above the middle, subtruncated below; cardinal margin regularly curved, sloping downwards posteriorly, uniting with the posterior end, which, from lines of growth, seems to have been faintly truncated. Surface marked only by lines of growth.

Figure, natural size.

Locality: A single specimen, found near Fort Téjon by Dr. Horn (Division B.).

This species appears to be closely allied to *M. lens*, from Chico Creek, in Division A. It is, however, a thicker, more robust shell, is more convex; the beaks are larger and are of a different shape, and the shell is altogether more regularly elliptical.

M. CALIFORNICA, Con.

(*M. Californica*, Con. Pacific R. R. Rep., vol. 5, p. 320, pl. 2, fig. 4.)

ALTHOUGH I searched thoroughly the locality from which this species was reported, and spent several days collecting fossils there, and although Dr. Horn has been collecting there for months, I have not seen even a single fragment that could by any possibility be referred to this species.

DOSINIA, Scopoli.

D. ELEVATA, G.

Pl. 30, Fig. 252.

(*D. alta*, Con. (non Dkr.) Pacific R. R. Report, vol. 5, p. 320, pl. 2, fig. 2.)
(Not *D. alta*, Con., Proc. Phila. Acad. Nat. Sci., 1856, p. 315.)

SUBCIRCULAR, convex, thick; beaks prominent, placed in advance of the middle, and strongly inclined forwards; base and ends regularly rounded; cardinal margin strongly arched and uniting with the posterior end by a faint angle; immediately adjoining the ligament there is an inward truncation of the cardinal border, which runs from the beaks to the posterior angle, and is nearly a quarter of an inch broad at its widest part. Lunule very faint. Surface marked only by lines of growth.

Figure, natural size.

Locality: Near Fort Téjon. Dr. Horn.

Dosinia alta, Con. (not Dunker), was described, by Mr. Conrad, from the Miocene formation of Monterey, in 1856. Subsequently, he applied the name to the Cretaceous form from the Cañada de las Uvas, on the evidence of a specimen in even a more fragmentary condition than the present one. By comparing fig. 252 with his original description, or with the figures in vol. 6, Pacific R. R. Report, pl. 3, fig. 13 *a*, 13 *b*, it will be seen at once that the two species are not of the same form.

This form approaches *D. inflata*, from Chico Creek, but is larger, thicker, broader, and less convex. That species also wants entirely the truncation of the cardinal margin.

D. PERTENUIS, n. s.

Pl. 30, Fig. 253.

SHELL broad, very thin, subcircular; anterior and basal margins forming a regular curve, cardinal margin nearly straight; posterior end obtusely subangulated; beaks small, in advance of the middle and inclined forwards. Surface marked by fine lines of growth. The cardinal margin is faintly truncated in a similar manner to *D. elevata*, though in a less degree.

Figure, natural size.

Locality: On the north side of the Siskiyou Mountains, in Southern Oregon, where it is not rare, though usually found as casts in the sandstone.

This shell is about the size of, and resembles somewhat, *D. tenuis*, Meek, from Vancouver Island, but is less convex, broader, and not so high as that species. It resembles it also in being very thin.

D. GYRATA, n. s.

Pl. 23, Fig. 148.

SHELL lenticular, nearly circular; beaks small, central, inclined anteriorly; cardinal line curved, sloping downwards, and uniting with the posterior margin; length and breadth about equal. Surface marked by numerous irregular lines of growth, crossed by a few indistinct, radiating lines. Lunule small, deeply impressed.

Figure, natural size.

Localities: Common at Marsh's, southeast of Mount Diablo; also found at Martiñez and near San Diego; and a single cast was found near the mouth of Cañada de las Uvas, at Alizos Creek (Division B.).

The extremely compressed form of this shell is one of its most prominent characters. The thickness of the specimen figured, measured from the external surfaces of the shell, is not more than three-tenths of an inch.

D. INFLATA, n. s.

Pl. 23, Fig. 149.

SHELL subcircular, very convex; beaks small, prominent, inclined strongly in advance; height a little greater than the width; margins all regularly and nearly equally convex. Lunule none. Hinge robust, internal margin plain. Surface marked by irregular, concentric lines of growth.

Figure, natural size.

Locality: Chico Creek, Butte County (Division A.).

TAPES, Megerle.

T. Conradiana, n. s.

Pl. 32, Fig. 282.

Shell long, narrow, very inequilateral, oblique; beaks prominent, and placed between a third and a fourth of the distance from the anterior end; cardinal margin sloping nearly straight to the posterior extremity, which is narrow and regularly rounded; basal margin most prominent under the beaks, very broadly rounded posteriorly, sloping upwards rapidly in advance to the anterior end. Lunule small, bordered by a simple impressed line. Surface ornamented by regular concentric ribs, nearly uniform throughout, rounded above, abruptly truncated on the side towards the beaks, and sloping towards the basal margin, so as to present an imbricated appearance, the overlapping being upwards.

Figure, natural size.

Localities: Alizos Creek, near Fort Téjon; abundant, and associated with *Meretrix Uvasana.*

? T. quadrata, n. s.

Pl. 30, Fig. 249.

Shell small, compressed, subquadrate, somewhat variable in shape; cardinal and basal margins convex, subparallel; beaks anterior, nearly terminal; anterior margin deeply excavated under the beaks, narrowly rounded below; posterior extremity obliquely truncated. Lunule long, narrow, and bordered by a sharp, impressed line. Surface marked by very fine lines of growth, sometimes obsolete.

Figure, natural size.

Localities: Division B., at Fort Téjon; and Martiñez: not abundant.

TRAPEZIUM, Mühlfeld.

T. carinatum, n. s.

Pl. 23, Fig. 150.

Shell subquadrate, elongate; the length is to the breadth as seven to five; beaks anterior, nearly terminal; anterior end concave under the beaks, convex and prominent below; cardinal margin slightly convex, nearly horizontal, uniting by a curve with the posterior end, which is obliquely truncated; basal margin broadly and regularly convex; a prominent, angular ridge passes from the beak to the posterior basal angle; in advance of this ridge the surface is gently convex; behind it, it is concave, and descends rapidly to the posterior margin. Surface marked only by a few minute lines of growth. Hinge slender; the teeth are all small and narrow, the most anterior two of the cardinal teeth are placed almost perpendicularly.

Figure, twice natural size.

Locality: Division A., Texas Flat, Placer County. Rare.

From the cabinet of the California Academy of Natural Sciences; collected by Dr. Trask.

CYPRINELLA, N. Gen.

Animal unknown. Shell regular, equivalve, subcordiform. Hinge with three diverging cardinal teeth, and one anterior and one posterior lateral tooth in each valve. Pallial sinus shallow.

This genus appears to be closely allied to *Cyprina*, but is sufficiently distinguished by the presence of a second lateral tooth, as large as the single one of that genus.

C. tenuis, n. s.

Pl. 23, Fig. 151, and 151 *a*.

Shell moderately large, very thin, subcordate; beaks small, prominent, strongly curved inwards and forwards; cardinal margin convex, curving rapidly downwards to meet the posterior end; anterior end sinuous, prominent below; basal margin broadly and regularly convex. Surface marked by concentric lines of growth, which are very regular towards the beaks. Hinge stout; lateral teeth about equal in size; middle cardinal tooth largest, robust, and grooved on the upper surface; posterior cardinal tooth long, linear. Lunule rather large, but only defined by an impressed line.

Figures, natural size.

Locality: In beds, either belonging to the newest Cretaceous, or possibly Tertiary, south side of Corral Hollow; associated with *Corbula primorsa* (supra), an Oyster, and two or three other species, none of which were found sufficiently perfect to be properly characterized. I have also received specimens from Dr. Frick, labelled "Contra Costa County."

All of the specimens were more or less distorted; so that it is possible that figure 151, which was taken from one of the best specimens, may not illustrate, with perfect accuracy, the proper form of the species. However, the inaccuracy, at the worst, cannot be very great.

CARDIUM, Linn.

C. (LÆVICARDIUM) ANNULATUM, n. s.

Pl. 23, Fig. 152.

SHELL thin, moderate in size, cordate, convex, nearly equilateral, length and breadth about equal; beaks large, prominent, and strongly incurved and directed forwards; anterior and posterior ends regularly convex, the posterior a little the broadest; base regular. Surface highly polished and ornamented by very minute, waved lines of growth, and small dots composed of circular or elliptical impressed lines, arranged in radiating series; these rings are placed at variable distances, usually about a tenth of an inch apart.

Figure 152, natural size; 152 *a*, magnified view of a portion of the surface.

Locality: Curry's, south side of Mount Diablo, from a very hard gray sandstone, in Division A. A single imperfect specimen, collected by Mr. Brewer.

C. Rémondianum, n. s.

Pl. 23, Fig. 153.

Shell small, subcordate, inequilateral, wider than long; beaks central, large, prominent, slightly inclined forward, with the sides sloping rapidly towards both ends; anterior end broadly and regularly convex; posterior end abruptly truncated; basal margin rounded, most prominent posteriorly; a rounded angle passes from the beaks to the posterior basal angle; in advance of this, the surface is prominently convex; behind it, it is flattened and descends abruptly to the posterior margin. Surface marked by about forty square, radiating ribs, with flat interspaces; these ribs are very large on the umbonal angle, and decrease gradually in size in front and behind, until they are mere lines. Internal edge crenulated.

Figure, about three times natural size.

Localities: From near Benicia, Division A.; also at "Wright's Gulch," near Shasta City; collected by Mr. Rémond.

C. Cooperii, n. s.

Pl. 24, Fig. 154, and 154 *a*.

Shell broad, cordate, equilateral; beaks small, central, prominent; cardinal margins sloping, rounded, not very abruptly, on both sides; ends symmetrical; base regularly convex. Surface marked by a large number of minute, rounded, radiating ribs; these ribs are a little larger on the posterior face of the shell, but the surface so covered is not separated from the rest by any angle or carina.

Figures, natural size.

Localities: From Division B., at Martiñez; San Diego; also near Cañada de las Uvas.

Closely related to *C. multiradiatum*, nob., of Alabama and (?) New Jersey; but distinguished by the broader outline, and the difference in size of the ribs on the posterior face, from those on the rest of the surface.

C. Brewerii, n. s.

Pl. 24, Fig. 155.

Shell moderate in size, subequilateral, subquadrate, a little wider than long; beaks central, strongly incurved; hinge-line nearly straight; anterior and basal margins forming a regular curve; posterior end abruptly truncated. Surface, in advance of a rounded, umbonal ridge, regularly convex; posterior slightly concave and sloping rapidly towards the posterior margin; ornamented by about twenty-five uniform subflattened ribs, with perfectly flat interspaces; the surface of these ribs is sometimes plain, sometimes faintly grooved longitudinally; the interspaces are crossed by numerous minute, squamose lines, which occasionally are visible on the ribs themselves.

Figure, natural size.

Localities: This beautiful shell is abundant in the beds of Division B., east of the north end of Cañada de las Uvas; also found in the same formation around Martiñez, although always small at the latter locality.

C. (Protocardium) Placerensis, n. s

Pl. 24, Fig. 156.

Shell small, subcircular, nearly equilateral; beaks central, moderately prominent, with the posterior end faintly subtruncated obliquely outwards; anterior end regularly convex. Surface marked by minute, irregular, concentric lines, and by seven or eight radiating ribs on the posterior face; the largest of these is on the umbonal angle, and is bounded by two deep grooves; the others are placed between it and the margin of the shell, and decrease regularly in size, leaving a narrow space between the last one and the margin plain. Internal margin plain. Hinge slender.

Figure, magnified three times.

Locality: Texas Flat, Placer County. Collection of the California Academy of Natural Sciences; collected by Dr. Trask.

CARDITA, Brug.

C. Hornii, G.

Pl. 24, Fig. 157.

(*C. planicosta*, Con. (not Lam.) Pacific R. R. Report, vol. 5, p. 321, pl. 2, fig. 6.)

Shell large, thick, convex, subquadrate, oblique; beaks prominent, anterior, subterminal; cardinal margin broadly arched, sloping slightly, and uniting with the posterior end with a regular curve; base broadly rounded, most prominent in the middle, from which point it runs upwards rapidly towards the anterior end, which is broadly and regularly curved; posterior end obliquely subtruncated, angular below. Surface marked by twenty-two broad rounded ribs, a little the smallest posterior to the umbonal angle; these ribs are somewhat flattened above, especially towards the base, have acute interspaces, and are crossed by numerous coarse, irregular lines of growth. Hinge very thick, robust, and resembling that of *C. planicosta* of the Eocene.

Figure, natural size.

Localities: Abundant near Fort Téjon; also found at Martiñez, and near Clayton.

I dedicate this magnificent species to my friend, Dr. Horn, U. S. A., in recognition of the valuable assistance he has rendered me, in collecting Cretaceous fossils in the vicinity of Fort Téjon.

It is not so surprising as might appear at first glance, that Mr. Conrad should have referred this shell to Lamarck's species. The form figured is probably an extremely oblique one, although all of the *adult* specimens show more or less of an approach to this shape. The young shells, of which I have examined a large number, approach much more nearly to *C. planicosta* in outline. Add to this the fact that whenever the shell is weathered so as to lose the outside layer, the ribs become quite flat, angular on the sides, and with broad, flat interspaces. Wherever the surface is preserved intact, however, the rotundity of the ribs, and the narrow, acute interspaces, show a character entirely incompatible with the other form. A further resemblance is in the hinge, which, as well as my memory serves me, is nearly, if not quite, undistinguishable from that of *C. planicosta*.

LUCINA, Brug.

L. NASUTA, n. s.

Pl. 24, Fig. 158.

SHELL small, very thin, subcompressed, inequilateral; beaks small, acute, not prominent, placed a little behind the middle; anterior end broadly rounded and very prominent; posterior cardinal margin straight, sloping downwards to unite with the posterior end, which is narrow, produced, and subtruncate; basal margin convex, most prominent in advance of the middle, slightly sinuated posteriorly; umbonal ridge subangular, straight. Surface polished, marked by faint, concentric lines of growth, and by almost imperceptible radiating lines.

Length, .55 inch.

Locality: A single specimen, from Division A., near Martiñez; collection of Mr. Mathewson.

L. POSTRADIATA, n. s.

Pl. 24, Fig. 159.

SHELL very small, suboval, compressed, inequilateral; beaks small, moderately prominent, placed behind the middle; hinge margin excavated anteriorly, straight, and sloping downwards posteriorly; anterior and basal margins regularly rounded, the latter most prominent in advance of the middle; posterior end rounded, subtruncate; a sharp ridge passes from the beaks to the posterior basal margin, behind which the surface falls suddenly as if dislocated, and then continues in a parallel plane with the rest of the surface to the posterior margin. Surface ornamented by moderately large, regular, concentric ribs, and on the posterior portion by two or three radiating ribs.

Figure, three times the natural size.

Locality: Division A., Texas Flat, Placer County; collection of the California Academy of Natural Sciences; collected by Dr. Trask.

The peculiar character of the posterior end of this little fossil will at once distinguish it. The umbonal ridge is not an exsert angle, but a mere dislocation of the surface; as if the shell had been broken along that line, and then set back a short distance.

L. SUBCIRCULARIS, n. s.

Pl. 24, Fig. 160.

SHELL small, subcircular, compressed; beaks small, central, pointing anteriorly; cardinal margin slightly excavated in front of the beaks, straight, acute, and sloping gently downwards posteriorly; anterior and basal margins forming a nearly perfect semicircle; posterior end faintly subtruncated; a faint umbonal ridge, behind which the surface is gently concave. Surface marked by small, regular, concentric ribs, which become nearly obsolete posterior to the umbonal ridge; these ribs are acute and sublamellar near the beaks, and rounded on the lower portion of the shell.

Figure, slightly magnified.

Locality: Collected with the preceding.

L. CUMULATA, n. s.

Pl. 24, Fig. 254.

SHELL minute, subcircular, thick; beaks large, subcentral; ends and base regularly rounded; anterior end slightly emarginate immediately under the beaks; cardinal margin nearly straight, uniting with the posterior end by a rounded angle. Surface marked by four or more enormous, rounded, concentric ribs, giving the shell the appearance of being composed of a number of independent masses laid one over another; besides these ribs there are a few small, oblique, divaricating, impressed lines, most marked near the apex.

Figures, about two and a half times the natural size.

Locality: Near Fort Téjon; very rare. The figure and description are from a single specimen.

I have seen but one fragment of another from the same locality.

? L. CRETACEA, n. s.

Pl. 30, Fig. 255.

SHELL thin, flattened, subquadrate; beaks subcentral; ends and base broadly rounded, subtruncate. Surface marked only by fine lines of growth.

Figure, twice natural size.

Localities: From Clayton to Marsh's, vicinity of Mount Diablo.

I have not seen the hinge of this little shell, and therefore refer it doubtfully to the above genus. It is not rare at Marsh's, fifteen miles east of Mount Diablo.

LORIPES, Poli.

? L. DUBIA, n. s.

Pl. 24, Fig. 170, and 171.

SHELL subcircular, inflated; beaks moderately large, prominent, strongly incurved and inclined forwards; margins regularly convex; basal margin sometimes nearly straight. Surface, in small specimens, marked by regular, concentric ribs, which, in larger ones, become irregular and sometimes quite coarse. Margin thin, not crenulated. Lunule apparently absent.

Figures, natural size.

Localities: Texas Flat, Placer County (Fig. 170); Chico Creek, Butte County (Fig. 171); and Tuscan Springs, Tehama County (Division A.).

This shell may prove to be the type of a new genus of *Lucinidæ*. The hinge resembles that of *L. anatellinoides;* but the apparent absence of a lunule and some other characters may serve to separate it from that species. The ligament appears to have been decidedly external. Adams says: "No external ligament;" while Chenu says: "Ligament logé dans un sillon oblique du bord cardinal;" and his figure of *L. edentula* shows it fully as external as it is in the present species.

MYSIA, Leach, 1819.

Diplodonta, Bronn, 1831.

? M. POLITA, n. s.

Pl. 30, Fig. 256.

SHELL small, thin, subglobose; beaks between the middle and anterior end; base and sides form about three-fourths of a nearly perfect circle; anterior end slightly excavated, immediately under the beaks; cardinal margin variable, arched, or sometimes nearly straight. Surface polished and marked by faint concentric lines of growth.

Figure, about three times the natural size.

Locality: Not rare about Martiñez; and also found at Clayton, near the coal-mines (from Division B.).

I have referred this shell to the above genus entirely from the external form, not having succeeded in exposing the hinge of any of the specimens.

ASTARTE, Sow.

A. CONRADIANA, n. s.

Pl. 24, Fig. 161.

SHELL moderate in size, elongate, subquadrate, compressed; beaks small, overhanging the anterior end, which is sinuous and not prominent; cardinal margin convex and slightly inclined downwards posteriorly; anal extremity convexly and obliquely truncated; basal margin broadly and regularly convex, most prominent at or a little behind the middle. Surface ornamented by small, regular, concentric ribs, which, when weathered, are replaced by finer radiating lines. Lunule small, deep.

Figure, natural size.

Locality: Texas Flat, Placer County: collected by Dr. Trask.

A. Mathewsonii, n. s.

Pl. 30, Fig. 258.

Shell small, compressed, subquadrate, length and breadth about equal; beaks very prominent, strongly incurved, presented forwards, and overhanging the anterior end; cardinal margin straight and sloping downwards; posterior truncated; anterior deeply emarginate above, narrowly and prominently rounded below. Surface marked by fine, irregular, concentric lines, variable in different specimens, but usually most prominent near the beaks. Lunule deeply impressed.

Figure, natural size.

Locality: Near Martiñez. All the specimens I have seen were collected by Mr. Mathewson.

A. Tuscana, n. s.

Pl. 30, Fig. 257.

Shell thick, narrow, cuneate; beaks small, incurved; cardinal margin straight, sloping downwards to the posterior end, which is obliquely and convexly truncated; anterior end straight and sloping outwards above, rounded below; base most prominent below the beaks, nearly straight behind, rounded upwards in advance. Lunule small, deeply sunken. Surface marked with regular, rounded, concentric ribs.

Figure, natural size.

Localities: From Division A., at Tuscan Springs; also at Pence's Ranch, Butte County.

Allied to *A. Conradiana;* but narrower posteriorly, more sloping on the cardinal border; the beak is also less terminal, and the anterior end is of an entirely different shape. Two specimens in the collection of the Survey, from Chico Creek, resemble this species in most of the essential characters, except that they are twice as large, are more robust, wider from beak to base, and slightly excavated on the anterior end, immediately under the beaks. They are also proportionally narrower posteriorly than the present species, and may prove to be distinct; but, without more material, I would not venture to name them.

ERIPHYLA, N. Gen.

Animal unknown. Shell subtrigonal. Surface of valves concentrically ribbed or striated. Hinge composed of two primary teeth in the right valve, and one in the left, and an anterior and posterior lateral tooth in each valve. Ligament external; lunule deep. Pallial line unknown.

This shell is closely allied to *Astarte* and *Gouldia*, but differs from both, in the presence of a well-marked posterior tooth in each valve. On the left valve there is a rudiment of a second cardinal tooth, which enters a depression on the opposite side, behind the large, posterior, cardinal tooth of that valve. Other species may show two well-defined cardinal teeth on each side.

E. umbonata, n. s.

Pl. 24, Fig. 162, and 162 *a*.

Shell subtrigonal, inequilateral; beaks prominent, subcentral, inclined in advance; posterior cardinal line rapidly sloping convexly; basal half of the shell nearly semicircular; anterior end rounded, excavated under the beaks. Lunule profound, subcordate. Internal margin with a minute rim or thickening running parallel with the edge. Surface ornamented with numerous regular concentric ribs, which, in some specimens, become obsolete on the middle of the shell.

Figure 162, natural size; 162 *a*, magnified view of the hinge.

Localities: Cow Creek, Shasta County; also Curry's, south side of Mount Diablo (Division A.).

CRASSATELLA, Lam.

C. GRANDIS, n. s.

Pl. 24, Fig. 163.

(*Crassatella alta*, Con. Pacific R. R. Report, vol. 5, p. 321.)
(Not *C. alta*, Con. Tert. Foss, p. 21, pl. 7.)

SHELL very large, subtrigonal, a little longer than wide; beaks moderate in size, prominent, with the sides sloping rapidly, most abrupt in advance, slightly convex behind; anterior end broadly rounded; posterior rounded, subtruncated; base nearly straight, and sloping upwards from directly below the beaks to the posterior end; umbonal ridge faint, broad, rounded. Surface marked only by a few small lines of growth. Inner margin minutely crenulated.

Figure, natural size of a small perfect specimen. One cast, with a portion of the shell preserved, measures over four inches from beaks to base.

Localities: From Division B., near Clayton; also from Alizos Creek, near Cañada de las Uvas.

This species was referred to *C. alta*, by Mr. Conrad, from fragments. I have been fortunate enough to procure two casts at the same locality, one of which still retains a large portion of the shell; and have before me a perfect specimen, although small, found by Mr. Rémond near the Mount Diablo coal-mines. The specific distinctness is obvious on comparing the outline of fig. 163 with plate 7 of "Tertiary Fossils." The shell is thicker than in *C. alta*, and the pallial impression is much more nearly parallel with the margin of the shell, wanting almost entirely the abrupt recurve posteriorly. The ligament area runs out gradually below, instead of ending abruptly; and the hinge-plate is equally massive, and even broader than in Mr. Conrad's species.

ANTHONYA, N. Gen.

SHELL equivalve, very inequilateral, long, narrow; beaks anterior, nearly terminal. Hinge composed of two strong, oblique teeth in each valve; those in the right valve articulating in front of those in the left. Muscular scars and pallial line unknown.

This genus is apparently allied to the group of *Megalodon* and *Opis* in the family *Crassatellidæ*, the form approaching remotely to *M. carinatus;* while the hinge differs in all of its details so strongly as to permit no doubts of its generic difference.

Named in honor of Mr. J. G. Anthony, a gentleman whose name is intimately connected with American fresh-water conchology.

A. CULTRIFORMIS, n. s

Pl. 30, Fig. 236, and 236 *a*.

SHELL long, narrow, compressed, slightly curved and tapering posteriorly; beaks acute, prominent, and placed very near the anterior end, which is obliquely truncated above, regularly rounded below; posterior extremity truncated obliquely upwards and inwards; cardinal margin concave, basal broadly convex. Surface marked by fine lines of growth, most marked near the beaks, where they assume the character of distinct undulations.

Figure 236, natural size; 236 *a*, a magnified view of the hinge.

Locality: Half a dozen specimens, mostly fragmentary; were found by Mr. Mathewson, near Martiñez.

UNIO, Retzius.

U. PENULTIMUS, n. s.

Pl. 24, Fig. 164.

SHELL moderately large, subquadrate, compressed, bialate, length and breadth nearly equal; beaks subcentral (?); wings nearly equal in height, the posterior a little the longest, slightly curved on their upper margin and rounded at the ends, so as to unite with the ends of the shell without forming an angle; anterior, posterior and basal margins regularly curved, the posterior basal portion being more produced than the anterior. Surface marked by faint lines of growth, rarely so distinct as to produce ridges. Ligament robust.

Figure, natural size.

Locality: From a bed of fine clay adjoining the "Peacock," or lower vein of coal, in the Peacock coal-mine, Mount Diablo District, Contra Costa County (Division B.).

This is the only undoubted fresh-water shell that has thus far been discovered in the California Cretaceous. I detected it in a vein of fine-grained clay, occupying a "fault" in the Peacock or Cumberland vein. All the specimens are more or less distorted, and I was only fortunate enough to get a single comparatively good one. The testaceous substance had apparently lost all of its animal matter, although the ligament of one specimen is still perfectly preserved. The diagnosis of the outline was obtained from the lines of growth on the surface.

MYTILUS, Linn.

M. PAUPERCULUS, n. s.

Pl. 25, Fig. 165.

SHELL small, thin, oblique; beaks terminal, acute; cardinal line slightly arched, uniting in a regular curve with the posterior side, which is broadly subtruncated above and rounded below; anterior margin nearly straight. Surface broadly convex, flattened above and somewhat abrupt on the sides near the beak; ornaments none; a few faint lines of growth visible near the margins towards the beaks.

Figure, magnified to nearly twice natural size.

Locality: Not rare in Division A., west of Martiñez.

M. ASCIA, n. s.

Pl. 30, Fig. 259.

SHELL long, narrow, oblique, convex; anterior margin nearly straight, abruptly truncated parallel with the border; cardinal margin slightly arched; anterior and posterior margins parallel, basal truncated somewhat convexly and at right angles to the two adjoining sides, uniting with them by rounded angles. Surface marked only by a few indistinct lines of growth.

Figure, natural size.

Locality: Found at Fort Téjon; but rare.

M. HUMERUS, Con.

(*M. humerus*, Con. Pacific R. R. Report, vol. 5, p. 321, pl. 2, fig. 10.)

I AM only acquainted with this species through the figure and description of Mr. Conrad, quoted above.

MODIOLA, Lam.

M. SISKIYOUENSIS, n. s.

Pl. 30, Fig. 260.

SHELL long, narrow, subcompressed; cardinal and basal margins nearly straight, diverging posteriorly; beaks anterior, subterminal; anterior end prominent, narrowly rounded; posterior very obliquely truncated above, rounded below. A well-marked, rounded, umbonal ridge passes from the beaks to the posterior basal angle. Surface marked by moderately distinct, concentric ribs, most prominent posteriorly, and ending in fine lines in advance.

Figure, natural size.

Localities: Siskiyou Mountains, California and Oregon; and Jacksonville, Oregon. Collection of the Survey and of Prof. Whitney.

This species is of the type of *M. concentrice-costellata*, Roem., from Texas, but is more compressed; the anterior end is narrower and of a different form; the posterior end is more obliquely truncated, broader and more acute below; and the cardinal and basal margins are straighter. The ribs are smaller and more numerous.

M. ORNATA, n. s.

Pl. 24, Fig. 166.

SHELL thin, broad, deep; beaks small, anterior, subterminal; anterior end narrow, rounded, produced; cardinal margin nearly straight, uniting by a broad curve with the posterior extremity; anterior basal edge broadly emarginate; umbonal ridge prominent, rounded, curved downwards and widening out posteriorly, until it becomes lost in the general swell of the surface.

In advance of this the surface is gently concave; behind, it is nearly flat. Surface marked by numerous, fine, dichotomous ribs, except on a small space under the beaks, where they sometimes become obsolete. Internal edge minutely crenulated.

Figure, natural size, from an unusually large specimen. Generally from an inch to an inch and a quarter long.

Localities: Division B., Martiñez, and Marsh's; most common at the latter locality.

M. CYLINDRICA, n. s.

Pl. 25, Fig. 167.

SHELL elongated, subcylindrical, sides nearly parallel; beaks anterior, nearly terminal, broad, not very prominent; anterior end broadly rounded; base nearly straight, sloping upwards slightly in advance; posterior end obliquely truncated; a broad, rounded, umbonal ridge, passes down from the beaks, gradually losing itself in the general convexity of the shell. Surface marked by a few faint, concentric lines of growth, which sometimes become slightly lamellar.

Figure, natural size.

Localities: Pence's Ranch, Butte County; Tuscan Springs; also near Martiñez (Division A.).

LITHOPHAGUS, Mühlf.

L. OVIFORMIS, n. s.

Pl. 25, Fig. 168.

SHELL small, ovoid, very gibbous; beaks large, anterior, overhanging; cardinal margin slightly arched; anterior and posterior ends round, basal slightly excavated, nearly straight. Surface unknown.

Figure, magnified to about three times the natural size.

Locality: Found embedded in the oyster, fig. 191; from Cow Creek, Shasta County (Division A.).

This species differs from *L. Ripleyanus* (nob.) in its smaller size, more robust form, more prominent beaks, and in being more compressed laterally behind.

SEPTIFER, Recluz.

S. DICHOTOMUS, n. s.

Pl. 30, Fig. 261.

SHELL small, oblique, subquadrate; cardinal margin straight, anterior and posterior margins subparallel, basal irregularly convex; anterior side abruptly truncated at an acute angle to the rest of the surface. Surface marked, posterior to this angle, by a few large, irregular, radiating ribs, dichotomous, or with smaller ones interpolated.

Figure, natural size.

Locality: A single specimen was obtained near Fort Téjon.

CRENELLA, Brown.

C. CONCENTRICA, n. s.

Pl. 24, Fig. 169.

SHELL small, long, narrow, very convex, inequilateral; beaks prominent, strongly incurved; sides subparallel, the anterior side being most prominent, the posterior curving above gradually into the cardinal margin; base rounded. Surface polished, and marked by regular, concentric lines.

Figure, magnified one-third more than natural size.

Locality: A single specimen, from Division B., at Martiñez.

The distinct, concentric lines, entire absence of radiation, and the more parallel sides, distinguish this species from *C. serica*, Con.; and the convex, narrow form, from *C. elegantula*, M. and H.

AVICULA, Klein, Lam.

A. PELLUCIDA, n. s.

Pl. 25, Fig. 172.

SHELL oblique, subcompressed, broad-linguæform; ears very unequal; beaks moderate, anterior; cardinal line straight; anterior ear short, angular, posterior ear broad, acuminate; anterior and posterior margins nearly parallel for a short distance below the ears; base forming an excentric curve, most produced behind; there is no distinct division between the body of the shell and the ears. Surface polished, and exhibiting only faint, concentric undulations, corresponding to lines of growth, and a few microscopic, radiating lines, posteriorly.

Figure, natural size of the largest specimen.

Locality: Division B., near Martiñez, and Division A., at the Ranch of San Luis Gonzaga, Pacheco's Pass.

But few valves of this species have been found. The outline is approximately restored from undulations on a young specimen, the one figured being so decomposed as to show no lines of growth or other markings.

INOCERAMUS, Sow.

I. Piochii, n. s.

Pl. 25, Fig. 173, and 174.

Shell small, thin, inequivalve, high and narrow. Right valve, with the beaks large, prominent, incurved, and placed directly along the anterior margin; posterior margin, to the most prominent part of the base, forms a pretty regular, elliptic curve; anterior margin sinuated. Left valve, beak small, not projecting beyond the hinge-line, which is transverse and nearly straight; anterior margin nearly straight, except towards the lower end, where it bends round to meet the base; posterior margin slightly convex. Surface marked by small, concentric ribs, which sometimes take the form of moderately large undulations; this is most strongly marked in the large valve.

Figures, natural size.

Localities: Division A., north side of Mount Diablo; also Tuscan Springs.

Named in honor of Mr. Pioche, of San Francisco, who kindly loaned me the first good specimens of the species I met with.

Fragments and single valves of several large and moderate sized species have been found at various localities in the State; but, on account of the number of species already described without figures, and the consequent difficulty in distinguishing allied species, I have deferred their description until I can compare them with specimens or good figures of those already named, outside of California.

PINNA, Linn.

P. Breweri, n. s.

Pl. 25, Fig. 175, and 175 *a*.

Shell long, slender, section subrhomboidal; sides diverging at an angle of 18° or 20°. Surface marked by rounded radiating ribs, on at least one-half of each valve; other half apparently crossed by a few radiating lines and one or two oblique ones. The middle of each valve is elevated and, in the crest of this ridge, marked by a broad groove.

Figures, natural size.

Localities: Division A., Curry's, south side of Mount Diablo; Martiñez and Siskiyou Mountains.

A small specimen, one inch long, probably of this species, was found at Cottonwood Creek, Shasta County; and a fragment of a much larger one, three inches across, apparently distinct, is in the collection of Mr. Bayerque, from Division B., near Mount Diablo.

TRIGONIA, Brug.

T. Tryoniana, n. s.

Pl. 25, Fig. 176.

Shell elongate, subquadrate, narrowest behind; beaks anterior, not prominent, subterminal; hinge-line straight, obliquely sloping; anterior end rounded, base convex in front, straight and sloping upwards behind, posterior end convexly subtruncated. Surface marked by two radiating grooves, one of which passes from the beaks to the posterior basal angle; the other is above it; between the first and the anterior ends are arranged oblique series of elongated tubercles. These are all crossed by numerous, fine, concentric lines of growth, and occasional irregular undulations.

Figure, natural size.
Locality: Tuscan Springs, Tehama County; collected by Dr. Veatch.

T. Evansii, Meek.

Pl. 25, Fig. 177.

(*T. Evansii*, Meek. Trans. Albany Institute, vol. 4, p. 42.)

Shell trigonal, produced behind; beaks anterior, subterminal, very prominent, strongly incurved; anterior end convexly truncated, very broad laterally; basal margin prominently rounded in the middle, sloping upwards posteriorly straight to the posterior end, which is narrow and round; cardinal margin concave, nearly straight behind. Corselet bordered by a rounded double rib crossed by small transverse lines, and marked on its surface by about eighteen or twenty small oblique ribs; remainder of the surface marked by from eighteen to twenty-two large, prominent ribs, slightly radiating, but nearly parallel posteriorly; on very young shells, these ribs are pretty regularly nodose, but become plain when the shell attains a medium size; sometimes the three or four posterior ribs show a faint groove; interspaces between the ribs regularly concave, and marked only by the lines of growth which cross the whole surface.

Figure, natural size. One specimen before me is between three and four inches long; but this size is rare.

Localities: Common in Division A. Found at Tuscan Springs, Tehama County; Chico Creek, Butte County; Curry's, south of Mount Diablo; Benicia; Martiñez; Rancho de San Luis Gonzaga, Pacheco's Pass; Jacksonville and Siskiyou Mountains, Oregon; and Nanaimo, Vancouver Island. The specimen figured, from Tuscan Springs, shows but eighteen ribs, and the lower portion of the buccal margin is unusually prominent. There can be little doubt, however, of the identity of the species, since I have found it very abundant at almost every locality of the lower member of the Cretaceous of the west slope, from Nanaimo, whence it was described, to Pacheco's Pass, a range of over seven hundred miles in length.

T. Gibboniana, Lea?

Pl. 17, Fig. 178, and Pl. 31, Fig. 262.

(*T. Gibboniana*, Lea. Trans. American Philosophical Soc., 1840, p. 255, pl. 9, fig. 7.)

(*T. Hondaana*, Lea. Id., p. 256, pl. 9, fig. 9.)

(*T. Hondaana*, D'Orb. Prodrome, vol. 2, p. 106, Etage 17, No. 711.)

Shell rounded, subquadrate, compressed; beaks anterior, subterminal; cardinal and basal margins nearly parallel, the former nearly straight, the latter broadly convex; anterior end broadly rounded, straight near the beaks; posterior end truncated obliquely above, vertically below.

Surface in adult specimens marked by about thirteen nodose ribs, starting from a line drawn from the beaks to the posterior basal angle, and running obliquely downwards and forwards; those nearest the beaks becoming more oblique and somewhat curved; above are some smaller pustular ribs, or rows of small tubercles, running parallel with the corresponding posterior margin of the shell. In very young specimens all of the ribs are reduced to rows of distinct tubercles, and those on the cardinal border change their direction somewhat. Besides these, on two specimens from Martiñez, is a single row of small, isolated tubercles, placed between the two rows of ribs.

Figures, natural size.

Localities: Near Martiñez, and Jacksonville, Oregon.

D'Orbigny, in his Prodrome de Paléontologie Stratigraphique, refers *T. Hondaana* to the Neocomien. Our specimens are undoubtedly from the equivalent of the lower part of the Upper or White Chalk of Europe, the Sénonien of D'Orbigny. Should I be correct in my reference of this shell to Lea's species, it will prove either an unusually wide stratigraphical range for the species, or some mistake on the part of the French author. Be that as it may, I can find no valid characters, in the poor figures and meagre description given by Mr. Lea, by which I can separate his species from the present one. It is also possible, although there is no present means of deciding, that his *T. Tocaimana* may be the same as *T. Evansii;* and that *Natica Gibboniana*, figured on the same plate, may be *Amauropsis alveata*, *Natica id.*, Con.

MEEKIA, N. Gen.

SHELL equivalve, inequilateral, gaping at both extremities; anterior end produced, and terminating in a hook-like angle above. Surface plain, or marked only by lines of growth. Hinge composed of two robust, triangular teeth on the right valve, and one large and one small one on the opposite side, the large one being received between the two of the right valve; posteriorly, on each side, is an indistinct lateral tooth. Ligament subexternal; lunule moderate, lanceolate. Muscular scars two; pallial line simple, or not more emarginate posteriorly than in *Trigonia* or *Tancredia*.

A short, robust plate separates the anterior muscular scar from the cavity of the beak.

The family relations of this shell are by no means obvious. The hinge is not unlike that of Lycett's genus, *Tancredia*, and the pallial line is also of the same form. A marked difference exists, however, in the gaping anterior end, and the angle at the junction of the cardinal and anterior margins. It is probable that these two genera will form the types of a new family.

It is with pleasure that I dedicate this curious genus to my friend, Mr. F. B. Meek, of Washington, D. C.

M. SELLA, n. s.

Pl. 25, Fig. 179.

SHELL robust, subquadrate; beaks subcentral, small, nearly touching, and inclined forwards; cardinal margin strongly arched, descending rapidly, and uniting by a regular curve with the posterior margin, which is sometimes faintly truncated; anterior end produced, laterally compressed, rounded and retreating below, and terminating above in a sharp angle, between which and the beak the margin is broadly concave; base regularly rounded, usually most prominent a little behind the beaks. Lunule small, bordered by a single impressed line. The posterior margin is abruptly thickened, both externally and internally. This latter character is very variable even in specimens of the same size and from the same locality; the thickening being, in some specimens, twice as great as in others. Surface marked only by lines of growth.

Figure, natural size.

Localities: Abundant near Martiñez (Division A.). Also found at Tuscan Springs, Tehama County, and in the Siskiyou Mountains.

M. RADIATA, n. s.

Pl. 25, Fig. 179 *a*.

THIS little shell is almost a perfect miniature of the preceding species; but the points of difference, although small, seem to be constant, and I have ventured to elevate it to the rank of a distinct species, despite my first impressions.

The shell is proportionally more gibbous, the beaks are more prominent, the anterior end is more produced, the whole outline is less quadrangular, and the anterior fourth of the surface is marked by a few radiating lines. The most marked difference between the two forms is, that this one, although found at a number of localities, over a range of about five hundred miles, and in some places quite abundantly, never attains a size greater than the figure, which is from an unusually large specimen

Localities: From Division A., at the Rancho de San Luis Gonzaga, in Pacheco's Pass; Orestimba Cañon, Stanislaus County; Tuscan Springs, Tehama County; Siskiyou Mountains, Siskiyou County, and at Jacksonville, Oregon.

M. NAVIS, n. s.

Pl. 25, Fig. 180.

SHELL long, boat-shaped, thin; beaks small, central, not prominent; cardinal margin concave in front, convex and slightly sloping behind; anterior end angular above, sloping inwards, rounded below; posterior end regularly rounded; base slightly convex, nearly straight in some specimens. Surface marked only by a few faint lines of growth. Posterior end not thickened, as in the preceding species.

Figure, natural size.

Localities: Division A., near Martiñez; also at Chico Creek and Pence's Ranch, Butte County.

This species is very distinct from the preceding. The difference in outline is very marked; it is very much compressed; the shell is thin; the posterior thickening, so characteristic in the former, is entirely absent in this; and the internal plate in front of the beak is thinner, and is inclined more strongly forward. It is rare, five specimens only having been found.

ARCA, Lam.

A. Breweriana, n. s.

Pl. 25, Fig. 181.

Shell small, longer than wide; beaks prominent, incurved, approximate, and inclined forward, placed in advance of the middle; umbones broad; anterior end rounded and sloping inwards; posterior end obliquely truncated and uniting with the base by an abrupt angle; basal margin slightly rounded in front, straight behind, and parallel with the hinge or sloping upwards; umbonal angle sharp, with the surface in front of it very convex, behind it somewhat excavated; area narrow, almost as long as the shell; marked by a few small, closely placed angular lines. Surface marked by numerous small, variable ribs, smallest behind the umbonal ridge; four or five of these ribs on the anterior end of the shell are larger than the others, placed wider apart, and are sometimes slightly nodose; the others are occasionally obsolete; these ribs are crossed by numerous very irregular lines of growth. Hinge slender; the teeth below the beaks, to the number of two or three only, are transverse; those adjoining are oblique, the angle rapidly growing wider, and those at the extremities are all horizontal; this is most strongly marked posteriorly, the *upper* tooth on that side extending for nearly half the length of the hinge.

Figure, slightly magnified.

Localities: Division A., Cottonwood Creek, Shasta County; also Tuscan Springs, Tehama County.

A. Hornii, n. s.

Pl. 30, Fig. 263.

Shell minute, subequilateral; beaks subcentral, approximated; anterior end broadly rounded; basal most prominent below, or a little in advance of the beaks, nearly straight posteriorly, and inclined upwards towards the posterior, which is obliquely truncated; posterior side abruptly truncated behind the umbonal angle; area short and very narrow. Surface marked by very fine, radiating striæ, somewhat undulated laterally, and crossed by still finer lines of growth, with an occasional coarser line formed by a slight interruption in the growth.

Figure, magnified between three and four times.

Locality: This beautiful little shell appears to be quite abundant in the vicinity of Fort Téjon, from which place Dr. Horn has sent me numerous specimens.

A. gravida, n. s.

Pl. 30, Fig. 264.

Shell thick, oblique, convex, very inequilateral; beaks small, approximate, placed about one-third of the length from the anterior end; base broadly rounded, inclined upwards from the posterior end, and convexly truncated in advance; posterior end very obliquely truncated; umbonal ridge very prominent and rounded; posterior to this the surface is nearly flat and at a right angle with the rest of the shell; area short and narrow. Hinge composed of about half a dozen small, transverse teeth under the beaks, three or four large lateral ones in front, and five or six behind. Surface apparently plain, or marked only by fine lines of growth.

Localities: "Rag Cañon," Napa County; and San Luis Gonzaga Ranch, Pacheco's Pass (Division A.).

All of the specimens are more or less rolled, so as to obliterate any very fine markings.

A. DECURTATA, n. s.

Pl. 31, Fig. 265, and 265 *a.*

SHELL thick, convex, triangular; beaks high, very approximate, subcentral; base broadly and regularly convex, most prominent in the middle; anterior end rounded below; posterior end straight, oblique and truncated behind the umbonal ridge, at an acute angle with the rest of the surface. Hinge very short; area short and broad. Surface marked only by indistinct lines of growth.

Figures, natural size.

Locality: A single specimen, found at Rag Cañon with the preceding.

CUCULLÆA, Lam.

C. MATHEWSONII, n. s.

Pl. 31, Fig. 266.

SHELL large, thin, gibbous, subquadrate, rounded in front and on the base, and truncated behind; beaks large, prominent, subcentral, incurved, and somewhat remote; area long, narrow; hinge-line nearly as long as the greatest length of the shell. Surface marked by a large number of small, regular ribs, rounded on the surface, sometimes grooved longitudinally and with acute interspaces; posterior to the umbonal angle these ribs are much smaller than on the rest of the surface; the whole surface is crossed by fine lines of growth. Inner margin of the valves crenulated; inner plate well marked, but not very elevated.

Figure, natural size.

Localities: Martiñez, collected by Mr. Mathewson; and a single specimen from Clayton, below the coal-veins.

This species cannot be confounded with *C. truncata.* It is thinner, more convex, less oblique, less produced behind, and the ornamentation of the surface is entirely different.

C. TRUNCATA, n. s.

Pl. 25, Fig. 182.

SHELL large, thick, subquadrate, obliquely truncate behind, rounded in front, and varying from nearly straight to prominently convex below; beaks moderate in size, very prominent, nearly central, distant and inclined slightly forwards. Surface of young specimens marked by pretty regular, fine, radiating lines, slightly elevated, and sometimes exhibiting a tendency to alternation in size; these lines usually become nearly obsolete in large specimens, and the lines of growth, which in the young shells are barely visible, then form the most obvious character of the surface; area broad, and marked by eight or ten angular lines. Hinge robust, broad at the ends and narrow in the middle; composed of three or four long, angular teeth at each end, and a few small, variable, transverse ones in the centre. Internal plate robust, but not very elevated.

Figure, average size.

Localities: Abundant in Division A., at Curry's, south of Mount Diablo; found also at Tuscan Springs, Tehama County; Benicia; Martiñez; Texas Flat, Placer County, and at many points in the Coast Range, on the east side between Mount Diablo and Pacheco's Pass; also at Jacksonville, Oregon.

This shell is allied to *C. Nebrascensis,* Owen; but differs in the smaller beak, proportionally longer form, more oblique truncation posteriorly, and in being more produced in the anterior basal region. There is also a difference in the hinge. In *C. Nebrascensis* the lateral teeth radiate, as it were, from an imaginary point; while in the present species they are parallel with each other and with the upper edge of the hinge-plate, and their inner ends are bent at a right angle.

For aid in the above comparisons I am indebted to Mr. F. B. Meek, who furnished me with sketches of Dr. Owen's species, much more accurately drawn than the published figures in Owen's Report, pl. 7, fig. 1.

Except *C. Maconensis,* Con., this is the largest *Cucullæa* found in America. A specimen before me, from the south side of Mount Diablo, measures three inches from beak to base; and I have seen fragments which appeared to belong to even larger shells

AXINÆA, Poli.

A. VEATCHII, n. s.

Pl. 25, Fig. 183, and 183 *a*.

SHELL thick, subglobose, equivalve and nearly equilateral; beaks large, incurved, central, approximate, with the sides sloping downwards; anterior and basal margins regularly rounded; posterior end rounded or subtruncate. Surface marked by from thirty-six to forty radiating ribs, very regular in size, a little the smallest anteriorly and obsolete behind; a faint depression usually exists on the posterior side of the umbones, which passes down and strikes the middle of the posterior margin. Internal margin coarsely crenulated. Hinge robust; teeth arranged radiately; the lateral teeth largest and most widely separated. Area very narrow and short.

Figures, natural size.

Localities: Tuscan Springs, Tehama County; collected by Dr. Veatch; very abundant. Also found at Texas Flat, Placer County; Pence's Ranch, Butte County; Cow Creek, Shasta County; Orestimba Cañon, Stanislaus County; and San Diego. Mr. Rémond has specimens in his collection, labelled "Antelope Creek," Tehama County.

A. (LIMOPSIS ?) SAGITTATA, n. s.

Pl. 31, Fig. 267, and 267 *a*.

SHELL subcircular, thin, equivalve, very slightly inequilateral; base regularly convex, sides unequally so, the posterior being a little the most prominent. Surface marked by numerous faint, radiating lines, which, on weathered surfaces, develop into strongly impressed grooves; along these lines are small pits, from which proceed downwards fine, impressed, diverging lines. Hinge composed of robust, radiating teeth. Inner margin finely crenulated. Area?

Figures, natural size, and a magnified view of the surface to show the markings.

Localities: Abundant near Fort Téjon, and also found near Martiñez.

I have been unable to discover the ligament area of this shell; which, if it exist, must be unusually small. On one specimen, in which the hinge is partially uncovered, there is an appearance which may prove to be the ligament pit of the genus *Limopsis.* It is directly under the beak, and appears to produce an interruption in the continuity of the teeth.

A. cor, n. s.

Pl. 31, Fig. 268, and 268 *a*.

Shell small, cordate, equivalve, widest below; base broadly convex, sides nearly straight, diverging; beaks small, prominent, incurved; area small, narrow, impressed. Surface marked by fine, elevated, radiating ribs, with broad, flat interspaces, crossed by regular, concentric, impressed lines.

Figure, twice natural size.

Locality: Found only at Martiñez, where a few specimens have been collected by Mr. Mathewson.

NUCULA, Lam.

N. truncata, n. s.

Pl. 26, Fig. 184, and 184 *a, b*.

Shell moderate in size, oblique; anterior end abruptly truncated; posterior end produced, rounded; cardinal and basal margins subparallel, convex; beaks small, anterior, terminal, and nearly touching. Surface marked by divaricating ribs; these ribs separate along an imaginary line, drawn from the beaks to the posterior basal margin; near the beaks they are regular, but towards the base, especially near the posterior end, they become irregular, sometimes diverging among themselves, sometimes becoming dichotomous, and at times presenting a "hacked" appearance, from the crossing of small impressed lines at acute angles. Anterior end almost entirely occupied by a large, sunken, subcordate lunule, faintly marked by minute ribs.

Figures 184, and 184 *a*, natural size; 184 *b*, magnified, to show the ribs.

Localities: Division A., at Pence's Ranch, Butte County; Tuscan Springs, Tehama County; Ranch of San Luis Gonzaga, east end of Pacheco's Pass; and in Division B., not rare, at Martiñez.

Closely allied to *N. divaricata*, Con., Wilkes's Expedition, Geology, pl. 18, fig. 6; but differs in the abrupt anterior truncation, the front of Conrad's species being sinuous, and the lunular depression absent.

LEDA, Schum.

L. PROTEXTA? Gabb.

Pl. 26, Fig. 185.

(Id. Jour. Acad. Nat. Sciences, Phila., 2 ser., vol. 4, p. 303, pl. 48, fig. 23.)

SHELL small, elongated, narrow; anterior end produced, rounded; posterior end long, narrow, curved upwards; base broadly and pretty regularly convex; beaks small, subcentral, not prominent, with the cardinal margin somewhat convex in front, excavated behind. Surface marked by numerous, regular, concentric ribs.

Figure, somewhat magnified.

Localities: Common in the strata overlying the coal, from Clayton to Marsh's, also found at Martiñez; San Diego; Alizos Creek, near Cañada de las Uvas, and in the San Emidio Cañon, near the same place (Division B.). It also occurs in Division A., near Martiñez.

This shell resembles so closely the species described under the above name from New Jersey and Tennessee, that I have not ventured to separate it. A careful comparison of specimens from the two sides of the continent might bring to light differences of specific value.

L. TRANSLUCIDA, n. s.

Pl. 30, Fig. 269.

SHELL minute, inequilateral, convex; beaks about two-fifths from the anterior end, which is produced and acutely rounded; base regularly convex; posterior side produced, acute below, forming nearly a straight line from the angle to the beak; this margin is, however, somewhat variable, being sometimes sinuous, and in other specimens concave below, so that the extremity is turned up. Surface highly polished, and marked by very faint lines, slightly undulated in the middle, running subparallel with the base, the lower four or five running to the margin of the shell before reaching the posterior angle. The substance of the shell is translucent in all of the specimens.

Figure, nearly three times natural size.
Locality: Cow Creek, Shasta County.

LIMOPSIS, Sassi.

L. TRANSVERSA, n. s.

Pl. 26, Fig. 186.

SHELL oblique, rounded, subquadrate, widest near the posterior end, which is broadly rounded; anterior end produced, convex; base straight or slightly sinuous; beaks anterior, subterminal, small, approximate; area obliquely triangular, small, divided into three unequal portions by two radiating ridges. Hinge curved, edentate in the middle, and with small oblique teeth at each end. Surface most convex in a line running from the beaks to the posterior basal region; marked by fine radiating lines, sometimes obsolete, crossed by concentric lines of growth.

Figure, slightly magnified.
Locality: Texas Flat, Placer County; collection of the California Academy of Natural Sciences,

PECTEN, Brug.

P. TRASKII, n. s.

Pl. 26, Fig. 187, and 187 *a*.

SHELL compressed, elongate, outline of the lower half forming two-thirds of a circle; margins of the body, above the curve, rapidly converging and straight. Right valve, anterior auricle long, truncated at the end, deeply excavated below; posterior auricle broad and obliquely truncated. Surface marked by numerous, radiating, squamose ribs, with sometimes smaller intermediate ones; the interspaces are marked by oblique lines, producing, under a glass, a woven appearance. These lines are represented too numerously in the figure 187 *a*.

Figure 187, natural size.

Locality: Texas Flat, Placer County (Division A.); collection of the California Academy of Natural Sciences; presented by Dr. Trask, after whom the species is named.

The species seems to be rare, as there are remains of but two valves in the collection. One is very young; the other consists of the internal cast and its corresponding mould, the substance of the shell having decomposed. The drawing is from a wax cast of this mould.

P. OPERCULIFORMIS, n. s.

Pl. 26, Fig. 188.

SHELL very much compressed, lenticular; basal half of the outline elongated, subsemicircular above; sides converging, straight. Left valve, auricles equal, outer margins converging, upper edges inclined upwards from the beak. Surface polished, showing under a glass minute, equal, concentric ribs. Right valve unknown.

Figure, natural size.

Localities: Cottonwood and Huling Creeks, Shasta County; and Curry's, south of Mount Diablo (Division A.).

This shell is allied to *P. orbicularis*, Sow. (*P. laminosus*, Mant.); but is proportionally longer, the ears are equal and narrower, and the concentric lamellæ are very much smaller, being invisible to the naked eye.

P. CALIFORNICUS, n. s.

Pl. 31, Fig. 270.

SHELL minute, subcircular, nearly equilateral, inequivalve; lower valve somewhat convex, upper valve nearly flat; sides and base regularly rounded; ears moderate; the right ear of the lower valve long, narrow, and deeply emarginate; left ear obliquely truncated. Surface marked by very fine, concentric lines.

Figure, two and a half times the natural size.

Locality: Cottonwood Creek, Shasta County (Division A.).

This shell is allied to *P. operculiformis*, but is smaller, the lower valve is more convex, there is a difference in outline, and the emarginated ear differs widely from the corresponding one of that species.

A small Pecten, of about the same size with the present, but sculptured like *P. Traskii*, is found at Martiñez. I have not ventured to name it.

LIMA, Brug.

(*Ctenoides*, *Radula*, Klein.)

L. MICROTIS, n. s.

Pl. 26, Fig. 189.

SHELL oblique, compressed; anterior side prominent, forming a subelliptical curve; posterior nearly straight; base rounded; beaks small; anterior ear small, obliquely truncated; posterior unknown, probably nearly obsolete; surface nearly flat, with a very gentle convexity, except near the posterior margin, where it is abruptly bent down, forming a marked truncation; ornamented by numerous flat, radiating, entire ribs, not dichotomous; the interspaces forming shallow grooves, serrated on the sides and marked in the middle by series of small pits or punctations.

Figure, natural size.

Localities: Two specimens only have been found. The one figured is from Cottonwood Creek; the other was associated with the specimen of *Meretrix longa*, ut supra (Division A.).

This shell resembles *L. ovalis*, Desh. (*Plagiostoma ovalis*, Sow.); but is more slender, the ribs are broader and flat, wider than the interspaces, and the intercostal punctæ are much smaller and more distant.

L. APPRESSA, n. s.

Pl. 31, Fig. 271.

SHELL thin, flattened, elongated, irregularly oval; anterior margin straight, or very slightly convex; posterior irregularly curved, most prominent in the middle; ears unequal. Surface marked near the base by a few faint, radiating undulations, crossed by fine lines.

Figure, natural size.

Locality: San Luis Gonzaga Ranch (Division A.). A single cast retaining but a small portion of the shell.

PLICATULA, Lam.

P. VARIATA, n. s.

Pl. 26, Fig. 190.

SHELL variable, usually somewhat curved. Lower valve attached by a portion of the surface, deep, radiately costate, ribs occasionally dichotomous. Upper valve flat or concave, plicate like the lower, but not so strongly, the ribs being sometimes obsolete. Hinge robust; muscular scar large; internal margin of the upper valve crenate; lower valve marked with pits corresponding with the teeth above.

Average length, about .7 inch.

Locality: Abundant in a hard, gray, calcareous sandstone, from Battle Creek, Shasta County (Division A.).

This little shell is extremely variable in outline and convexity; one of the commonest forms is illustrated in the figure.

ANOMIA, Linn., Müll.

A. LINEATA, n. s.

Pl. 26, Fig. 193.

SHELL thin, variable in shape; commonest form subcircular, often obliquely truncated on the right side; beak of upper valve small, distinct, marginal or submarginal. Surface marked by fine, linear, radiating ribs, often dichotomous, sometimes laterally undulated and crossed by concentric lines of growth, which sometimes become squamose. Muscular scar large. Under valve unknown.

Figure, natural size.

Localities: Division A., Texas Flat; Pence's Ranch; Chico Creek, &c.

OSTREA, Linn.

O. Brewerii, n. s.

Pl. 26, Fig. 191.

Shell large, thick, elongated, tapering pretty regularly towards the beak. Surface squamose, not plicate. Ligament pit subquadrate to triangular, median depression broad and deep, a cross section forming from a fourth to a fifth of a circle; upper end strongly curved towards the left side. Internal margin plain. Shell gregarious.

Figure, two-thirds of the natural size.

Locality: Cow Creek, Shasta County; collected by Mr. Brewer.

O. malleiformis, n. s.

Pl. 31, Fig. 272.

Shell auriculate, nearly equivalve, the lower valve a little the most convex, long, narrow, slightly curved to one side; hinge very small, cardinal margin descending on each side of the hinge at a broad angle, nearly straight; ear on the right side biangular, nearly square; opposite ear uniting with the side in a broad curve. Surface not squamose, marked by a few lines of growth. Muscular scar nearly central longitudinally, small.

Figure, natural size.

Localities: Siskiyou Mountains, in California and Oregon; also at Jacksonville, Oregon (Division A.).

GRYPHÆA, Lam.

G. VESICULARIS, Lam.

A FEW small specimens of this species were picked up, not *in situ*, near San Diego, by Dr. Cooper. It has not been found elsewhere on the west coast.

EXOGYRA, Say.

E. PARASITICA, n. s.

Pl. 26, Fig. 192, and 192 *a*, *b*, and Pl. 31, Fig. 273, and 273 *a*.

SHELL always attached by the lower valve, thin when young, thick and irregular in shape when adult. Lower valve shallow, oblique, elevated and overhanging on the right hand side, flat on the left; beak low, excentric, small; hinge small, oblique, curved; inner margin of both valves minutely crenulated; muscular scar long, narrow. Upper valve distinctly spiral in young specimens, somewhat oblique, flattened, or with an irregular angular ridge running from beak to base. Surface of upper valve very squamose; of the lower valve less so.

Figures 192, 192 *a*, and 192 *b*, are of young specimens from Texas Flat; 273, and 273 *a*, adult lower and upper valves, from opposite Folsom.

Localities: Found at the two above-quoted localities, and at Cottonwood Creek, Shasta County.

TEREBRATELLA, D'Orb.

T. OBESA, n. s.

Pl. 26, Fig. 194, and 194 *a*, *b*.

SHELL moderately large, broad, and very convex. Lower valve unknown, except the beak, which is acuminate, high, and with the sides nearly straight; area narrow, sloping slightly backwards from the foramen; foramen longer than wide, sides straight, and bordered on each side by a small impressed line.

Upper valve broad, suboval, very high; ends rounded, sloping, nearly straight above, base nearly straight, except in the median emargination; marked by from twenty-five to thirty radiating, subangular ribs, with nearly equal interspaces; from eight to ten of these ribs on the middle of the shell are a little shorter than the others, producing a straight, shallow emargination on the basal edge of the valve. Internal margin of the base deeply notched; hinge teeth of the upper valve robust; median plate rather long and prominent (in a young specimen); loop unknown.

A young upper valve, .6 of an inch wide, is straighter above and semicircular on the sides and base; it has but seventeen ribs, two or three of which are dichotomous, none so angular as in the adult shell, and there is no emargination of the base.

Adult shells vary very much in convexity and costation, one specimen having eight and another ten ribs in the median portion. But one fragmentary beak has been seen, as represented in the figure.

Figures, natural size, except 194 *b*, which is from a smaller specimen and is slightly magnified.

Localities: Division A., Texas Flat, Placer County.

ZOOPHYTA.

FLABELLUM, Lesson.

F. Rémondianum, n. s.

Pl. 26, Fig. 199.

Polypidom triangular, convex on the sides, acute and straight on the lateral margins; sides marked by eight or nine prominent radiating ribs, with regularly concave interspaces. Upper surface unknown.

Figures, natural size.

Locality: Between Mount Diablo and the coal-mines, in Division B.; a single specimen collected by Mr. Rémond.

This specimen was embedded in a soft sandstone, and the surface is somewhat corroded, so that any fine markings which may have existed are obliterated. The upper portion is still covered by the matrix, and, from the nature of the specimen, it is impossible to expose it without destroying the lamellæ.

TROCHOSMILIA, E. and H.

Subgen. ACROSMILIA, D'Orb.

T. striata, n. s.

Pl. 26, Fig. 195.

Elongate, slender, curved, section circular or subcircular; epithelium rudimentary; surface marked by numerous prominent striæ, usually rounded, of variable size, and often showing a well-marked alternation of larger and smaller ones. Surface of calicle unknown.

Figure, twice natural size.
Locality: Division B., near the coal-mines at Mount Diablo.

SUBGEN. ELLIPSOSMILIA, D'Orb.

? T. GRANULIFERA, n. s.

Pl. 26, Fig. 196, and 196 *a*.

POLYPIDOM trochiform, robust, elliptical above, attached by a broad base; surface marked by impressed striæ, each one corresponding to the space between two of the septa; between these striæ the surface is finely granulated. Septa thick, not very numerous, granular on the sides, as seen from above, narrow on the upper margin.

Figure, three times natural size.
Locality: Rare in Division A., near Chico Creek.

ASTROCŒNIA, E. and H.

? A. PETROSA, n. s.

Pl. 31, Fig. 274, and 274 *a*.

POLYPIDOM dendroid and massive, the branches subcylindrical and dichotomous; cells circular, disposed irregularly, somewhat remote, surrounded by thick walls; columella projecting beyond the edges of the septa, but not reaching as high as the top of the cup. Septa twenty-four in number, thin, somewhat irregular; walls between the cells massive, solid, striated.

Figures, natural size and magnified.
Locality: All of the specimens were obtained from a single mass of limestone, a mile west of Martiñez.

Doubtful Species.

Figure 197, plate 26, and figure 275, plate 31, represent interesting forms, which I have been unable to refer to any genera with certainty, from not being able to expose the hinges. Figure 198, plate 26, is probably a Trigonia; but I have deferred further determination until more perfect specimens shall have been discovered. It has been found at Orestimba Cañon, Stanislaus County; Cottonwood Creek, Shasta County; and Jacksonville, Oregon. The shell figured at 197 is from Martiñez, and is very rare. Figure 275 is from a Mactra-like shell; but, from the remains of the impression of the hinges on the matrix, it seems to have had two or three heavy cardinal teeth, and to have wanted entirely the cartilage-pit of that genus. Two specimens were found at Marsh's, east of Mount Diablo.

Besides these, there are imperfect remains of twenty or thirty species in the collection of the Survey, of which I have not sufficient material for determination. One of the most interesting is a single Echinoderm, belonging apparently to the *Spatangidæ*, the only representative of the class yet discovered in the formation in California. It was found near Clayton by Mr. Bromley, and is in too imperfect a condition for determination.

APPENDIX TO SECTION IV.

SINCE the above species were described, a few additional ones have been received, which are described below, together with one or two which had been overlooked before.

FICUS, Rousseau.

F. MAMILLATUS, n. s.

Pl. 32, Fig. 276.

SHELL moderate in size, thin, rounded; spire low; whorls five, rapidly increasing in size, the first one smooth and rather prominent, presenting a mamillated appearance; suture distinct. Surface marked by numerous small, sharp, revolving ribs, crossed by finer longitudinal lines. Columellar lip sinuous, emarginate above, convex below; outer lip simple.

Figure, drawn from a smaller specimen to the scale of the largest fragment.

Locality: Near Fort Téjon; Dr. Horn.

This beautiful species resembles, in its sculpture, *Fusus* (*Hemifusus*) *Rémondii*, found at the same locality; but the shell can be at once distinguished by its more convex whorls and shorter spire. There is a difference also in the sculpture; the revolving ribs in this species are larger than the longitudinal ones; while in the other species both sets are nearly of the same size.

NATICA, Adanson.

N. Uvasana, n. s.

Pl. 32, Fig. 277.

Shell small, subglobose; spire somewhat elevated; whorls four; suture distinct; mouth subcircular; inner lip incrusted above; umbilicus somewhat open, with a small revolving callus. Surface smooth, showing a few lines of growth.

Figure, magnified.
Locality: Near Fort Téjon; Dr. Horn.

SCALARIA, Lam.

Subgen. OPALIA, H. and A. Ad.

S. Mathewsonii, n. s.

Pl. 32, Fig. 278.

Shell robust, turriculate; whorls numerous, convex; suture distinct. Surface marked by about eighteen or twenty large ribs, with broad, convex interspaces, crossed by fine revolving lines; lower angle of the body whorl bordered by a prominent rib, the lower surface being flattened and marked only by striæ similar to those on the sides of the whorl. Mouth subcircular, truncated below.

Figure, natural size.
Locality: A single specimen, from near Martiñez; collected by Mr. Mathewson.

TURRITELLA, Lam.

T. infra-granulata, n. s.

Pl. 32, Fig. 279.

Shell elongated, tapering, scalariform; whorls numerous, sloping straight, or somewhat concavely outwards above, angulated and obliquely truncated below; suture impressed. Surface marked by numerous fine, revolving, thread-like lines, sometimes alternating in size, and on the angle near the lower margin of the whorl, by coarse granulations. Aperture subquadrate.

Figure, natural size.
Locality: Near Martiñez; Mr. Mathewson; very rare.

SOLEN, Linn.

SUBGEN. SOLENA, Browne.

S. DIEGOENSIS, n. s.

Pl. 32, Fig. 280.

SHELL thick, subconvex; cardinal and basal margins nearly parallel; beaks placed near the anterior end; ends gaping; anterior end somewhat dilated; base straight. Surface marked by rather distinct lines of growth.

Figure, natural size.
Locality: San Diego; very near if not at the top of the Cretaceous of the State; collected by Mr. Morse.

CHIONE, Mühlf.

? C. ANGULATA, n. s.

Pl. 32, Fig. 281.

SHELL small, thin, compressed, triangular; beaks small, acute, prominent, placed about two-fifths of the length from the anterior end, which is produced and narrowly rounded below, broadly emarginate above; the cardinal margin slopes nearly straight from the beaks to the posterior end; base broadly rounded. Passing from the beaks to the posterior angle is a sharp ridge, very near the margin; posterior to which the surface drops at an acute angle to the edge of the shell, making a well-marked, abrupt truncation. Surface ornamented by fine, numerous, regular, concentric lines. Lunule bordered by a fine impressed line.

Figure, magnified to nearly twice natural size.

Locality: A single specimen was found by Mr. Mathewson, in Division A., west of Martiñez.

This shell resembles very closely *Crassatella Uvasana*, Con., in general outline. It is very much thinner, however, is more produced posteriorly, the anterior end is not so deeply excavated under the beaks, is more compressed, and the surface ornaments and lunule are entirely different.

I have not succeeded in uncovering the whole of the hinge of the specimen described; but, from what I can see, it seems to resemble more nearly that of *Chione* than any other genus. I have, therefore, referred it so provisionally.

TAPES, Megerle.

? T. CRETACEA, n. s.

Pl. 32, Fig. 283.

SHELL large, robust, quadrate; cardinal and basal margins nearly parallel; beaks small, approximate, anterior; anterior end broadly rounded; posterior convexly subtruncated. Surface convex above, flattened towards the base, marked only by lines of growth.

Figure, natural size.

Locality: North of Corral Hollow, Alameda County.

CRASSATELLA, Lam.

C. UVASANA, Con.

Pl. 32, Fig. 284.

(*C. Uvasana*, Con. Pacific R. R. Rep., vol. 5, p. 320, pl. 2, fig. 5.)

SHELL thick, robust, triangular, convex; beaks broad, prominent, and strongly incurved; cardinal margin sloping a little convexly to the posterior end, which is subangular; anterior end broadly rounded below, deeply excavated above; lunule large, lanceolate, and deeply impressed. Surface marked by a variable number of strong, concentric ribs, near the beaks, which become obsolete within a half or three-fourths of an inch from the apex, and below which the rest of the shell is marked only by very fine lines of growth.

Figure, natural size of the largest specimen.

Locality: Near Fort Téjon; Dr. Horn.

By a comparison of the figure published in the Pacific R. R. Report with the present one, it will be observed that there are a number of important discrepancies. My figure is critically correct, and I can only account for the inaccuracy of Mr. Conrad's by supposing that his was made from a mutilated specimen. There can be no doubt but that I have identified his species, this being the only shell that approaches in the most remote manner to the figure and description quoted above, out of many hundreds of specimens collected at the original locality. The outline of the posterior end of figure 284 is restored from lines of growth and from smaller specimens.

CARDITA, Brug.

C. VENERIFORMIS, n. s.

Pl. 32, Fig. 285, and 285 *a*.

SHELL small, very convex, subquadrate; beaks rather large, strongly incurved; cardinal margin nearly straight; posterior end obliquely and convexly truncated; anterior end deeply excavated under the beaks, produced and narrowly rounded below; base broadly rounded; lunule broad, deeply impressed. Surface marked by about forty fine, acute, radiating ribs, with sometimes an intercalated one arising in the middle of the shell, and becoming as large as the others before it reaches the base; these are most numerous anteriorly, where all of the ribs are smaller than on the middle; margin strongly crenulated.

Figure 285, magnified to about three times natural size. Fig. 285 *a*, magnified view of surface.

Locality: West of Martiñez; Mr. Mathewson.

BARBATIA, Gray.

B. Morsei, n. s.

Pl. 32, Fig. 286.

Shell small, thin, subcompressed, oblique, broadest posteriorly; beaks small, approximate, anterior; area long and very narrow, shorter than the shell; anterior end short and broad; posterior end oblique above, rounded below; base sinuous, slightly gaping. Surface depressed in the middle and towards the ends, ornamented by numerous fine radiating ribs, alternating pretty regularly in size in the middle of the shell. Hinge slender, composed of numerous small, oblique teeth.

Figure, natural size.

Locality: San Diego; collected by Mr. Morse.

YOLDIA, Möller.

Y. nasuta, n. s.

Pl. 32, Fig. 287.

Shell thin, convex, elongate; beaks subcentral, a little posterior; cardinal margin concave in advance, sinking convexly behind; anterior end produced, most prominent above. Hinge composed of uniform teeth, largest in advance of the beaks. Surface polished.

Figure, natural size.

Locality: A single specimen in the collection of the California Academy of Natural Sciences, labelled "Los Angeles," and associated with Cretaceous fossils. This shell may be Cretaceous, or possibly Tertiary. The discovery of better authenticated specimens will be necessary to determine its true age.

PLACUNANOMIA, Brod.

P. INORNATA, n. s.

Pl. 32, Fig. 288, and 288 *a*.

SHELL thin, irregular, inequivalve; upper valve convex, usually narrowest near the beaks, broad towards the base; hinge-margin thickened; surface marked by fine radiating lines, or smooth, usually concentrically undulated; lower valve concave, without the radiating lines; hinge-line but little, if at all, thickened; foramen small, bordered on one side by a thickened margin.

Figures, natural size.

Localities: Near San Diego, Mr. Morse; and north of Corral Hollow. Abundant at both localities.

TABULAR STATEMENT

OF THE PRINCIPAL

LOCALITIES OF CRETACEOUS FOSSILS

FOUND IN CALIFORNIA AND THE ADJACENT TERRITORIES, AND DESCRIBED OR NOTICED IN THIS VOLUME.

	Jacksonville, Oregon.	Siskiyou Mountains.	Cottonwood Creek.	North of Yreka.	Pence's Ranch.	Tuscan Springs.	Cow Creek, Shasta Co.	Weaverville.	Chico Creek.	Folsom.	Texas Flat.	Arbuckle's Diggings.	Rag Cañon.	Suisun.	Benicia.	Martiñez, Division B.	Martiñez, Division A.	Clayton.	Marsh's.	Curry's, S. of Diablo.	Puerto Cañon.	Orestimba Cañon.	S. L. Gonzaga Ranch.	Téjon.	San Diego, Upper.	San Diego, Lower.	Vancouver I.	Miscellaneous Localities.
Callianassa Stimpsonii, G.									*									*						*				
Belemnites impressus, G.			*															*										
Nautilus Texanus, Shum.																		*										Alderson's Gulch, Shasta Co.
Aturia Mathewsonii, G.																	*	*						*				
Ammonites subtricarinatus, G.																												Battle Creek. Tehama Co.
" Newberryanus, Meek.			*														*	*		*							*	
" Brewerii, G.			*																									
" Haydenii, G.			*																									
" Peruvianus?, von Buch.						*																						
" Traskii, G.												*																
" ramosus, Meek.			*																									
" Hoffmanii, G.																												Horsetown, Shasta Co.
" Rémondii, G.			*																									
	1	2	3	4	5	6	7	8	9	10	11	12	13	14	15	16	17	18	19	20	21	22	23	24	25	26	27	

	1	2	3	4	5	6	7	8	9	10	11	12	13	14	15	16	17	18	19	20	21	22	23	24	25	26	27	
" Batesii, Trask.			*									*			*					*								
" Chicoensis, Trask.		*	*		*				*														*					
" complexus, H. & M.										*																		
? " Cooperi, G.																										*		
Hamites Vancouverensis, G.																											*	
Helicoceras vermicularis, G.																	*											
" Brewerii, G.					*																							
" declive, G.					*																							
Turrilites sp. ?	*																											Alderson's Gulch, and Eagle Cr'k, Shasta Co.
Ptychoceras æquicostatus, G.			*																									
P. (Hamites?) quadratus, G.					*																							
Crioceras Rémondii, G.			*																									
" latus, G.								*																				
" percostatus, G.			*									*					*											
Ancyloceras sp. undet.			*									*																
Baculites Chicoensis, Trask.		*	*		*	*	*		*		*	*			*		*			*		*				*		
" sp. indet.																											*	
Typhis antiquus, G.																*												
Fusus Martiñez, G.																*												

	Jacksonville, Oregon.	Siskiyou Mountains.	Cottonwood Creek.	North of Yreka.	Pence's Ranch.	Tuscan Springs.	Cow Creek, Shasta Co.	Weaverville.	Chico Creek.	Folsom.	Texas Flat.	Arbuckle's Diggings.	Rag Cañon.	Suisun.	Benicia.	Martiñez, Division B.	Martiñez, Division A.	Clayton.	Marsh's.	Curry's, S. of Diablo.	Puerto Cañon.	Orestimba Cañon.	S. L. Gonzaga Ranch.	Téjon.	San Diego, Upper.	San Diego, Lower.	Vancouver I.	Miscellaneous Localities.
	1	2	3	4	5	6	7	8	9	10	11	12	13	14	15	16	17	18	19	20	21	22	23	24	25	26	27	
Fusus Mathewsonii, G.																*	*	*		*								
" Averillii, G.						*																						
" Diaboli, G.																		*										Cochran's east of Mount Diablo.
" flexuosus, G.																	*											
" aratus, G.																	*											
" Kingii, G.			*																									
" Californicus, Con.																		*						*				Cochran's east of Mount Diablo.
Hemifusus Hornii, G.																*								*				
" Cooperi, G.																									*			Cochran's east of Mount Diablo.
" Rémondii, G.																*		*						*				Cochran's.
Neptunæa curvirostris, G.							*																					
" ponderosa, G.		*			*	*	*								*		*											
" perforata, G.			*																									

	1	2	3	4	5	6	7	8	9	10	11	12	13	14	15	16	17	18	19	20	21	22	23	24	25	26	27	
? " supraplicata, G.																		*							*			
" Hoffmanni, G.			*																									
" gracilis, G.																*												
Perissolax brevirostris, G.					*	*											*											
" Blakei, Con., sp.																*		*						*				
Turris Claytonensis, G.																		*										Cochran's.
" varicostata, G.																		*										
Cordiera microptygma, G.																								*				
Tritonium Hornii, G.																								*				Cochran's.
" Diegoensis, G.																									*			
" paucivaricatum, G.																								*				
" Whitneyi, G.																								*		*		
Buccinum liratum, G.																*		*	*									
Nassa cretacea, G.																*												
" antiquata, G.																*												
Haydenia impressa, G.					*	*																						
Pseudoliva lineata, G.																*												
" volutæformis, G.																								*				
Olivella Mathewsonii, G.																*								*				

	Jacksonville, Oregon.	Siskiyou Mountains.	Cottonwood Creek.	North of Yreka.	Pence's Ranch.	Tuscan Springs.	Cow Creek, Shasta Co.	Weaverville.	Chico Creek.	Folsom.	Texas Flat.	Arbuckle's Diggings.	Rag Cañon.	Suisun.	Benicia.	Martinez, Division B.	Martinez, Division A.	Clayton.	Marsh's.	Curry's, S. of Diablo.	Puerto Cañon.	Orestimba Cañon.	S. L. Gonzaga Ranch.	Téjon.	San Diego, Upper.	San Diego, Lower.	Vancouver I.	Miscellaneous Localities.
	1	2	3	4	5	6	7	8	9	10	11	12	13	14	15	16	17	18	19	20	21	22	23	24	25	26	27	Cochran's.
Ancillaria elongata, G.																*		*							*			
Fasciolaria læviuscula, G.																*		*								*		
" sinuata, G.																								*	*			
? " Io, G.																								*				
Volutilithes Navarroensis, Shum.	*	*			*	*	*		*								*											
Mitra cretacea, G.																*												
Whitneya ficus, G.																								*				
Morio tuberculatus, G.																*		*							*			
? Ficus cypræoides, G.						*																						
Lunatia avellana, G.			*																									
" Shumardiana, G.																*												
" Hornii, G.																							*					
" nuciformis, G.																		*					*					

	1	2	3	4	5	6	7	8	9	10	11	12	13	14	15	16	17	18	19	20	21	22	23	24	25	26	27
L. (Gyrodes ?) Conradiana, G.																							*				
Gyrodes expansa, G.	*	*	*		*	*			*		*						*										
Neverita secta, G.																								*			
Naticina obliqua, G.																*								*			
Amauropsis oviformis, G.						*																					
" alveata, Con. sp.																*		*		*				*		*	
Cinulia obliqua, G.		*	*		*	*			*		*						*										
" Mathewsonii, G.																	*					*					
" pinguis, G.																	*										
Ringicula varia, G.							*																				
Nerinæa dispar, G.			*																								
Actæonina pupoides, G.			*																								
" Californica, G.				*											*		*										
Globiconcha Rémondii, G.															*												
Cylindrites brevis, G.																	*										
Chemnitzia Spilmani ? Con.					*																						
Niso polita, G.																*								*			
Cerithiopsis alternata, G.																*											
Architectonica Veatchii, G.						*																					

	1 Jacksonville, Oregon.	2 Siskiyou Mountains.	3 Cottonwood Creek.	4 North of Yreka.	5 Pence's Ranch.	6 Tuscan Springs.	7 Cow Creek, Shasta Co.	8 Weaverville.	9 Chico Creek.	10 Folsom.	11 Texas Flat.	12 Arbuckle's Diggings.	13 Rag Cañon.	14 Suisun.	15 Benicia.	16 Martiñez, Division B.	17 Martiñez, Division A.	18 Clayton.	19 Marsh's.	20 Curry's, S. of Diablo.	21 Puerto Cañon.	22 Orestimba Cañon.	23 S. L. Gonzaga Ranch.	24 Téjon.	25 San Diego, Upper.	26 San Diego, Lower.	27 Vancouver I.	Miscellaneous Localities.
Architectonica cognata, G.																*		*										
" Hornii, G.																								*				
" inornata, G.						*											*											
Margaritella crenulata, G.																										*		
" globosa, G.															*													
Discohelix Leana, G.											*																	
Straparollus paucivolvus, G.											*																	
" lens, G.											*																	
Angaria ornatissima, G.						*					*																	
Conus Rémondii, G.																*		*						*	*			
" Hornii, G.																								*				
" sinuatus, G.																								*				
Rimella canalifera, G.																*								*				

	1	2	3	4	5	6	7	8	9	10	11	12	13	14	15	16	17	18	19	20	21	22	23	24	25	26	27	
" simplex, G.																		*							*			
Pugnellus hamulus, G.																	*											
" manubriatus, G.			*																									
Tessarolax distorta, G.						*																						
Aporrhais falciformis, G.					*	*	*		*		*																	
" angulata, G.																	*											
" Californica, G.		*															*				*	*						
" exilis, G.																*												
? Cypræa Bayerquei, G.																		*										
Potamides diadema, G.			*																									
" tenuis, G.					*																							
? Littorina compacta, G.											*															*		
Turritella infralineata, G.			*																			*						
" seriatim-granulata, G.		*	*			*																						
" Veatchii, G.						*																						
" Chicoensis, G.									*																			
" Uvasana, Con.																*		*										
" Saffordii, G.														*			*											Clear Lake.
" robusta, G.						*																						

	1. Jacksonville, Oregon.	2. Siskiyou Mountains.	3. Cottonwood Creek.	4. North of Yreka.	5. Pence's Ranch.	6. Tuscan Springs.	7. Cow Creek, Shasta Co.	8. Weaverville.	9. Chico Creek.	10. Folsom.	11. Texas Flat.	12. Arbuckle's Diggings.	13. Rag Cañon.	14. Suisun.	15. Benicia.	16. Martiñez, Division B.	17. Martiñez, Division A.	18. Clayton.	19. Marsh's.	20. Curry's, S. of Diablo.	21. Puerto Cañon.	22. Orestimba Cañon.	23. S. L. Gonzaga Ranch.	24. Téjon.	25. San Diego, Upper.	26. San Diego, Lower.	27. Vancouver I.	Miscellaneous Localities.
Galerus excentricus, G.																*		*						*	*			
Crypta pileum, G.																								*				
Nerita deformis, G.			*																									
" cuneata, G.			*																									
Lysis duplicosta, G.											*																	
Dentalium pusillum, G.						*?										*								*				
" Cooperii, G.		*																		*				*	*			
" stramineum, G.																*				*					*			
Emarginula radiata, G.											*																	
Patella Traskii, G.											*																	
Helcion circularis, G.																	*											
" dichotoma, G.											*																	
" Anisomyon Meekii, G.			*																									

	1	2	3	4	5	6	7	8	9	10	11	12	13	14	15	16	17	18	19	20	21	22	23	24	25	26	27	Corral Hollow.
Actæon impressus, G.			*																									
Bulla Hornii, G.																								*				
Cylichna costata, G.					*	*					*					*	*	*	*				*	*				
Megistostoma striata, G.																*												
Martesia clausa, G.					*	*					*																	
Turnus plenus, G.			*																				*?					
Solen parallelus, G.																*			*					*				
Pharella alta, G.																	*											
Siliqua Oregonensis, G.		*																										
Panopæa concentrica, G.			*														*											
Corbula primorsa, G.																												
" Traskii, G.					*	*					*																	
" cultriformis, G.																	*											
" Hornii, G.																								*				
" parilis, G.																*			*						*			
Anatina Tryoniana, G.																	*											
" inequilateralis, G.		*																										
? " lata, G.					*																							
Pholadomya Brewerii, G.					*																							

	Jacksonville, Oregon.	Siskiyou Mountains.	Cottonwood Creek.	North of Yreka.	Pence's Ranch.	Tuscan Springs.	Cow Creek, Shasta Co.	Weaverville.	Chico Creek.	Folsom.	Texas Flat.	Arbuckle's Diggings.	Rag Cañon.	Suisun.	Benicia.	Martiñez, Division B.	Martiñez, Division A.	Clayton.	Marsh's.	Curry's, S. of Diablo.	Puerto Cañon.	Orestimba Cañon.	S. L. Gonzaga Ranch.	Téjon.	San Diego, Upper.	San Diego, Lower.	Vancouver I.	Miscellaneous Localities.
Pholadomya nasuta, G.																*												
Neæra dolabræformis, G.																*												
Mactra Ashburnerii, G.		*			*	*			*		*				*	*	*		*			*	*	*				
Lutraria truncata, G.					*				*																			
Asaphis undulata, G.											*																	
? Gari texta, G.																*												
Tellina longa, G.																*			*					*				
" Rémondii, G.																								*				Cochran's.
" Hoffmanniana, G.					*												*											
" monilifera, G.											*																	
" ooides, G.					*												*											
" decurtata, G.					*																							
Mathewsonii, G.																	*											
	1	2	3	4	5	6	7	8	9	10	11	12	13	14	15	16	17	18	19	20	21	22	23	24	25	26	27	

	1	2	3	4	5	6	7	8	9	10	11	12	13	14	15	16	17	18	19	20	21	22	23	24	25	26	27	
? Tellina quadrata, G.						*																						
" Ashburnerii, G.					*																							
" Whitneyi, G.	*																											
" parilis, G.																	*											
" Hornii, G.																		*						*				
" Californica, G.																			*					*				
Venus varians, G.	*	*			*	*	*		*	*	*				*		*			*		*						
" Veatchii, G.						*																						
" lenticularis, G.															*													
" tetrahedra, G.																	*											
Meretrix Uvasana, Con.																*								*				
" lens, G.									*																			
" Hornii, G.																								*				
" nitida, G.							*		*								*					*						
" longa, G.																												Shasta?
" arata, G.		*		*																		*						
" ovalis, G.																								*				
" Californica, Con.																												
Dosinia elevata, G.																								*				

	1 Jacksonville, Oregon.	2 Siskiyou Mountains.	3 Cottonwood Creek.	4 North of Yreka.	5 Pence's Ranch.	6 Tuscan Springs.	7 Cow Creek, Shasta Co.	8 Weaverville.	9 Chico Creek.	10 Folsom.	11 Texas Flat.	12 Arbuckle's Diggings.	13 Rag Cañon.	14 Suisun.	15 Benicia.	16 Martinez, Division B.	17 Martinez, Division A.	18 Clayton.	19 Marsh's.	20 Curry's, S. of Diablo.	21 Puerto Cañon.	22 Orestimba Cañon.	23 S. L. Gonzaga Ranch.	24 Téjon.	25 San Diego, Upper.	26 San Diego, Lower.	27 Vancouver I.	Miscellaneous Localities.
Dosinia pertenuis, G.		*																										
" gyrata, G.																*		*						*	*			
" inflata, G.									*																			
Tapes Conradiana, G.																*								*				
" quadrata, G.																*								*				
Trapezium carinatum, G.											*																	
Cyprinella tenuis, G.																												Corral Hollow.
Cardium annulatum, G.																	*			*								
" Rémondianum, G.															*													Wright's Gulch
" Cooperii, G.																*								*	*			
" Brewerii, G.																*								*				
" Placerensis, G.										*																		
Cardita Hornii, G.																*		*						*				

	1	2	3	4	5	6	7	8	9	10	11	12	13	14	15	16	17	18	19	20	21	22	23	24	25	26	27
Lucina nasuta, G,																	*										
" postradiata, G.											*																
" subcircularis, G.											*																
" cumulata, G.																								*			
? " cretacea, G.																		*	*								
? Loripes dubia, G.						*			*		*																
Mysia polita, G.																*	*	*									
Astarte Conradiana, G.											*																
" Mathewsonii, G.																*											
" Tuscana, G.					*	*																					
Eriphyla umbonata, G.							*													*							
Crassatella grandis, G.																			*					*			
" Uvasana, Con.																								*			
Anthonya cultriformis, G.																	*										
Unio penultimus, G.																		*									
Mytilus pauperculus, G.																	*										
" ascia, G.																								*			
" humerus, Con.																								*?			
Modiola Siskiyouensis, G.	*	*																									

	Jacksonville, Oregon.	Siskiyou Mountains.	Cottonwood Creek.	North of Yreka.	Pence's Ranch.	Tuscan Springs.	Cow Creek, Shasta Co.	Weaverville.	Chico Creek.	Folsom.	Texas Flat.	Arbuckle's Diggings.	Rag Cañon.	Suisun.	Benicia.	Martiñez, Division B.	Martiñez, Division A.	Clayton.	Marsh's.	Curry's, S. of Diablo.	Puerto Cañon.	Orestimba Cañon.	S. L. Gonzaga Ranch.	Téjon.	San Diego, Upper.	San Diego, Lower.	Vancouver I.	Miscellaneous Localities.
Modiola ornata, G.																*		*	*					*				
" cylindrica, G.					*	*																						
Lithophagus oviformis, G.							*																					
Septifer dichotomus, G.																								*				
Crenella concentrica, G.																*	*											
Avicula pellucida, G.		*														*							*					
Inoceramus Piochii, G.						*													*									
Pinna Brewerii, G.		*															*			*								
Trigonia Tryoniana, G.						*																						
" Evansii, Meek.	*	*	*		*	*			*		*		*	*	*		*			*		*	*				*	
" Gibboniana, Lea.	*	*															*											
Meekia sella, G.		*				*											*											
" radiata, G.	*	*															*					*	*					
	1	2	3	4	5	6	7	8	9	10	11	12	13	14	15	16	17	18	19	20	21	22	23	24	25	26	27	

	1	2	3	4	5	6	7	8	9	10	11	12	13	14	15	16	17	18	19	20	21	22	23	24	25	26	27	
" navis, G.					*				*								*											
Arca Breweriana, G.			*			*																						
" Hornii, G.																								*				
" gravida, G.													*										*					
Cucullæa Mathewsonii, G.																*		*										
" truncata, G.	*					*					*				*		*			*	*	*	*					
Axinæa Veatchii, G.					*	*					*											*				*		
" sagittata, G.																*								*				
" cor, G.																*								*				
Nucula truncata, G.					*	*																	*					
Leda protexta, G.																*		*	*				*	*				San Emidio.
" translucida, G.							*																					
Limopsis transversa, G.											*																	
Pecten Traskii, G.											*						*?											
" operculiformis, G.			*																	*								Huling Creek.
" Californicus, G.			*																									
Lima microtis, G.			*								*?																	
" appressa, G.																							*					
Plicatula variata, G.																												Battle Creek.

	Jacksonvill, Oregon.	Siskiyou Mountains.	Cottonwood Creek.	North of Yreka.	Pence's Ranch.	Tuscan Springs.	Cow Creek, Shasta Co.	Weaverville.	Chico Creek.	Folsom.	Texas Flat.	Arbuckle's Diggings.	Rag Cañon.	Suisun.	Benicia.	Martiñez, Division B.	Martiñez, Division A.	Clayton.	Marsh's.	Curry's, S. of Diablo.	Puerto Cañon.	Orestimba Cañon.	S. L. Gonzaga Ranch.	Téjon.	San Diego, Upper.	San Diego, Lower.	Vancouver I.	Miscellaneous Localities.
Anomia lineata, G.					*				*		*																	
Ostrea malleiformis, G.	*	*																										
" Brewerii, G.							*																					
Gryphæa vesicularis, Lan.																										*		
Exogyra parasitica, G.										*	*																	
Terebratella obesa, G.											*																	
Flabellum Rémondianum, G.																		*										
Trochosmilia striata, G.																		*										
? " granulifera, G.									*																			
Astrocœnia petrosa, G.																	*											

INDEX OF GENERA AND SPECIES.

PLATE I.

PAGE

Fig. 1. CLISIOPHYLLUM GABBI. 8

A large, somewhat weathered specimen.

1 *a.* A calice of a smaller individual, with its margins partly broken away, and the interior partly filled with stony matter, around the central boss.

1 *b.* Vertical section of a small specimen, showing the depth of the calice, and the prominence of the central boss, as well as the structure of the interior. The outer vesicular zone is not well seen in this specimen, which is too small to have it well developed.

Fig. 2. LITHOSTROTION? CALIFORNIENSE. 6

An external view of a part of a corallite.

2 *a.* Transverse section of the same.

2 *b.* A group of three young corallites, as seen in the matrix, apparently diverging from a common base, and showing the much-weathered calices.

2 *c.* Longitudinal section of one of the corallites, showing the internal structure.

Fig. 3. LITHOSTROTION MAMILLARE? 7

A fragment, showing the weathered lower extremities of the corallites.

3 *a.* Longitudinal section enlarged, showing the internal structure of same.

Fig. 4. LITHOSTROTION MAMILLARE, var. *sublævis.* 5

A group of corallites.

4 *a.* Longitudinal section a little enlarged, showing the internal structure of one of the same.

4 *b.* Transverse section of same, enlarged.

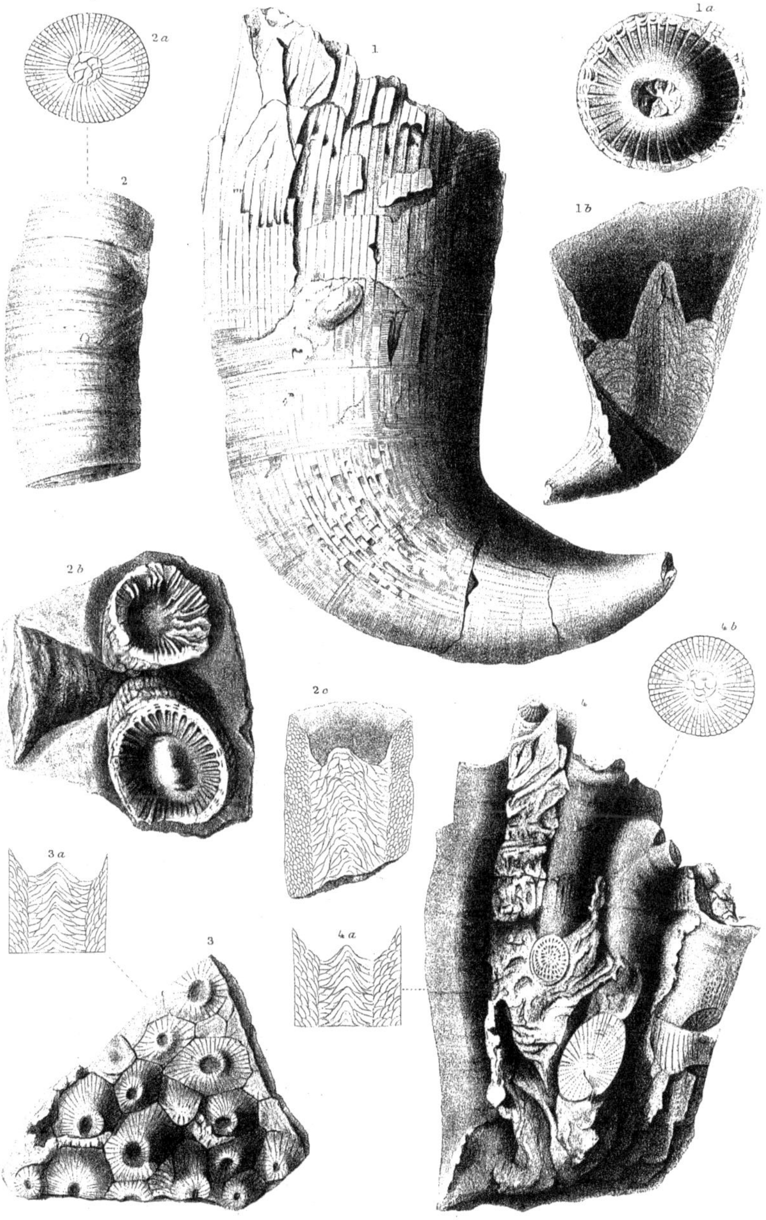

F.B. Meek, del.t J. Young.

PLATE II.

PAGE

Fig. 1. FUSULINA GRACILIS. 4

Natural size.

1 *a*. Same, enlarged.

1 *b*. Section of same, enlarged.

1 *c*. Enlarged view, showing the undulations of the septa, as seen in a longitudinal section.

Fig. 2. FUSULINA CYLINDRICA. 4

Natural size.

2 *a*. The same, enlarged.

Fig. 3. FUSULINA ROBUSTA. 3

A rather small specimen. Natural size.

3 *a*. Same, enlarged.

3 *b*. Transverse section of same, enlarged.

3 *c*. Enlarged view, showing the undulations of the septa, as seen in a longitudinal section.

Fig. 4. PRODUCTUS SEMIRETICULATUS. 11

View of ventral valve, much weathered and broken.

4 *a*. Side view of same.

Fig. 5. ORTHIS ——— ? 10

Ventral view. Natural size.

5 *a*. Dorsal view of same, enlarged.

5 *b*. Side view of same, enlarged.

5 *c*. Enlargement of a portion of the surface, showing the openings left by the breaking away of the minute tubular spines.

Fig. 6. SPIRIFER (*Martinia*) LINEATUS? 13

Dorsal view. Natural size.

6 *a*. Ventral valve of same. Profile view.

6 *b*. Another view of same.

6 *c*. Cardinal view of same, showing the foramen.

6 *d*. Enlarged surface markings of same species as seen on weathered specimens.

Fig. 7. RETZIA COMPRESSA. 14

Ventral valve. Natural size.

7 *a*. Same, enlarged.

7 *b*. Front view of same specimen, enlarged.

7 *c*. View of the beak (somewhat enlarged) of a ventral valve, as seen imbedded in the matrix.

Fig. 8. EUOMPHALUS (*Omphalotrochus*) WHITNEYI. 15

View of underside, showing the umbilicus. (The portion of the body whorl represented without striæ is restored in the figure.)

8 *a*. Side view, showing the aperture, &c.

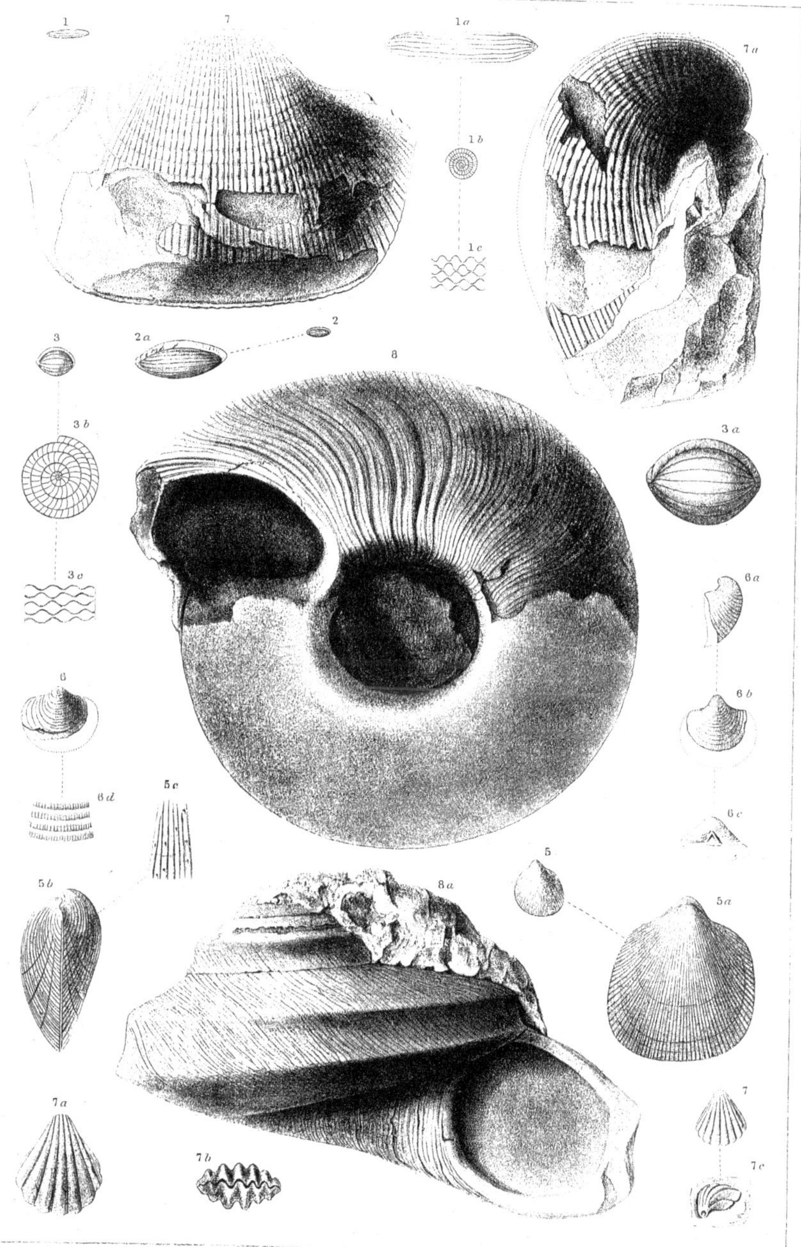

F.B. Meek, del[t].

J. Young.

PLATE III.

		PAGE
Fig. 1.	ORTHOCERATITES BLAKEI.	19
2.	NAUTILUS WHITNEYI.	19
3.	*id.*	
4.	——— MULTICAMERATUS.	20
5.	*id.*	
6.	GONIATITES LÆVIDORSATUS.	21
7.	*id.*	
16.	AMMONITES AUSSEANUS.	25
17.	*id.*	
18.	——— HOMFRAYI.	26
19.	*id.*	
21.	——— RAMSAUERI.	27
21 *a*.	*id.*	

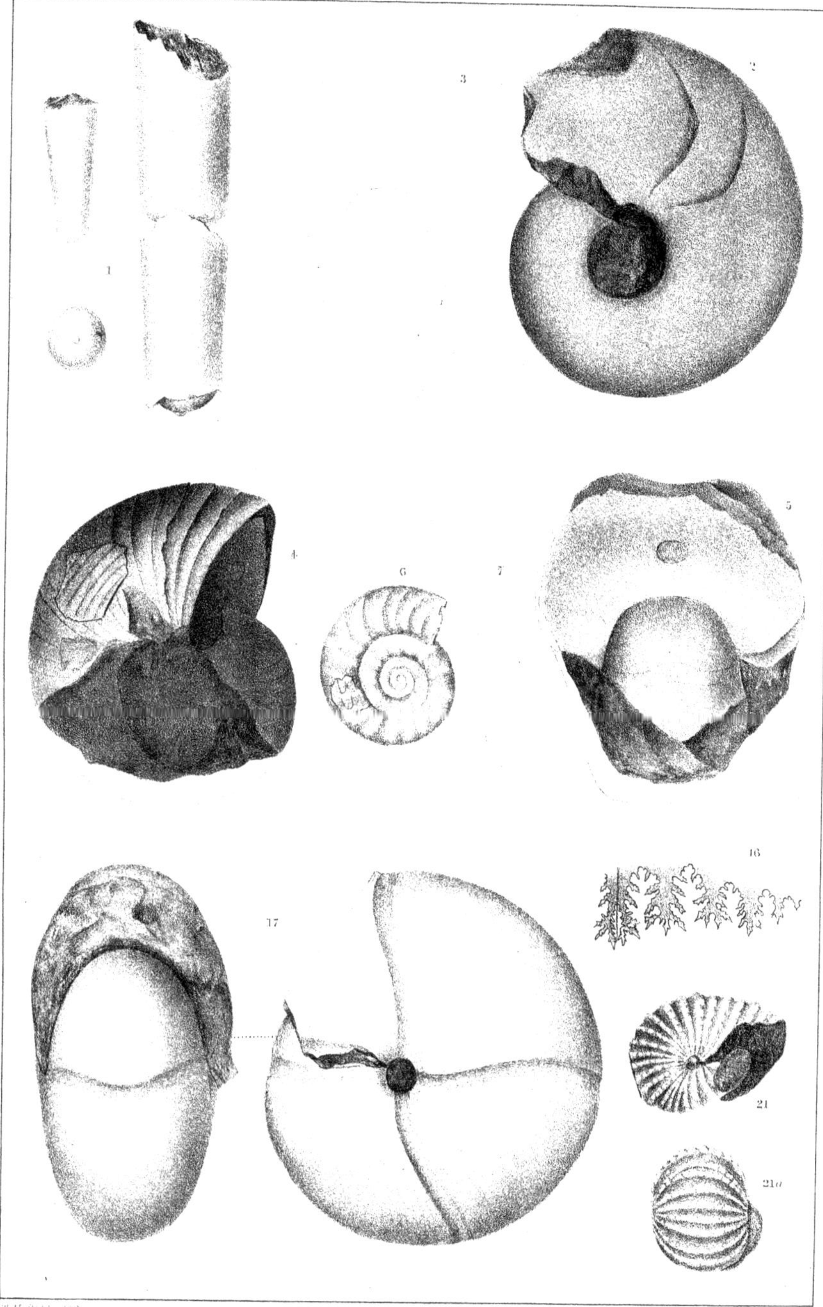

W. M. Gabb, del. T. Sinclair's lith, Phila. On stone by J. Getz

PLATE IV.

		PAGE
Fig. 9.	CERATITES HAIDINGERII.	22
11.	——— WHITNEYI.	23
12.	*id.*	
13.	*id.*	
14.	AMMONITES BLAKEI.	24
15.	*id.*	

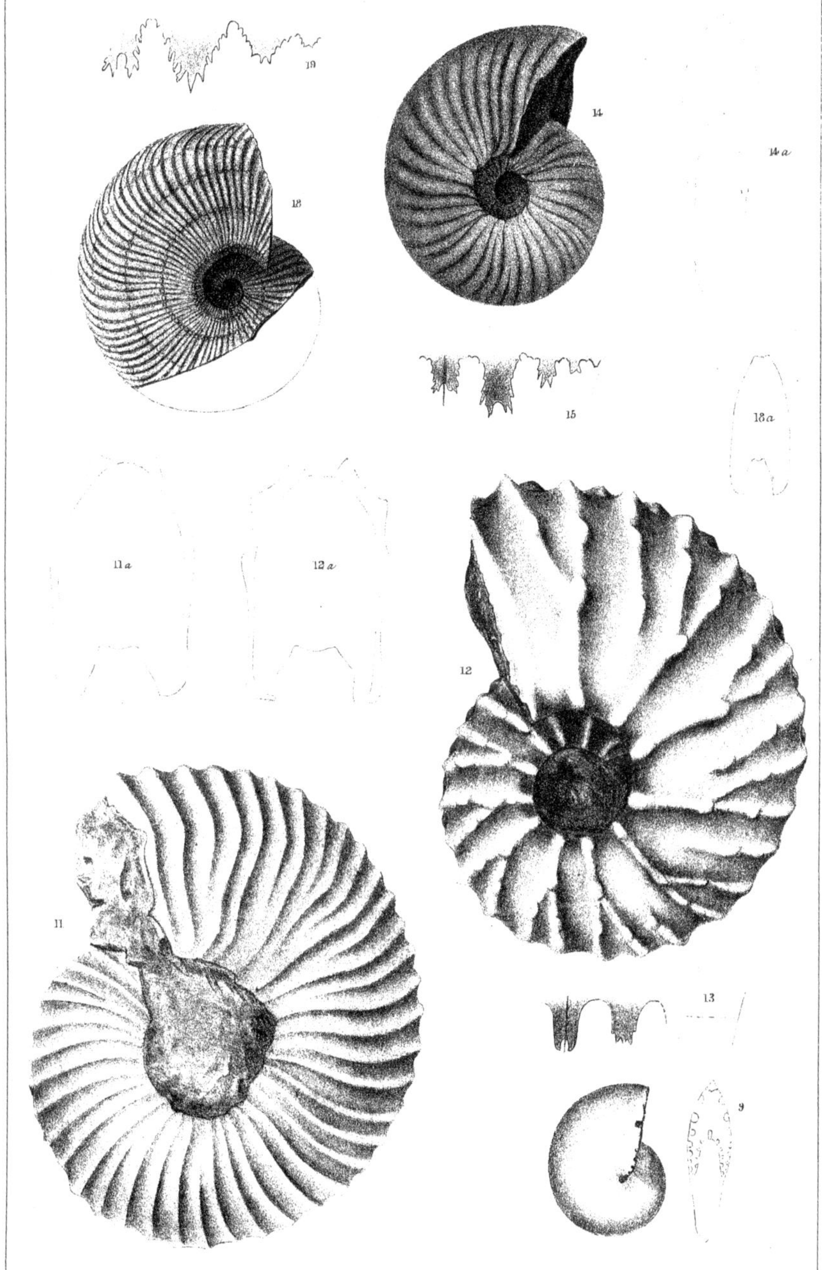

W. M. Gabb, del. T. Sinclair's lith, Phila. On stone by J. Golz

PLATE V.

		PAGE
Fig. 8.	CERATITES HAIDINGERII.	22
10.	*id.*	
20.	AMMONITES BILLINGSIANUS.	26
20 *a*.	*id.* Section of body whorl.	
22.	MYACITES HUMBOLDTENSIS.	28
23.	PANOPÆA (?) RÉMONDII.	28
24.	CORBULA BLAKEI.	29
27.	AVICULA MUCRONATA.	30
28.	? HALOBIA DUBIA.	30
28 *a*.	*id.* Inside of a fragment of a valve, the largest specimen collected; *b*, part of the surface of one of the most perfect specimens; *c*, magnified view of the ribs.	
30.	RHYNCHOPTERUS OBESUS.	32

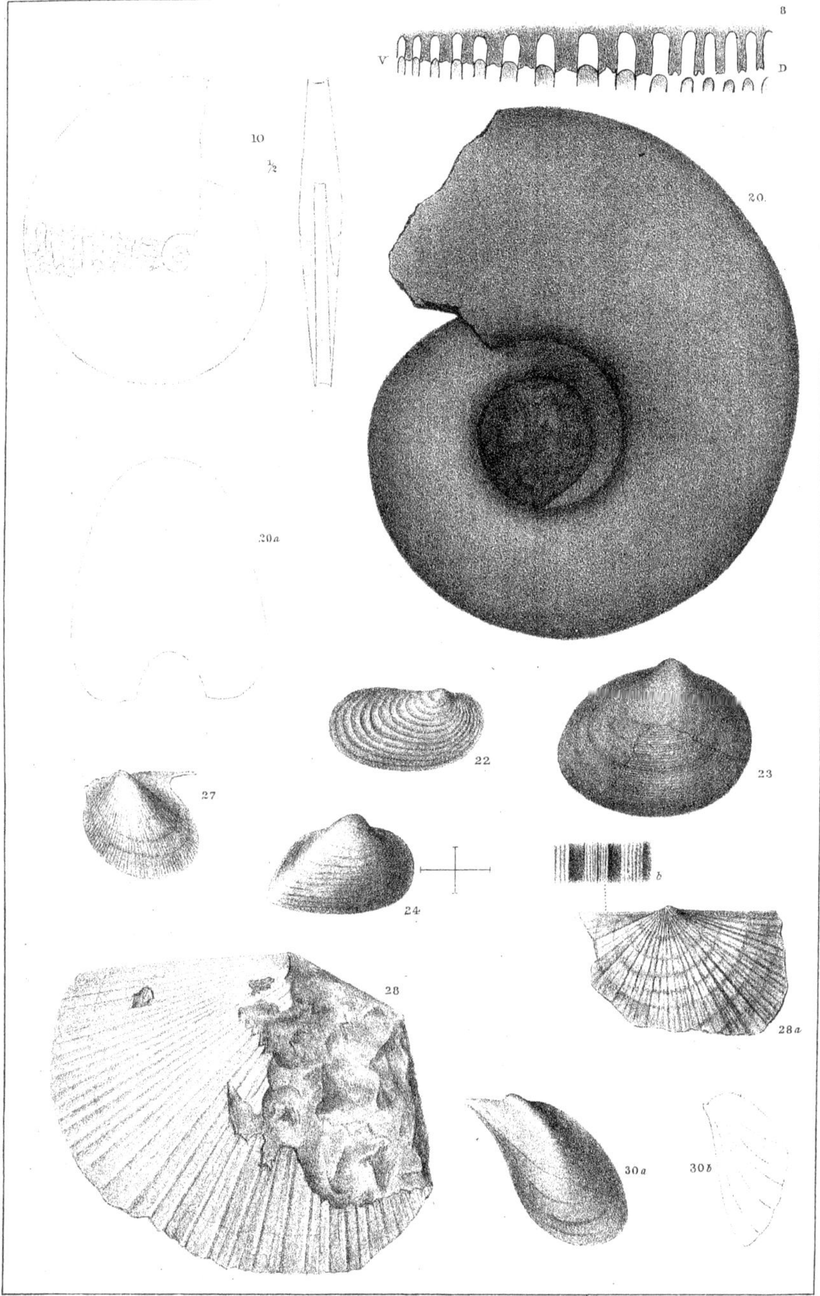

W. M. Gabb. del. T. Sinclair's lith, Phil^a On Stone by J. Golz

PLATE VI.

		PAGE
Fig. 25.	Mytilus Homfrayi.	29
26.	Avicula Homfrayi.	29
29.	Monotis subcircularis.	31
29 *a*.	*id.* Magnified view of the surface.	
31.	Posidonomya stella.	32
32.	——— Daytonensis.	32
33.	Myophoria alta.	33
34.	Pecten deformis.	33
35.	Terebratula Humboldtensis.	34
36.	Rhynchonella lingulata.	34
37.	——— æquiplicata.	35
38.	Spirifer Homfrayi.	35

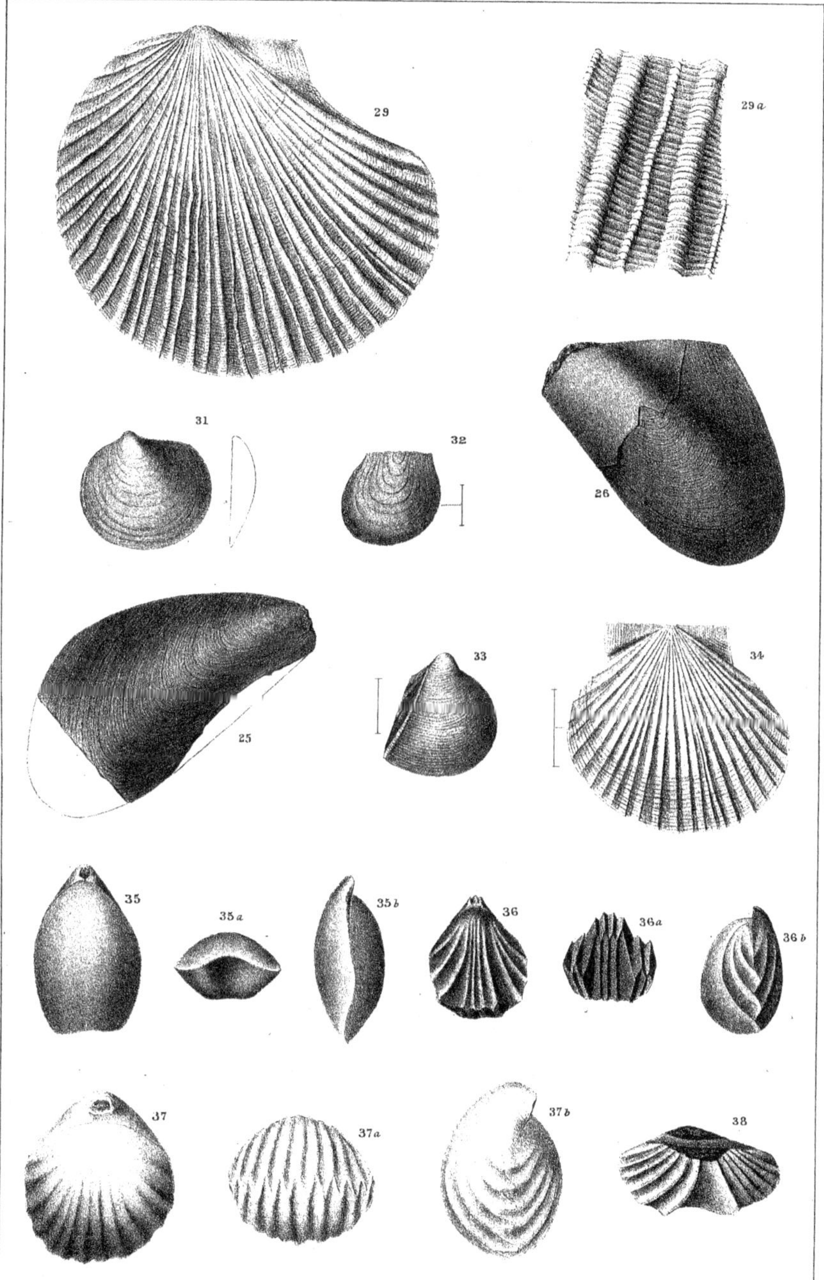

W. M. Gabb, delt. T. Sinclair's lith, Philª. On Stone by J. Golz

PLATE VII.

		PAGE
Fig. 1.	INOCERAMUS? RECTANGULUS.	47
	View of right valve.	
1 *a.*	Section of same, to show its convexity.	
Fig. 2.	INOCERAMUS? OBLIQUUS.	47
	View of right valve.	
2 *a.*	Section of same, to show its convexity.	
Fig. 3.	An undetermined bivalve.	
Fig. 4.	LIMA? SINUATA.	43
	View of a left valve, with the front of the beak broken away.	
4 *a.*	Anterior profile view of the same, to show its convexity, and gaping margin.	
Fig. 5.	LIMA? RECTICOSTATA.	44
	View of right valve.	
Fig. 6.	LIMA? CUNEATA.	44
	View of right valve, with beak and portions of the margin broken away.	
Fig. 7.	MYTILUS MULTISTRIATUS.	49
	View of right valve.	
7 *a.*	Magnified surface striæ of same.	

F. B. Meek, delt. J. Young, sc.

PLATE VIII.

PAGE

Fig. 1. RHYNCHONELLA GNATHOPHORA. 39

Dorsal view.

1 *a.* Ventral view of same.
1 *b.* Anterior view of same.
1 *c.* Profile of same.
1 *d.* Dorsal view of a wider, more compressed specimen.
1 *e.* Front view of same.
1 *f.* Front view of a gibbous specimen.

Fig. 2. TEREBRATULA ——— ? 41

2 *a.* Dorsal view of same, with beak broken.
2 *b.* Profile of same.

Fig. 3. PECTEN ACUTIPLICATUS. 46

A mould or impression left in the matrix, by apparently a left valve. The shell is not entirely dissolved out, but fills the portions of the mould.

Fig. 4. GRYPHÆA ——— ? 42

View of the under side of the lower valve of a small specimen.

4 *a.* View of the upper side of an upper valve, as seen in the matrix, showing also a little of the beak of the lower valve. The left margin of both valves imperfect.

Fig. 5. ASTARTE VENTRICOSA. 50

View of left valve, being from a plaster cast, taken from a mould left in the matrix.

5 *a.* An ideal section of the entire shell, to show its convexity.

Fig. 6. MYACITES DEPRESSUS. 51

View of left valve, broken a little in front.

6 *a.* Dorsal view of same.

Fig. 7. TRIGONIA PANDICOSTA. 48

View of a right valve imbedded in the matrix (outline may not be exactly correct).

Fig. 8. UNICARDIUM ? GIBBOSUM. 50

Posterior view.

8 *a.* View of right valve.

Fig. 9. BELEMNITES ——— ? 53

A longitudinal section of the upper extremity, showing the alveolar cavity filled with the stony matrix.

9 *a.* A transverse section of the same at the extremity of the cavity.

Geological Survey of California.

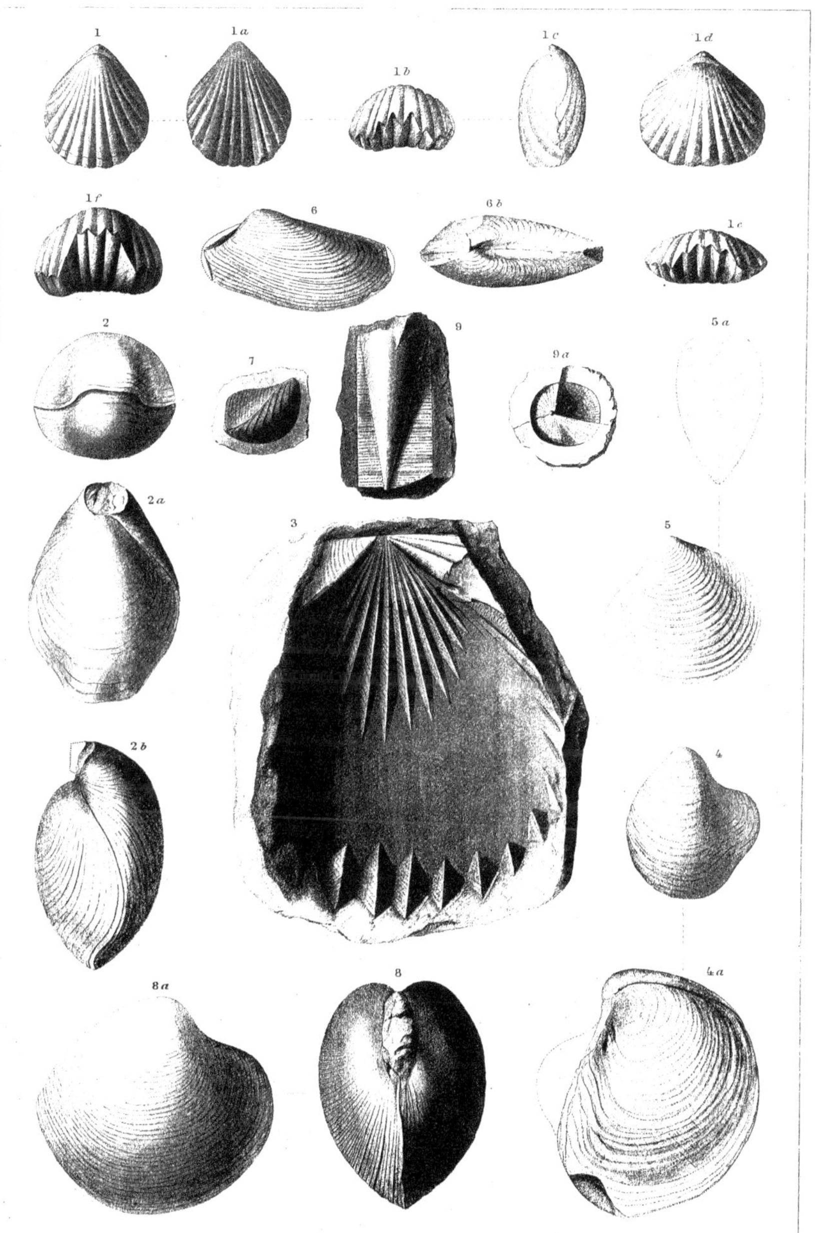

F. B. Meek del[t]. J. Young.

PLATE IX.

		PAGE
Fig. 1.	CALLIANASSA STIMPSONII.	57
	Natural size.	

a. Three segments of the abdomen, from Clayton.
b. A fragmentary hand from Chico Creek.
c. Part of a hand, from the same specimen as Fig. *a.*

Fig. 2.	BELEMNITES IMPRESSUS.	58
	Natural size.	

2 *a.* A section across the middle of Fig. 2.

Fig. 3.	NAUTILUS TEXANUS ?	59
	$\frac{2}{3}$ Natural size.	

a. Side view.
b. Front view.

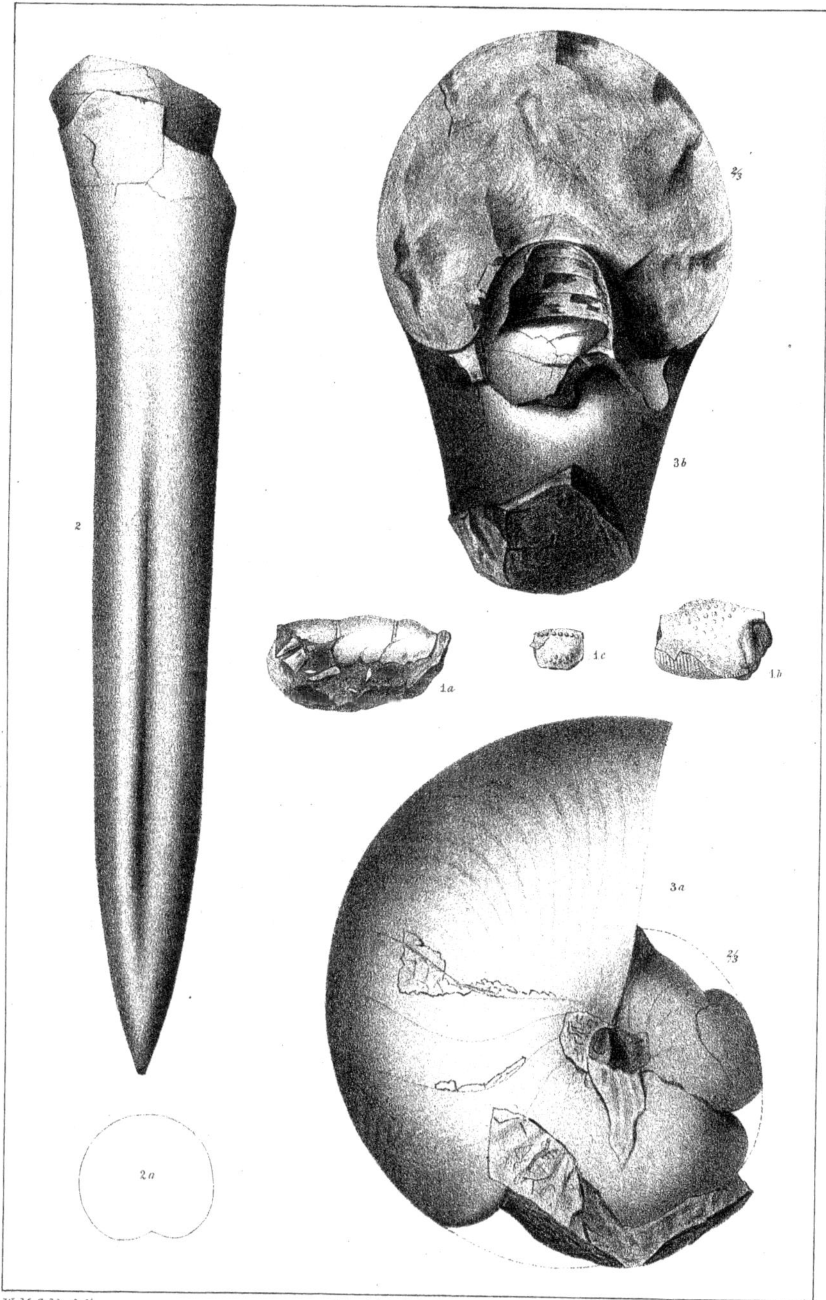

W. M. Gabb, del^t. T. Sinclair's lith, Phil^a. On stone by A. J. Ibbotson

PLATE X.

		PAGE
Fig. 4.	AMMONITES SUBTRICARINATUS.	60
	Natural size.	
4 *a*. End view of the fragment.		
Fig. 5.	A. NEWBERRYANUS.	61
	Natural size. Mount Diablo.	
Fig. 6.	A. NEWBERRYANUS.	61
	Natural size. Cottonwood Creek	
6 *a*. Front view.		
6 *b*. Septum.		
Fig. 7.	A. BREWERII.	62
	$\frac{2}{3}$ Natural size.	
Fig. 8, 8 *a*.	A. HAYDENII.	62
	$\frac{2}{3}$ Natural size.	
8 *b*. Septum.		
Fig. 9.	A. PERUVIANUS?	63
	Natural size	

W. M. Gabb, delt. T. Sinclair's lith, Phila. On stone by A. J. Ibbotson

PLATE XI.

		PAGE
Fig. 10.	AMMONITES TRASKII.	63
	Natural size.	
Fig. 12.	A. RAMOSUS.	65
	Slightly diminished in size.	
12 *a*.	Section of a volution.	
Fig. 13.	A. HOFFMANNII.	65
	$\frac{2}{3}$ Natural size.	
13 *a*.	Section of volution.	

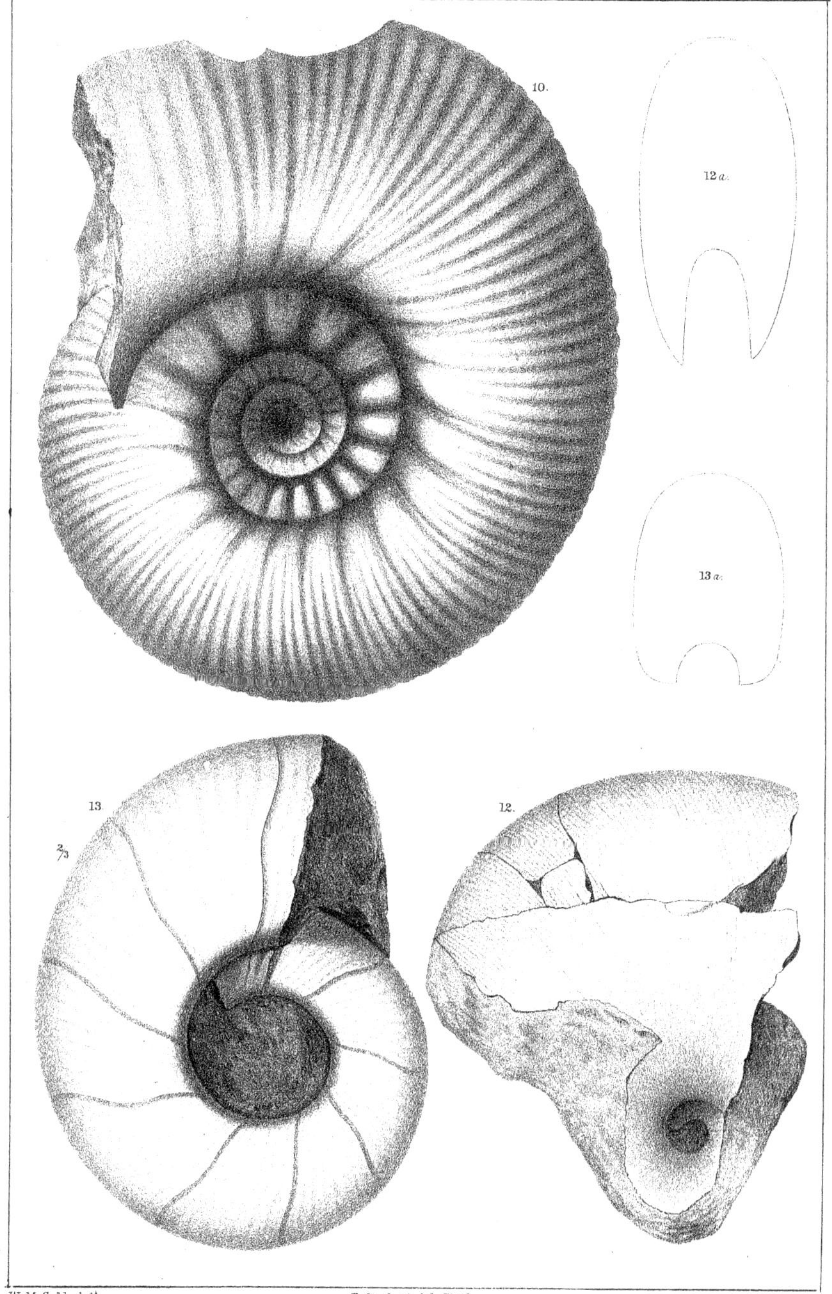

W. M. Gabb, delt. T. Sinclair's lith, Phila. On stone by A. J. Ibbotson.

PLATE XII.

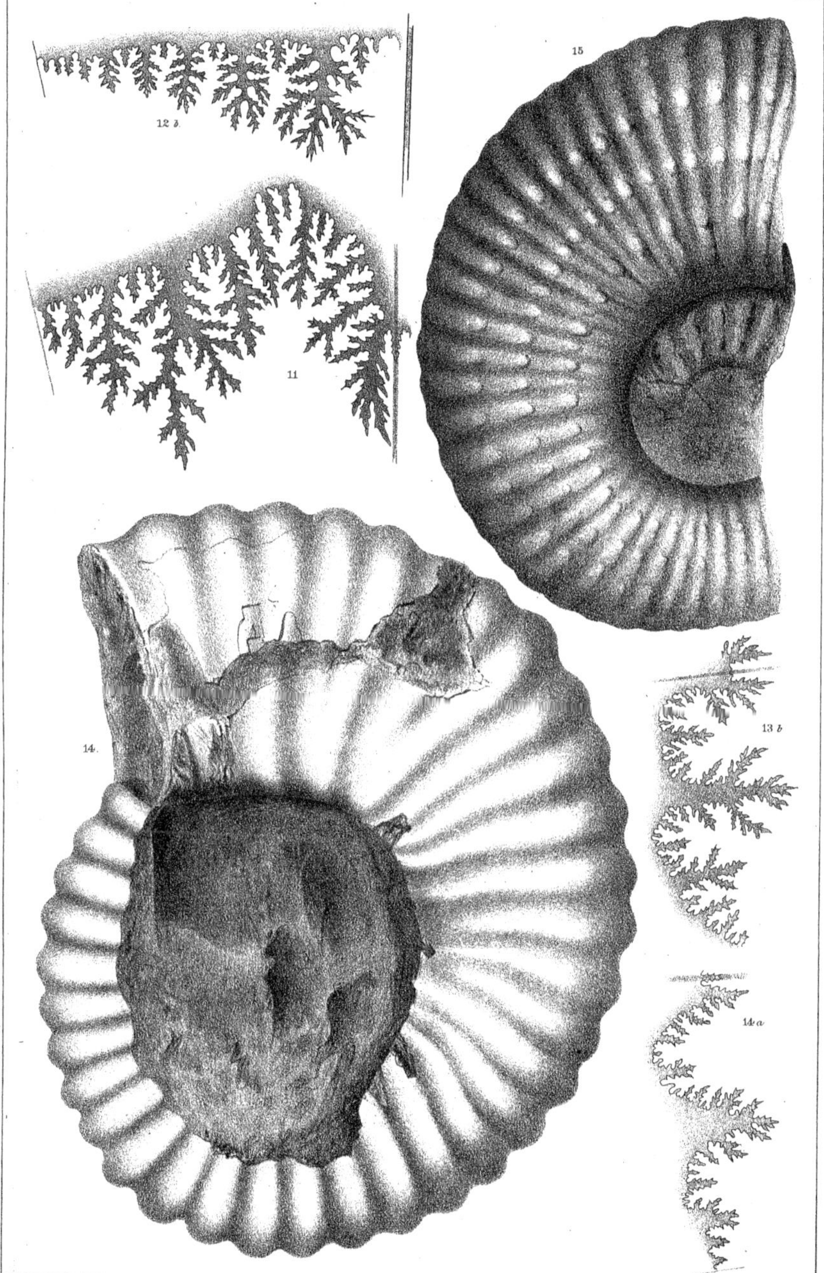

W. M. Gabb, del. T. Sinclair's lith, Phil[a] On stone by J. A. Ibbotson

PLATE XIII.

		PAGE
Fig. 16.	AMMONITES BATESII.	67
16 *a*.	Section of volution.	
b.	Septum.	
Fig. 17.	A. CHICOENSIS.	68
a.	Section of volution.	
b.	Septum.	
Fig. 18.	HAMITES VANCOUVERENSIS.	70
	½ Natural size.	
Fig. 19.	HELICOCERAS VERMICULARIS.	71
19 *a*.	Section.	
b.	Septum.	
Fig. 20.	PTYCHOCERAS ÆQUICOSTATUS.	74
	Natural size.	

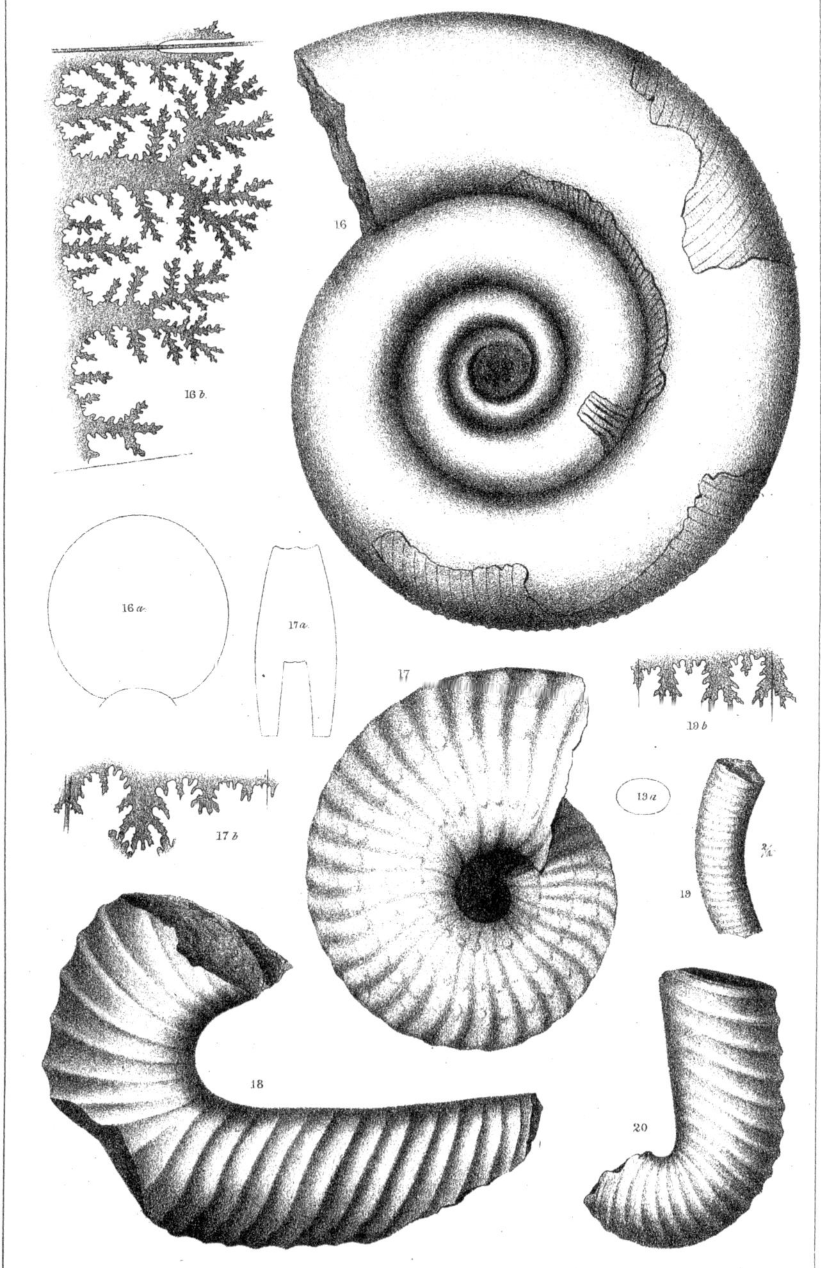

W. M. Gabb, delt. T. Sinclair's lith, Phila. On stone by A. J. Pobotsun

PLATE XIV.

		PAGE
Fig. 21 *a*.	Septum of PTYCHOCERAS (HAMITES?) QUADRATUS.	74
Fig. 22.	HELICOCERAS BREWERII. Natural size.	72
a.	Dorsal view.	
b.	Septum, showing the unsymmetrical character of the upper and lower sides.	
Fig. 23.	? AMMONITES COOPERII. Natural size.	69
a.	Septum.	
Fig. 24.	CRIOCERAS (? ANCYLOCERAS) RÉMONDII.	75
a.	Section of volution.	
Fig. 25 *b*.	Septum of C. LATUS.	76
Fig. 27 *b*.	Septum of BACULITES CHICOENSIS.	80
Fig. 28 *b*.	Septum of BACULITES. Sp. indet.	80
Fig. 29.	BACULITES CHICOENSIS. Variety.	80
a.	Section of same.	
Fig. 17 *c*.	AMMONITES CHICOENSIS. One of the original specimens.	68

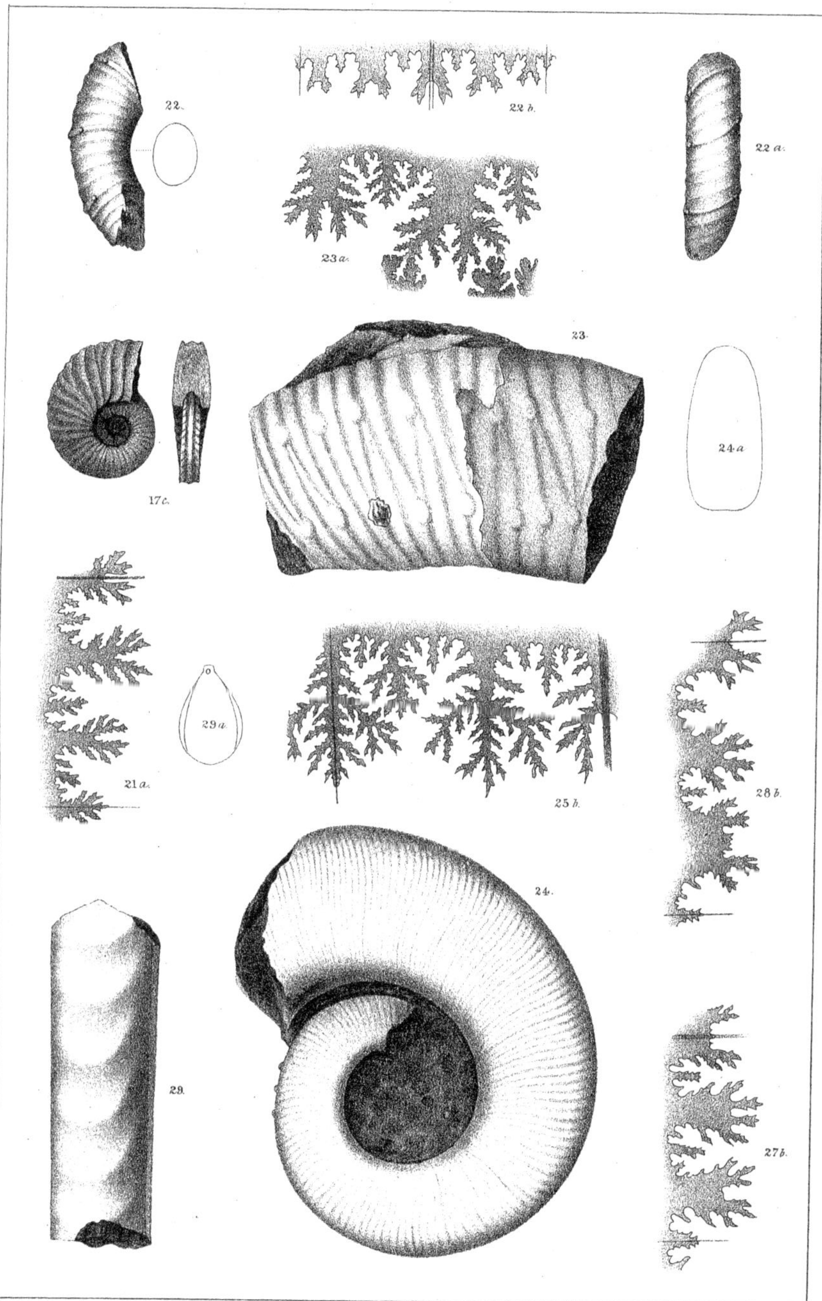

W. M. Gabb, delt. T. Sinclair's lith, Phila. On stone by A. J. Ibbotson

PLATE XV.

		PAGE
Fig. 21.	PTYCHOCERAS QUADRATUS. Natural size.	74
Fig. 25.	CRIOCERAS LATUS. $\frac{4}{5}$ Natural size.	76
a.	Section of volution.	
Fig. 30.	ANCYLOCERAS. Sp. indet. $\frac{2}{3}$ Natural size.	78
a.	Septum.	

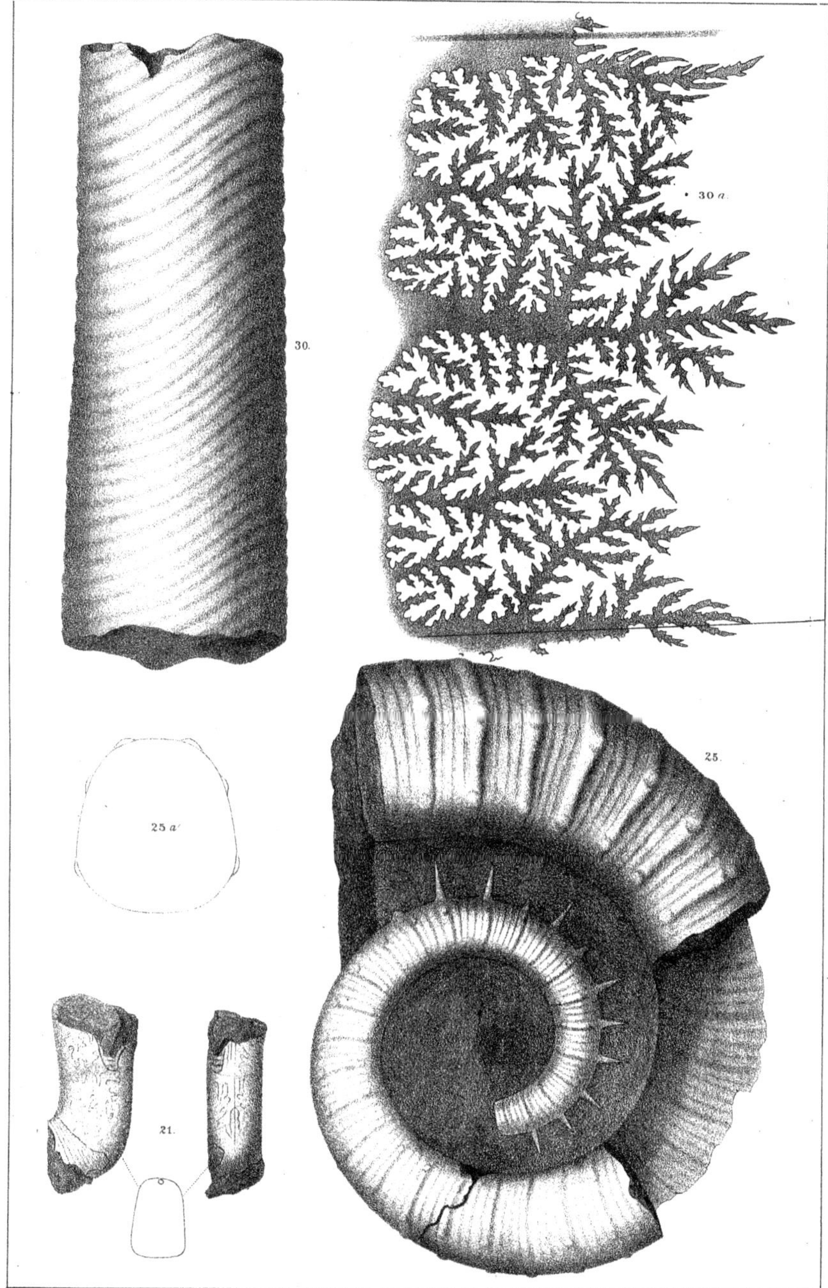

W. M. Gabb, del. T. Sinclair's lith, Phil^a. On stone by A. J. Ibbotson

PLATE XVI.

		PAGE
Fig. 26.	CRIOCERAS PERCOSTATUS. $\frac{1}{2}$ Natural size.	77

W. M. Gabb. del[t] T. Sinclair's lith, Phil[a] On stone by Ibbotson

PLATE XVII.

		PAGE
Fig. 26 *a*.	Section from CRIOCERAS PERCOSTATUS.	77
Fig. 27.	BACULITES CHICOENSIS. Natural size.	80
a.	Section.	
Fig. 28.	BACULITES, Sp. indet. Natural size.	81
Fig. 31.	ATURIA MATHEWSONII. Natural size.	59

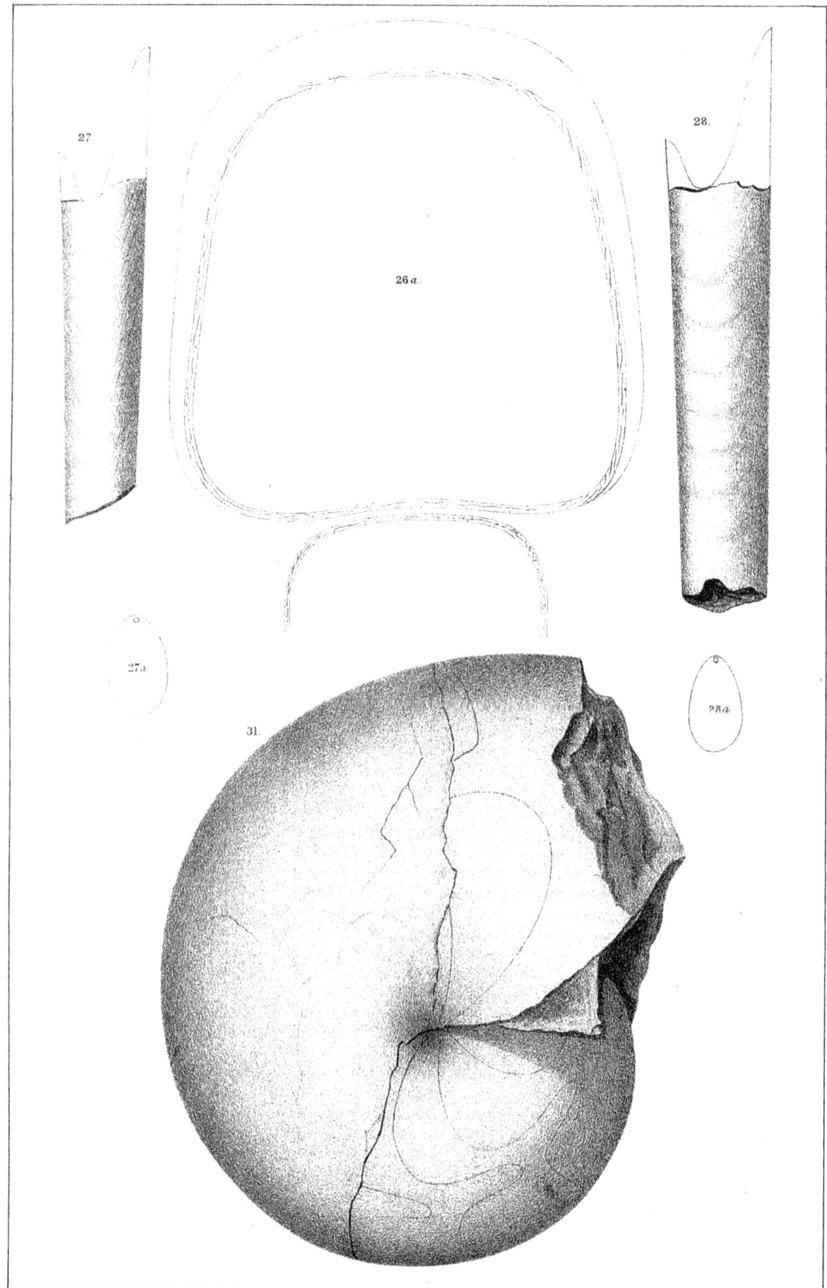

W. M. Gabb, delt. T. Sinclair's lith, Phila. On stone by A. J. Ibbotson

PLATE XVIII.

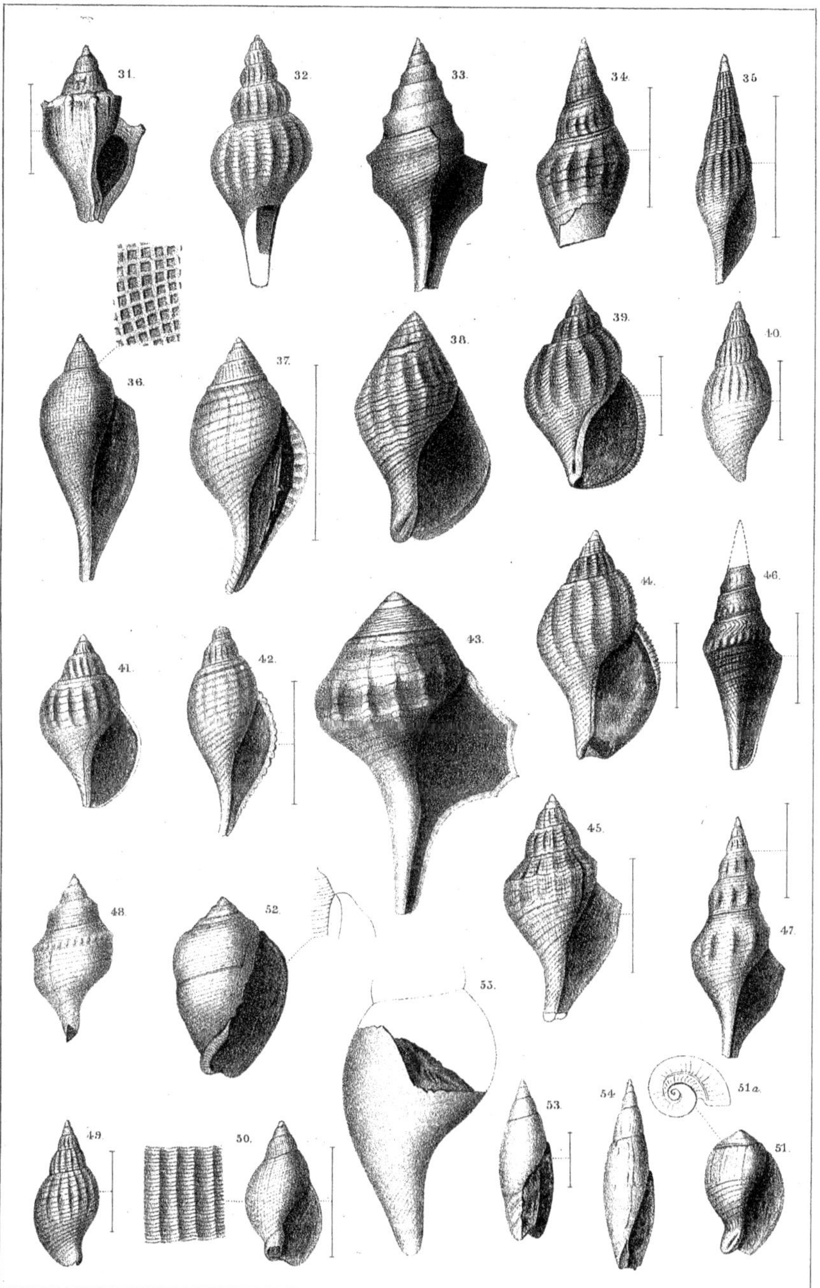

W. M. Gabb, del^t. T. Sinclair's lith. Phil^a. On stone by A. J. Ibbotson.

PLATE XIX.

Geological Survey of California.

PALÆONTOLOGY. VOL. 1. (Cretaceous) PLATE 19

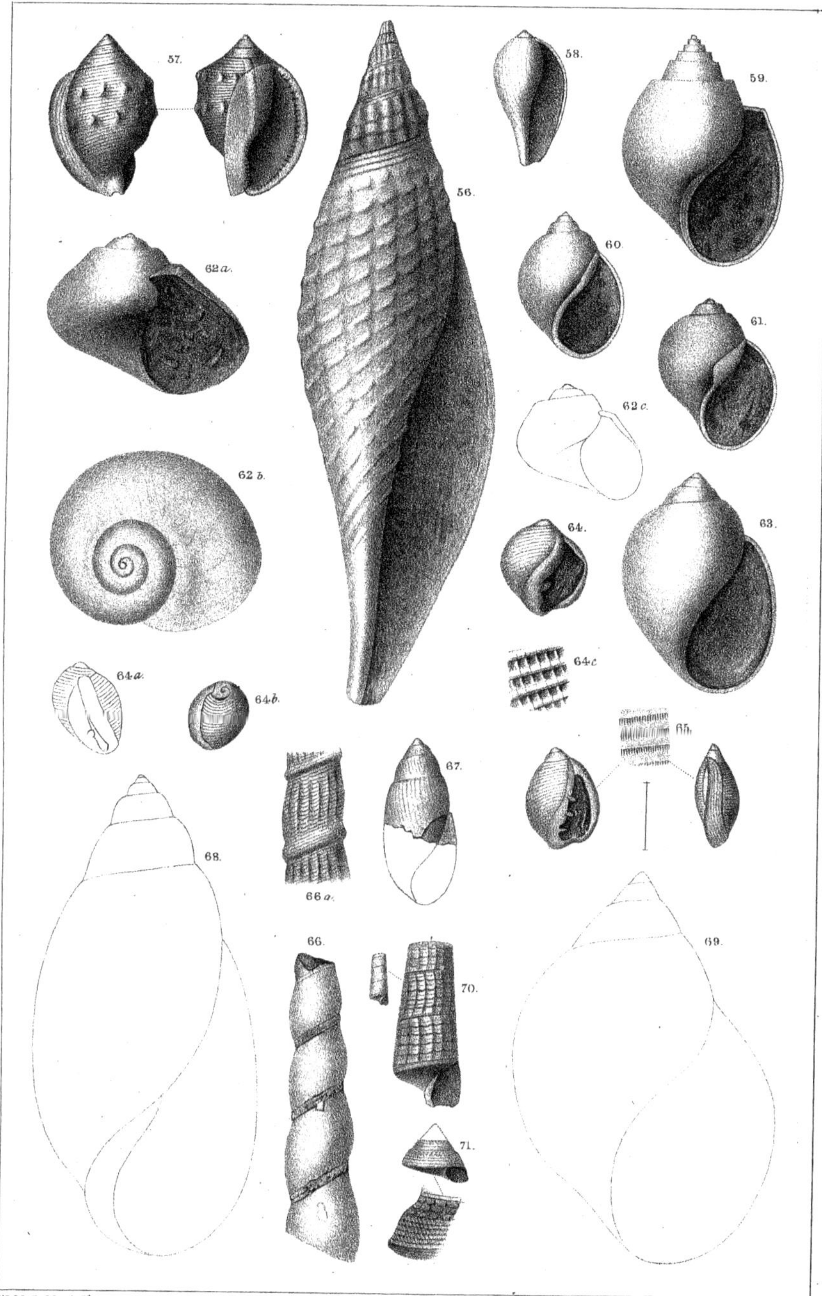

W. M. Gabb, delt. T. Sinclair's lith, Phila. On stone by Ibbotson

PLATE XX.

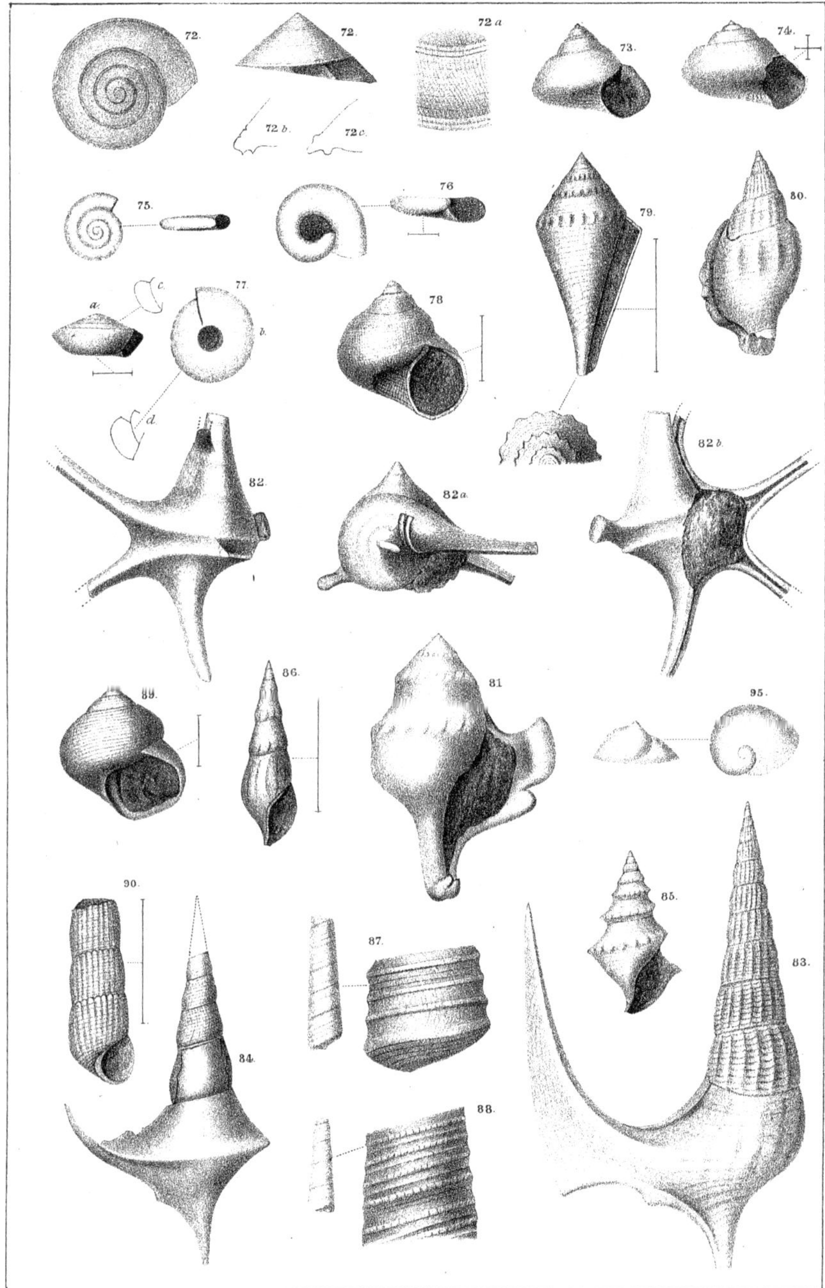

W. M. Gabb, delt. T. Sinclair's lith, Phila. On stone by A. J. Ibbotson

PLATE XXI.

		PAGE
Fig. 91.	Turritella chicoensis. Magnified.	133
Fig. 92.	T. Uvasana. Natural size.	134
Fig. 93.	T. Saffordii. Natural size.	135
Fig. 94.	T. robusta. Natural size.	135
Fig. 96.	Nerita deformis. Natural size.	137
Fig. 97.	N. cuneata. Natural size.	137
Fig. 98.	Lysis duplicosta. Natural size.	138
Fig. 99.	Dentalium (? Ditrupa) pusillum. Magnified.	139
Fig. 100.	D. Cooperii. Natural size.	139
Fig. 101.	D. stramineum. Natural size.	139
Fig. 102, *a*.	Emarginula radiata. Magnified.	140
Fig. 103.	Patella Traskii. Natural size.	140
Fig. 104.	Helcion dichotoma. Magnified.	141
Fig. 105.	Anisomyon Meekii. Natural size.	142
Fig. 106.	Actæon impressus. Magnified.	142
Fig. 107.	Cylichna costata. Natural size.	143
Fig. 108.	Megistostoma striata. Natural size.	144
	a. Back view.	
	b. Magnified view of surface.	
Fig. 109.	Fusus flexuosus. Magnified.	85
Fig. 110.	Perissolax Blakei. Natural size.	92
Fig. 111.	Amauropsis alveata. *Var*. Natural size.	110
Fig. 112.	Naticina obliqua. Magnified.	109
Fig. 113.	Niso polita. Magnified.	116
Fig. 114.	Cerithiopsis alternata. Natural size.	116
114, *a*.	Magnified view of body volution.	

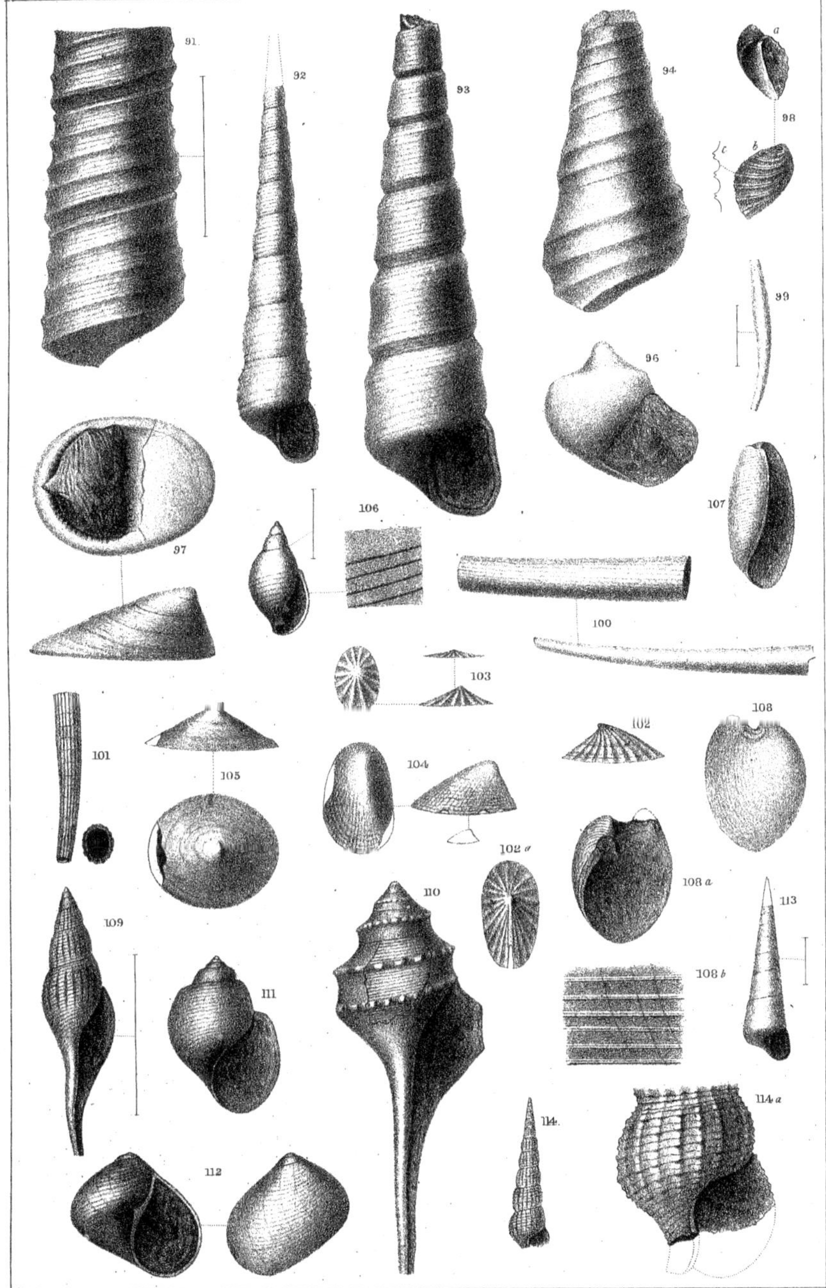

W. M. Gabb, delt. T. Sinclair's lith, Phila. On stone by A. J. Ibbotson

PLATE XXII.

		PAGE
Fig. 115.	Martesia clausa. Magnified.	145
Fig. 116.	Turnus plenus. Natural size.	146
Fig. 117.	Solen parallelus. Natural size.	146
Fig. 118.	Pharella alta. Magnified.	147
Fig. 119.	Panopæa concentrica. Natural size.	148
Fig. 120.	? Corbula primorsa. Magnified.	148
Fig. 121.	C. Traskii. Magnified.	149
Fig. 122.	C. cultriformis. Magnified.	149
Fig. 123.	Pholadomya Brewerii. Natural size.	152
Fig. 125.	Neæra dolabræformis. Magnified.	153
Fig. 126.	Anatina lata. Natural size.	151
Fig. 127.	Mactra Ashburnerii. Natural size.	153
Fig. 128.	Lutraria truncata. Natural size.	154
Fig. 129.	Asaphis undulata. Magnified.	154
Fig. 130.	? Gari texta. Natural size.	155
Fig. 131.	Tellina longa. Natural size.	155
Fig. 132.	T. Rémondii. Natural size.	156
Fig. 133, *a*.	T. Hoffmanniana. Natural size.	156
Fig. 134.	T. monilifera. Natural size.	157
	a. Magnified view of posterior end.	
Fig. 135.	T. ooides. Natural size Martiñez.	157
135, *a*.	Cast of same species from Pence's ranch.	

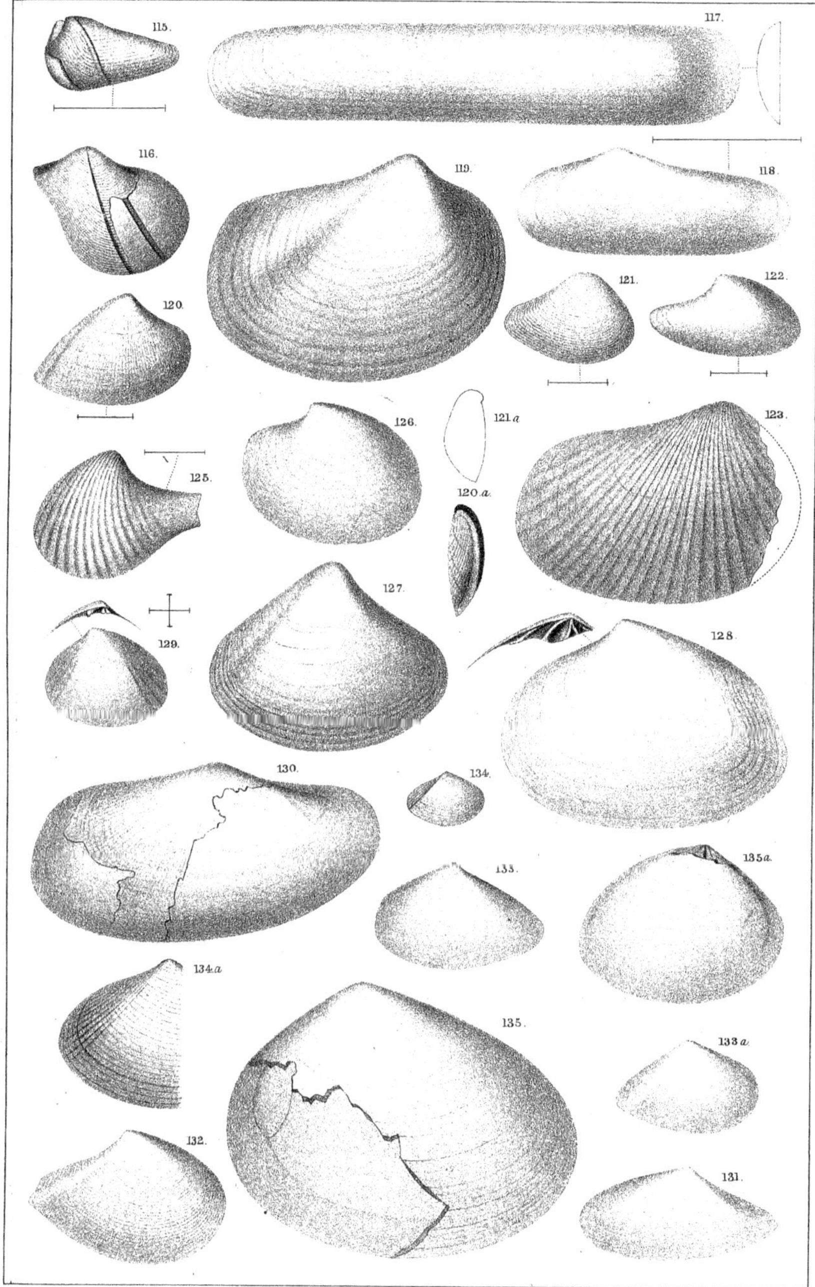

W. M. Gabb, del.t T. Sinclair's lith, Phil.a On stone by A. J. Ibbotson

PLATE XXIII.

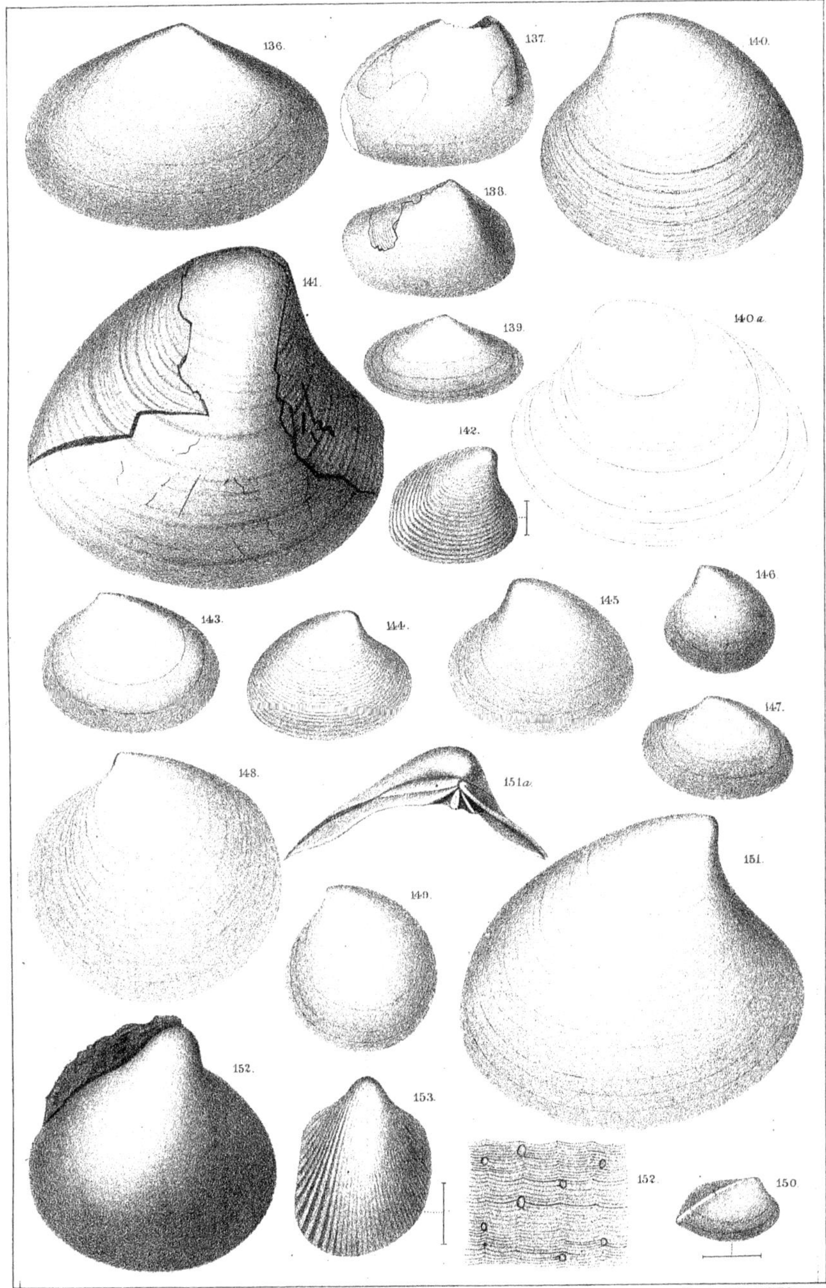

W. M. Gabb, delᵗ. T. Sinclair's lith, Philᵃ. On stone by A. J. Ibbotson

PLATE XXIV.

W.M.Gabb, del[t] J.Young, sc.

PLATE XXV.

		PAGE
Fig. 165.	MYTILUS PAUPERCULUS. Magnified.	183
Fig. 167.	MODIOLA CYLINDRICA. Natural size.	185
Fig. 168.	LITHOPHAGUS OVIFORMIS. Magnified.	185
Fig. 172.	AVICULA PELLUCIDA. Natural size.	186
Fig. 173.	INOCERAMUS PIOCHII. Large valve. Natural size.	187
Fig. 174.	*Id.* Small valve. Natural size.	187
Fig. 175.	PINNA BREWERII. Natural size.	188
175, *a*. Section.		
Fig. 176.	TRIGONIA TRYONIANA. Natural size.	188
Fig. 177.	T. EVANSII. Natural size.	189
Fig. 178.	T. GIBBONIANA, ? Young. Natural size.	190
Fig. 179.	MEEKIA SELLA. Natural size.	191
Fig. 179, *a*.	M. RADIATA. Natural size.	192
Fig. 180.	M. NAVIS. Natural size.	192
Fig. 181.	ARCA BREWERIANA. Magnified.	193
Fig. 182.	CUCULLÆA TRUNCATA. Natural size.	196
Fig. 183.	AXINÆA VEATCHII. Natural size.	197
Fig. 183, *a*. End view.		

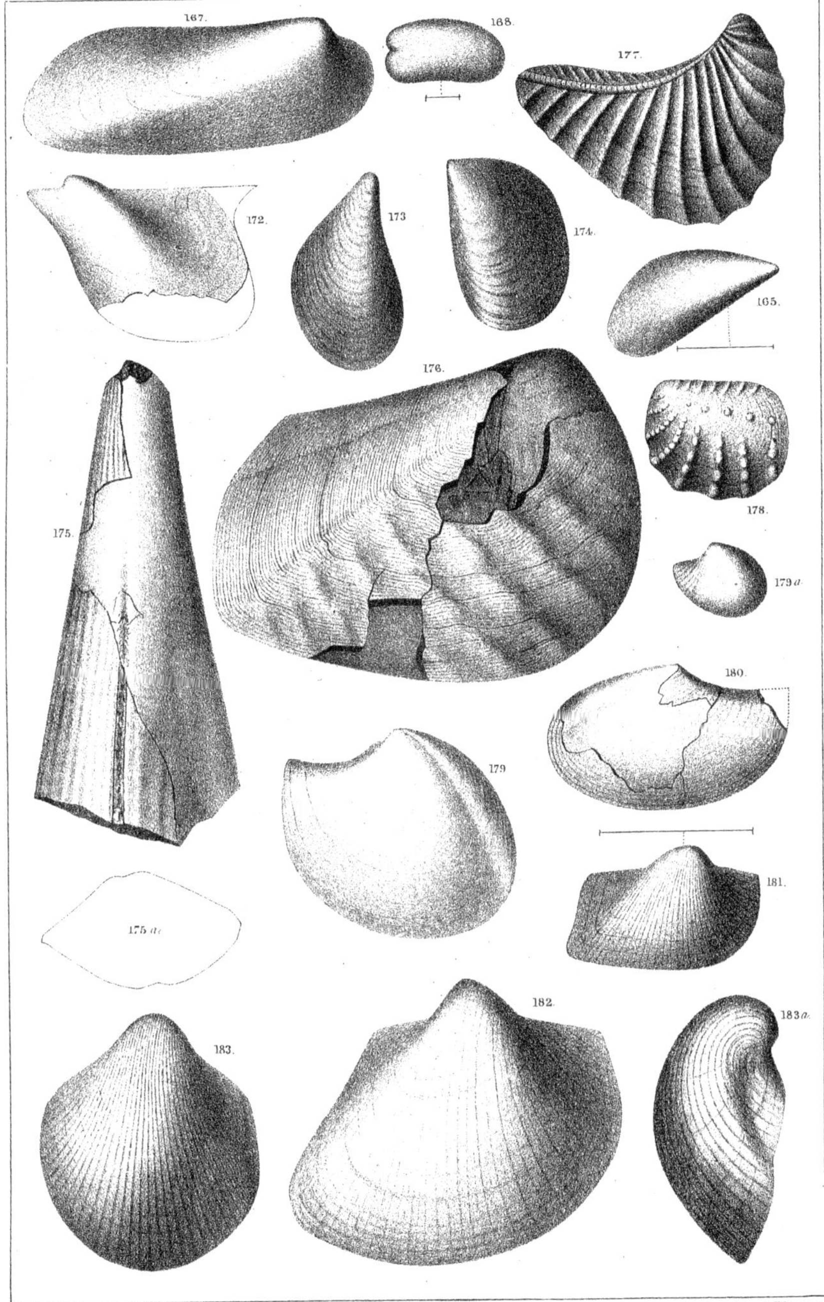

W. M. Gabb, del[t] T. Sinclair's lith, Phil[a] On stone by A. J. Ibbotson

PLATE XXVI.

		PAGE
Fig. 184.	NUCULA TRUNCATA. Natural size.	198
184, *a*.	*Id.* End view.	
184, *b*.	*Id.* Magnified view of the surface.	
Fig. 185.	LEDA PROTEXTA? Magnified.	199
Fig. 186.	LIMÓPSIS TRANSVERSA. Slightly magnified.	200
Fig. 187.	PECTEN TRASKII. Natural size.	200
187, *a*.	*Id.* Surface magnified.	
Fig. 188.	P. OPERCULIFORMIS. Natural size.	201
Fig. 189.	LIMA MICROTIS. Natural size.	202
Fig. 190.	PLICATULA VARIATA. Magnified.	203
Fig. 191.	OSTREA BREWERII. Natural size.	204
Fig. 192.	EXOGYRA PARASITICA. Young. Natural size.	205
192, *a*.	Upper valve.	
192, *b*.	Inside of lower valve.	
Fig. 193.	ANOMIA LINEATA. Natural size.	203
Fig. 194.	TEREBRATELLA OBESA. Natural size.	205
194, *a*.	Front view of upper valve.	
194, *b*.	Area of lower valve.	
Fig. 195.	TROCHOSMILIA STRIATA. Magnified.	207
Fig. 196.	? T. (ELLIPSOSMILIA) GRANULIFERA. Magnified.	208
196, *a*.	Upper view.	
Fig. 197.	Indet.	209
Fig. 198.	? TRIGONIA. Sp. indet.	209
Fig. 199.	FLABELLUM RÉMONDIANUM. Natural size.	207

Geological Survey of California.

PALÆONTOLOGY, VOL. I. (Cretaceous) PLATE 26

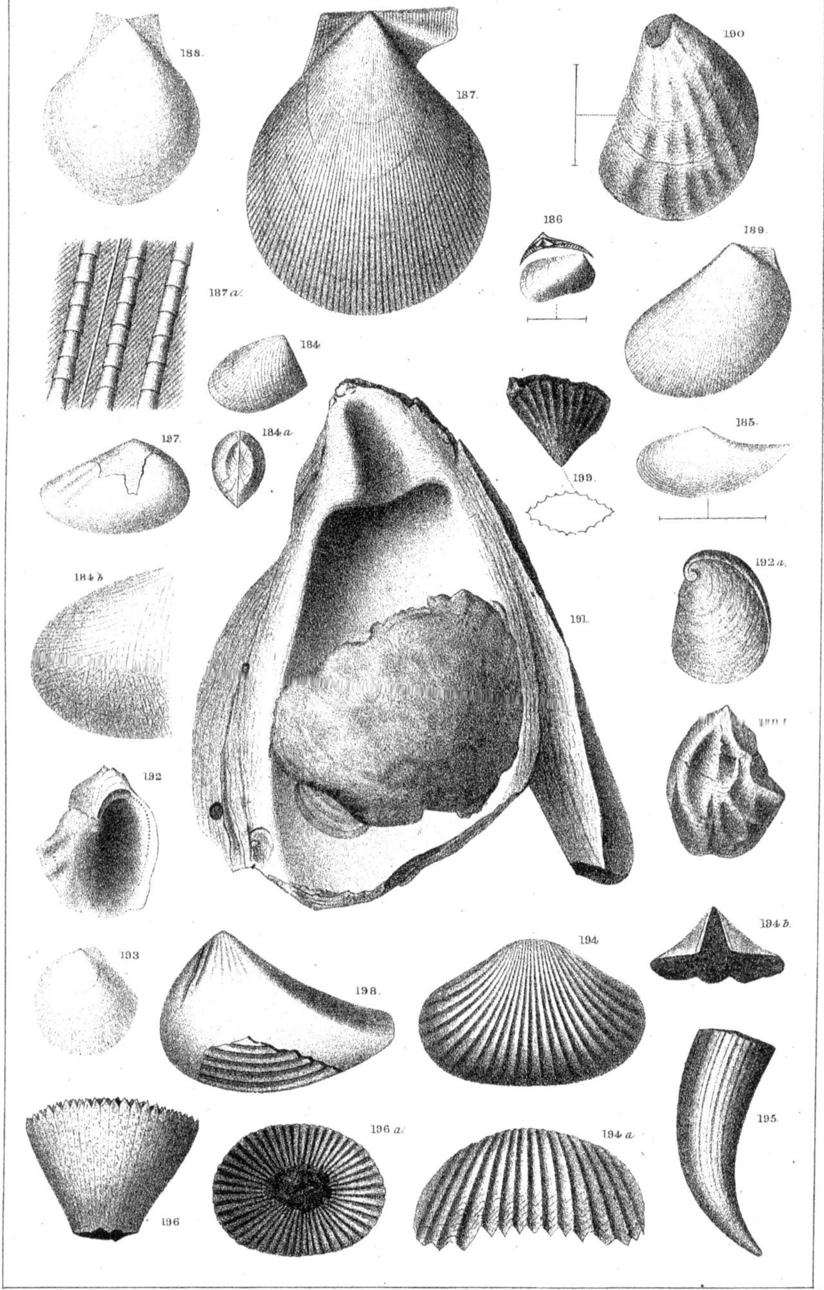

W. M. Gabb, del^t. T. Sinclair's lith, Phil^a. On stone by A. J. Ibbotson

PLATE XXVII.

PAGE

Fig. 199. Ammonites Newberryanus. Four-fifths of natural size. 61

Fig. 199, *b*. Septum, as far as the angle of the umbilicus.

Fig. 199, *c*. Surface magnified, to show the granulation.

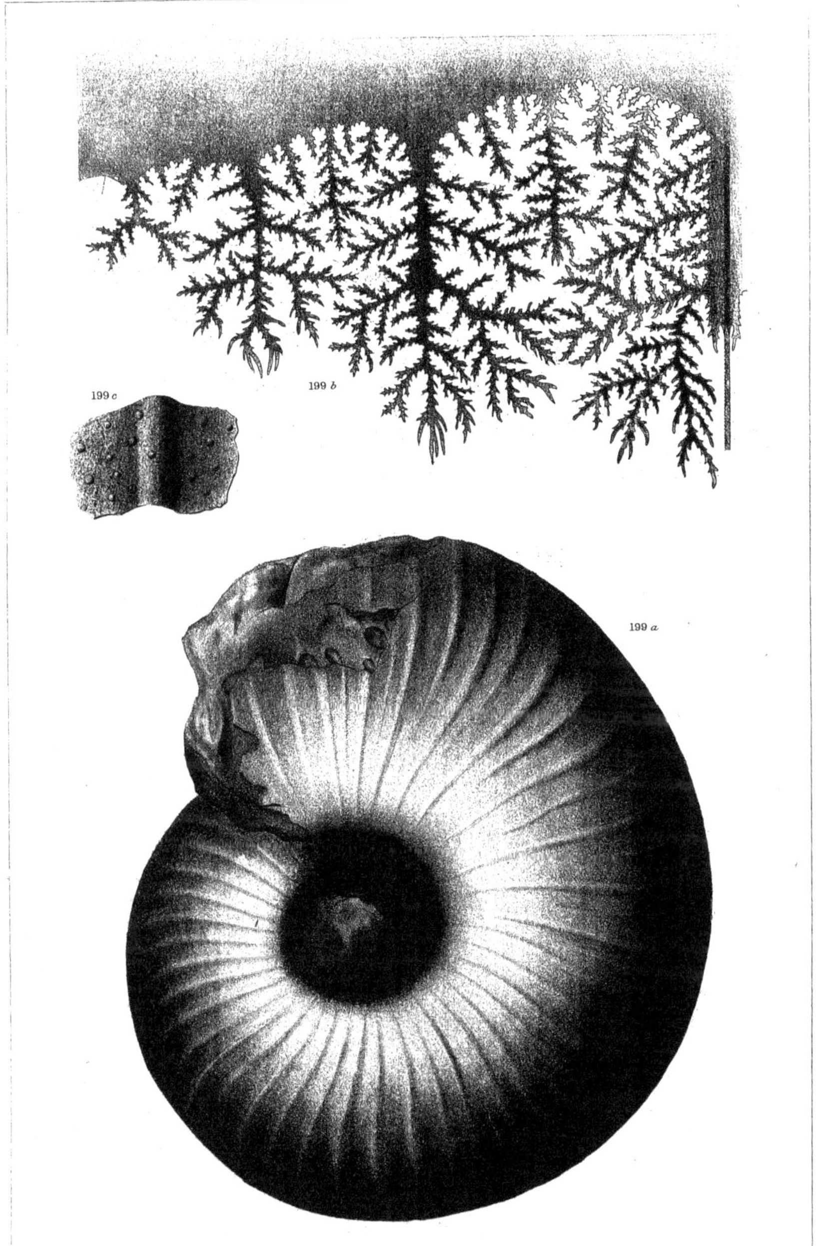

W. M. Gabb. del[t]

J. Young.

PLATE XXVIII.

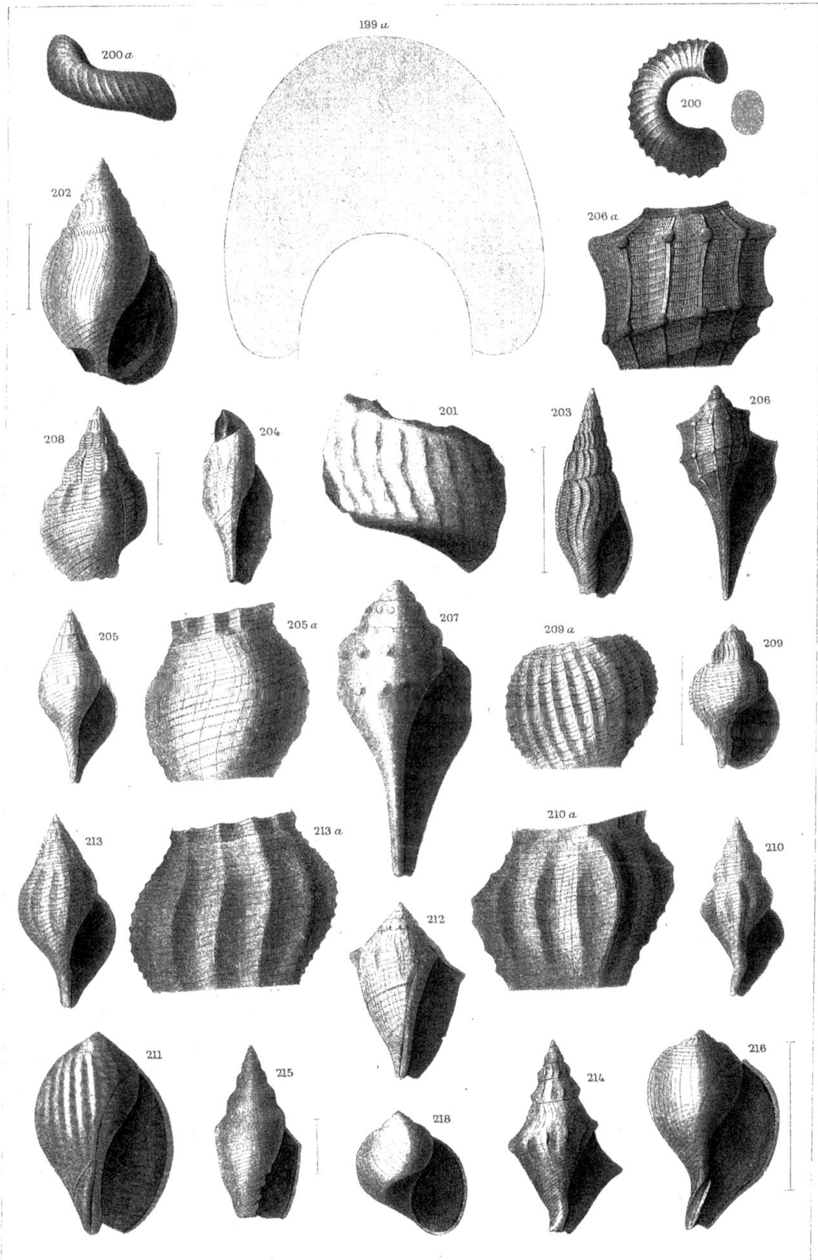

W. M. Gabb, delt. J. Young, sc.

PLATE XXIX.

W. M. Gabb, del[t]. J. Young, sc.

PLATE XXX.

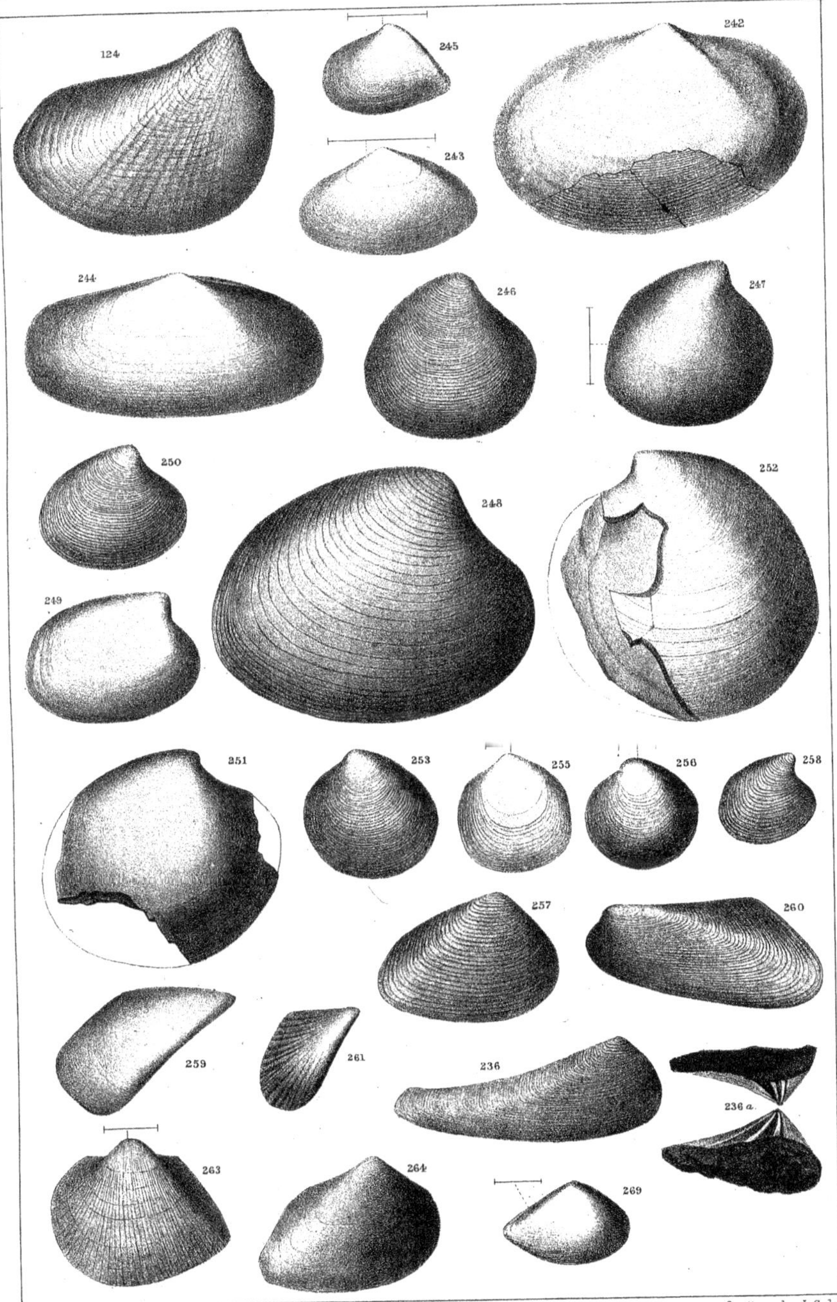

W. M. Gabb, del[t]. T. Sinclair's lith. Phil[a]. On stone by J. Golz

PLATE XXXI.

		PAGE
Fig. 262.	TRIGONIA GIBBONIANA. Natural size.	190
Fig. 265.	ARCA DECURTATA. Natural size.	195
265 *a*.	*Id.* Opposite side, exhibiting the truncation.	
Fig. 266.	CUCULLÆA MATHEWSONII. Natural size.	195
Fig. 267.	AXINÆA (? LIMOPSIS) SAGITTATA. Natural size.	197
267 *a*.	*Id.* Surface.	
Fig. 268.	A. COR. Magnified.	198
268 *a*.	*Id.* Surface.	
Fig. 270.	PECTEN CALIFORNICUS. Magnified.	201
Fig. 271.	LIMA APPRESSA. Natural size.	203
Fig. 272.	OSTREA MALLEIFORMIS. Natural size.	204
Fig. 273.	EXOGYRA PARASITICA. Natural size, lower valve.	205
273 *a*.	*Id.* Upper valve.	
Fig. 274.	? ASTROCŒNIA PETROSA. Natural size.	208
274 *a*.	*Id.* Surface magnified.	
Fig. 275.	Indet.	209

Geological Survey of California.

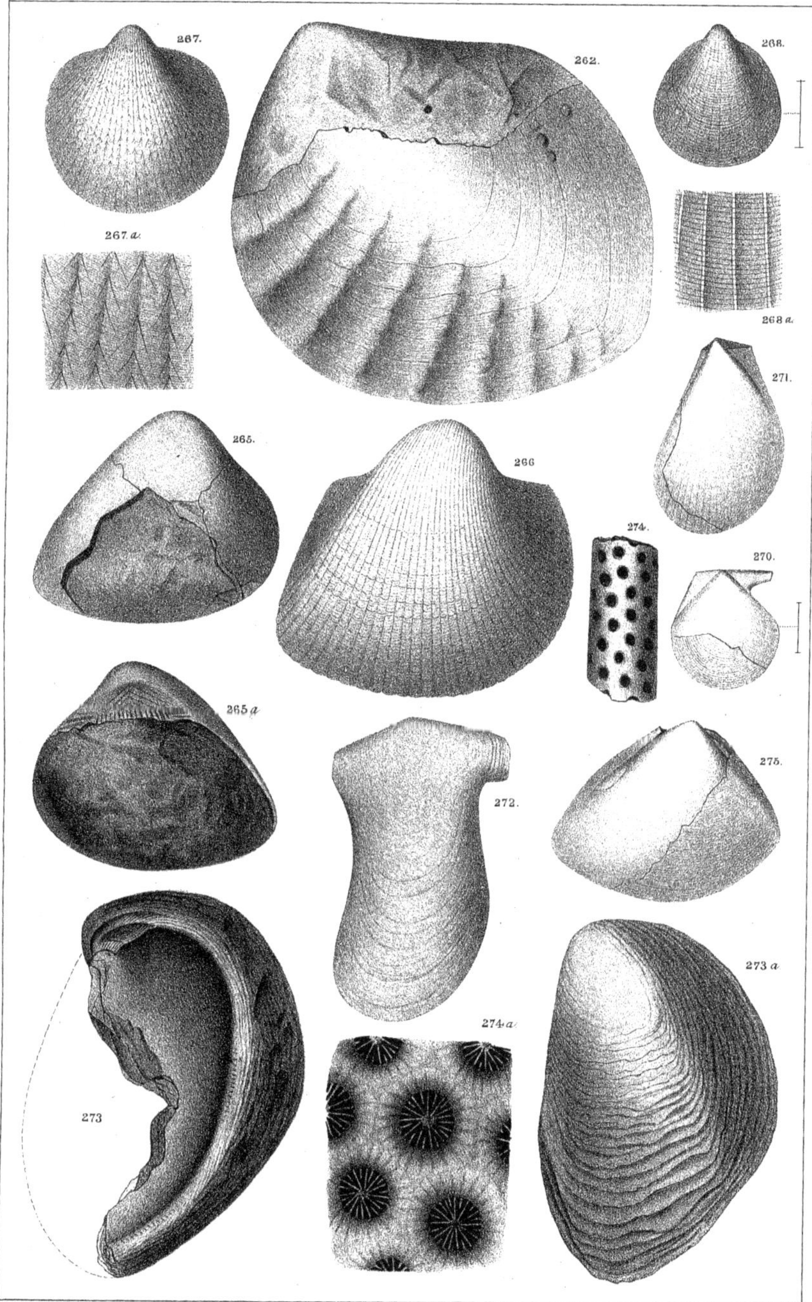

W. M. Gabb del^t. T. Sinclair's lith, Phil^a. On stone by A. J. Ibbotson

PLATE XXXII.

		PAGE
Fig. 276.	FICUS MAMILLATUS. Natural size.	211
Fig. 277.	NATICA UVASANA. Magnified.	212
Fig. 278.	SCALARIA MATHEWSONII. Natural size.	212
Fig. 279.	TURRITELLA INFRA-GRANULATA. Natural size.	212
Fig. 280.	SOLEN DIEGOENSIS. Natural size.	213
Fig. 281.	CHIONE ? ANGULATA. Magnified.	213
Fig. 282.	TAPES CONRADIANA. Natural size.	169
Fig. 283.	T. ? CRETACEA. Natural size.	214
Fig. 284.	CRASSATELLA UVASANA. Natural size.	214
Fig. 285.	CARDITA VENERIFORMIS. Magnified.	215
285 *a*.	Surface magnified.	
Fig. 286.	BARBATIA MORSEI. Natural size.	216
Fig. 287.	YOLDIA NASUTA. Natural size.	216
Fig. 288.	PLACUNANOMIA INORNATA. Natural size. Upper valve.	217
288 *a*.	*Id.* Lower valve.	

Geological Survey of California.

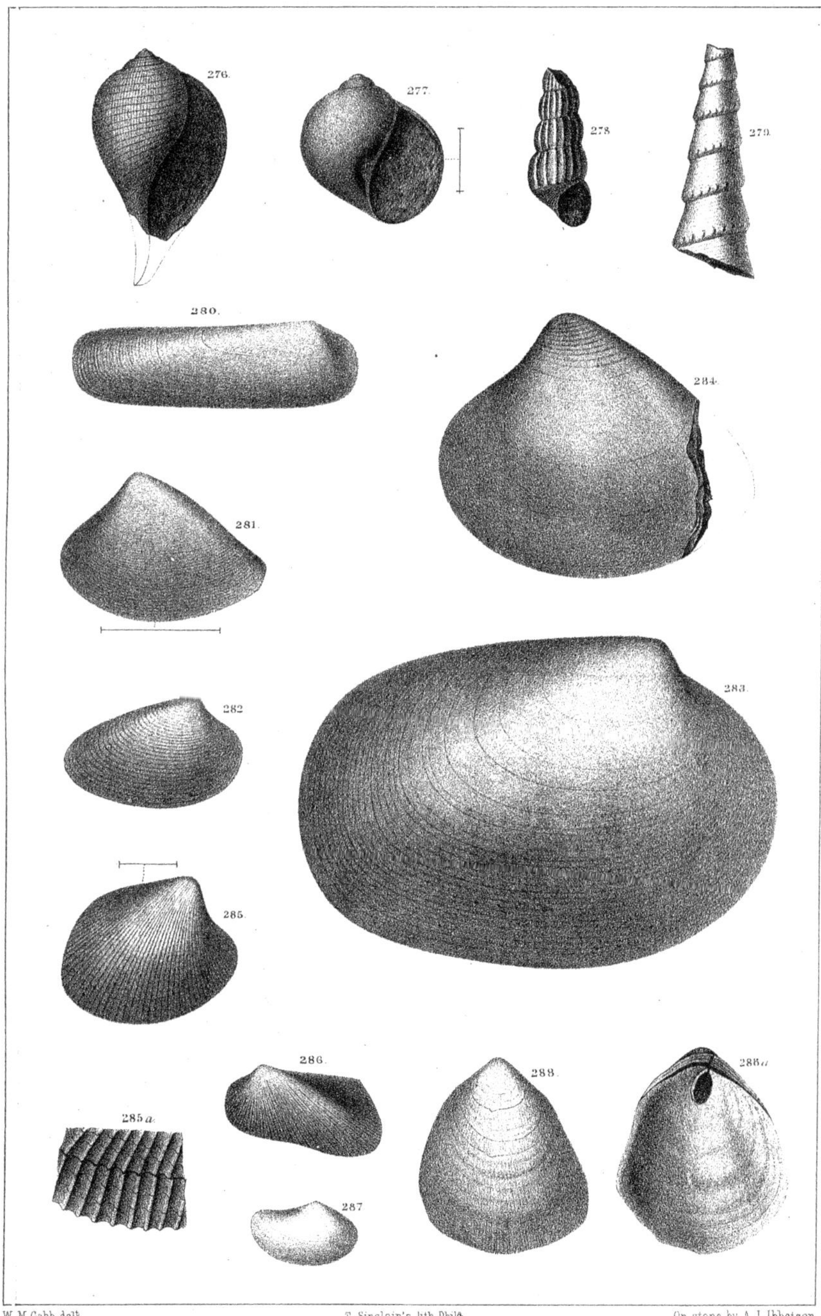

W. M. Gabb, del[t] T. Sinclair's lith, Phil[a] On stone by A. J. Ibbotson

www.ingramcontent.com/pod-product-compliance
Lightning Source LLC
LaVergne TN
LVHW020121110826
845151LV00001B/228

9781425542023